Method
in
Architecture

Method
in
Architecture

Tom Heath

Queensland Institute of Technology

JOHN WILEY & SONS

Chichester · New York · Brisbane · Toronto · Singapore

Library of Congress Cataloging in Publication Data:

Heath, Tom.
  Method in architecture.

  Bibliography: p.
  Includes index.
  1. Architecture—Methodology. I. Title.
NA2500.H38 1984   720'.1'8   84–3719
ISBN 0 471 90409 0

British Library Cataloguing in Publication Data:

Heath, Tom
  Method in architecture.
  1. Architecture—Methodology
  I. Title
  721'.0'8   NA2510

ISBN 0 471 90409 0

Typeset by Photo-Graphics, Honiton, Devon
and printed in Great Britain by Page Bros. (Norwich), Norwich

Contents

Preface

Once upon a time I believed, like most practising architects then and now, that the design of buildings was a process of exploration and discovery which each time followed a different path and revealed something entirely new. When I first encountered the idea that there might be something orderly or predictable about this process I rejected it. That was some twenty years ago; the occasion was a lecture by a visiting Fulbright Scholar, Professor Benjamin Handler. Handler was an economist and therefore accustomed to the idea of representing complex situations in mathematical form, and he argued that something of the sort could be done for architecture.

The opportunity (as it seemed) to refute this heresy came a year or so later with the announcement of the first international conference of the Design Methods Group. I set out to write a paper demonstrating that there was in fact no similarity between the processes used in designing different buildings, drawing on my recent experience of the design of office buildings in Sydney.

I proved myself wrong; analysis showed that the process had been essentially the same in each case. I had discovered an algorithm for the design of office buildings. There was, as it turned out, nothing new in this discovery; that same year Skidmore Owings and Merrill disclosed that they had developed a computer program which would design office buildings in any one of several American cities.

Having discovered that a method existed for one kind of building, I assumed that it would be of general application. So I set out to apply it generally, with very uneven results. Applied to office buildings it continued to work quite well. Applied to a technical college it was not particularly useful. When I attempted to use it in the design of a hospital, it was of no help at all.

I was much more baffled by this than I should have been. I was caught in a typical piece of dichotomized thinking; *either* there was no method for any type of design *or* one method must work for all designs. I had found both of these propositions to be untrue, and was thoroughly puzzled. Now however I came across the work of Rittel and his associates which distinguished between 'well-behaved' and 'wicked' problems. This distinction turned out to apply pretty well to the differences between those cases in which my 'office building' method would work and those in which it would not. I went on for some years working out the implications of this in relation to my continuing practice in the design of hospitals and large, complex buildings in general.

This work, which appeared in various published papers from time to time, might never have turned into a book had I not been asked to review Newell and Simon's *Human Problem Solving* for the Architectural Science Review. I was struck by the analogy between the various kinds of problem-solving methods which they had identified in laboratory studies and the kinds of design process which I had by then found to exist in architectural practice. This provided the theme which has given this book its structure, as the constant interaction between theory and practice has provided its content. My hope is that this ordering of my experience will help others to order theirs, and thus make for a better understanding of architecture amongst all those concerned with it.

Acknowkedgements

I would like to acknowledge the contribution, both direct and indirect, of my friends and former colleagues at McConnel, Smith and Johnson, to the genesis of this book. The final form is of course my own responsibility.

Section 4.3 of Chapter 4 was originally published in *Environmental Design: Research, Theory and Application* edited by Andrew Seidel and Scott Danford, and is reproduced by permission of the Environmental Design Research Association.

Section 5.7, including Figures 5.3 and 5.4, was published in a slightly different form in DMG-DRS Journal, Vol. 7, No.3 pp.201–206. It is reproduced by permission of the Design Methods Group.

Credits for illustrations

Architectural Press, London, pp.98, 198

Artemis, Zurich: pp. 154, 156

Design Methods Group, San Luis Obispo, Figures 5.3, 5.4

Diane Graham: p.153

Harvard University Fine Arts Library, p.118

G.E. Kidder Smith: pp. 3, 115

McConnel Smith and Johnson Pty. Ltd.: p.00 Figures 2.1, 5.1, 5.3

David Moore: pp.161, 163

Pitkin Pictorials Ltd., London: p.8

Jules Schick Photography, Inc., Philadelphia: p.155

W.D. Scott and Co. Pty. Ltd.: Figure 7.1

Sipen: pp.160

Urban Systems Corp., Figure 2.1

Yatanabe: p.4

Chapter 1

Introduction

1.1 What is architecture?

Whilst most writers on architecture take it for granted that they and their readers share some common notion as to what architecture is, this assumption is not by any means always justified. The definition of the terms of ordinary language is in general a useless practice, generating either aphorisms of limited applicability, or explanations so long and carefully qualified that they explain nothing. But it may prove useful to talk a little around the subject, with the object of indicating something of the scope and limits of the study of method. The view of architecture that will be taken here is that it is primarily a certain kind of activity, not a kind of building; in the currently fashionable terms, that it is a process and not a product. This is given some support by the derivation of the word: architect after all means master builder, and architecture might therefore be expected to mean the activity of such people and thence, by the kind of extension usual in the development of language, the buildings which they oversee.

  As against this view, we have the history of architecture, which characteristically deals with products rather than processes, though there are some notable exceptions. Partly this bias results from the way in which architectural history, as a subject, developed; its first concern was the taxonomy of styles. And partly it is a matter of documentation; the records of the process are often lacking or inadequate, while the product is self-recording. Nevertheless, architectural history, insofar as it has concentrated on products, has frequently encountered the question, What is to count as architecture? This difficulty is not too acute for periods before, let us say, the eighteenth century: the customary method is simply to include all buildings of any size which survive, giving special emphasis to those that have attracted the most admiration. The historian who deals with modern times, however, because of the superfluity of material, has to be more selective. And here the criteria used have been of one of two kinds: historicist or qualitative. Those writers who adopt historicist criteria take as their starting point some theory of history: a "mainstream" or "direction" of development; those works which contribute to this particular path are included as significant, and all others are excluded, or, if for other reasons they cannot be absolutely disregarded, at best reduced to the status of footnotes. The well known histories of Pevsner (1949) and Giedion (1941) have been criticized for unduly restricting the canon of modern architecture in this way. And in general there is good reason to be dubious of historicist criteria.

On the other hand, attempts to distinguish architecture from other kinds of building by way of some quality or group of qualities of the product have led to conclusions that are not merely dubious but absurd. This is the case, for example, of attempts to make architecture mean "good buildings". Here the term becomes both too inclusive, as in the paradoxical title of Rudofsky's *Architecture without Architects* (Rudofsky, 1965) and too exclusive, since we must conclude that if architecture means "good building", there can be no *bad* architecture; yet criticism, doubts and theoretical problems clearly arise just because some architecture is deemed to be bad.

Fortunately it is not essential to solve the historian's problem here. His selection, if he is a good historian, will no doubt be based both on complex qualitative judgements and on an equally complex apprecia-tion of the way in which a particular work fits into the web of history. The point here, however, is that this kind of appraisal does not determine whether or not something is architecture. So far it has been suggested rather vaguely that this distinction depends not on the product but on some undefined process; and more specifically that this process involves an architect. Since this character appears more concrete so far than the process he engages in, it may be of benefit to focus on him more closely. People who are recognizably architects occur very far back in history. Senmut, Queen Hatsheput's architect and subsequently her consort, flourished around 1500 BC. It may perhaps be argued that it is stretching the concept "architect" too far to project it into a culture so remote. But Senmut has the first, and only essential, qualification; he is mentioned in the records as having been in charge of major building works.

As we move through history and across cultures the education and social position, the class in fact from which architects so defined are drawn, inevitably varies; but it does so within certain surprisingly apparent limits. The range extends from the man of general culture, at one end, whose technical background may be limited and who may even be an amateur, to at the other end the man whose background is in the crafts and trades, the building technology of the period. Amongst the former we have already mentioned Senmut. Other similar

The tomb of Queen Hatsheput at Deir-el-Bahari, designed by Senmut. People who are recognizably architects occur very far back in history

figures are Sen-no-Riku, the teamaster designer of the Myoki-an and the Renaissance and Baroque architects such as Alberti, Perrault and Sir Christopher Wren. In modern times the increasing regulation of life and work has tended to discourage the amateur, but a much discussed case is Wittgenstein the philosopher, who designed his parents' home in Vienna; and there is also Rudolf Steiner's Goethaneum. As examples of the other extreme, the men whose background is in the crafts and trades, we may take mediaeval master builders such as Henry Yevele, carpenter to Henry VII, and Villard de Honnecourt of the sketchbook; and among the modern masters Mies van der Rohe, who was apprenticed as a stonemason and cabinet maker. The degree of formal education and the extent to which it was supplemented by apprenticeship likewise varies. Vitruvius, of course, sets out an ambitious programme (Vitruvius, 20 BC). According to Harvey (1950), the

The Myoki-an teahouse, designed by the teamaster Sen-no-Riku. The cultured amateur is a recurrent figure in architectural history, though the importance of the amateur has declined with the growing complexity of technology.

mediaeval architects in general received what was for the time an extensive education over and above their apprenticeship in their craft; some few, like Inigo Jones and Wright, are largely self-educated. And finally, the degree to which the architect is dependent on his profession for his means of existence varies too but not so symmetrically: some like Lord Burlington are wholly independent, a large number are partially independent and the majority depend on their professional earnings entirely, whether expressed as an annual salary or a fee for the job or some combination of these.

The introduction of formal education and legal status has restricted the range of distribution and increased the proportion of architects in the "modal" category. Yet degrees, diplomas and certificates of registration are not essential to the activity of architecture; nor is the ideology or the formal social structure of professionalism. If we put these several descriptions of the architect together to yield what is certainly not a formal definition but rather the description of the central tendency of a fuzzy set, we may say that the architect is a full-time designer of buildings, professional in the sense of deriving his living from such work, and having undergone some kind of specific training for his task, and that architecture is building designed by such men. This does distinguish architecture from building in general, but tells us nothing about the characteristics of the result, or about whether it is good or bad.

What sort of situation calls for such a designer? This question is most easily answered by exclusion. A professional designer will *not* be required in a traditional society where building problems are all solved by minor adaptation of a pre-established type. Nor is he required in similar circumstances in a modern society. The small speculative builder has long managed very well in Australia by making minor variations to traditional house plans (Boyd, 1952); and prefabricated buildings of various kinds are used in all kinds of situations from telephone boxes to schools to factories. What all these situations have in common is that nothing special or unusual is required; and conversely we can say that the architect, and architecture, is generally concerned with the special or unusual case, even if it be only the first case of a new type

The need for the professional designer arises because design becomes self-conscious; design becomes self-conscious because a demand has arisen, no matter how, for something special or unusual. The distinction between self-conscious and unselfconscious design was developed by Alexander in his *Notes on the Synthesis of Form* (Alexander, 1964). He distinguished between those artefacts (including buildings) that develop gradually over long periods, centuries perhaps, by the spontaneous adaptation of a type, making the minimum change necessary to deal with changed circumstances or some perceived failure, and those that are produced with the intention of making something new and distinctive; the former he calls the unselfconscious process, the latter the self-conscious process. Alexander believes this difference is a product of individualism on the part of the designer, that self-conscious cultures are produced by formal processes of education, by, for instance, the existence of architecture schools, which teach explicit rules, and by socioeconomic competition for trade on the part of designers, as with the carpenters who build Samoan guest-houses; while in unselfconscious cultures teaching will take place by the characteristic craft method of demonstration and specialization, and the associated economic competition will not exist. In this, however, he is mistaken. Self-conscious design would not have arisen, architects would not have been identified by activity and name, architecture schools would not have been established, had there not first of all been the wish and will to achieve something exceptional, to do something which differed sufficiently from the established types to require exceptional care and thought, something the form and execution of which must be planned in advance. Individualism, as is in fact clear enough from Alexander's account of the Samoan guest-houses, is a by-product of the expression of social significance; for otherwise why, when the home proper was built by the owner, was the guest-house built by a professional carpenter? Whether the social significance involved is mainly symbolic, related, that is, to the status of some activity or individual, or is mainly prudential, resulting from some pressing communal or personal problem, or from just the sheer size or complexity of the work to be undertaken, is unimportant. Indeed, until the relatively modern separation of architecture and engineering it is hardly possible to draw a line between symbolic and prudential building considered as activities. Roman aqueducts and bridges and mediaeval castles appear in the histories of architecture, and rightly so. The "art" of architecture and the "science" of engineering are not really separate even today, as the work of the artist engineers, Maillart, Nervi and Arup makes clear.

Self-conscious design not only arises from some special social demand; it requires large resources, at least in relation to the scale of the work. Building of any kind has always been expensive. Exceptional building has been proportionately more expensive, though its relative cost has declined greatly in modern times; the Parthenon bankrupted a nation and a region, while the Sydney Opera House merely overset a state government. And indeed a little reflection will show that it is only for the exceptional building that the luxury of a full-time designer can be afforded. It is the unusually large or unusually elaborate building (whether the elaboration be symbolic or technical) which both demands the skill of an architect and can absorb the cost of his services within its budget without gross distortion.

Summarizing, then, architecture, for the present purpose, will be taken to be the design, by a full-time professional designer trained for his work, of structures of some social importance to which, whether because of their large scale or their complexity, considerable resources must be devoted. This, it must be said again, is not a definition of a word: it is a description, in short form, of a kind of activity.

1.2 Why method?

Books on architecture, and no doubt on other serious topics, are written in the effort to cope with some state of affairs which the author, at least, perceives as a problem. Such perceived problems may be limited; the absence of a good textbook on timber construction, for example. Or they may be an individual's view of some more widespread or general unrest or ferment of ideas. At the moment of writing, doubts and fears about architecture, its nature and future, are widespread. Such doubts and fears are, perhaps, more common in architecture than in other professions, for economic reasons. Even slight changes in the general well-being of an economy may have dramatic effects on the demand for architecture; for architecture as we have seen demands both social commitment and considerable resources. These natural fluctuations in their worldly affairs, create in architects, as in other men, spiritual doubts. They ask themselves, what have we done to deserve this? And that is a question which, once asked, finds answers. In the late 70s and early 80s a relatively deep and worldwide depression has followed a long period of increasing affluence. It is not surprising that doubt and dismay are widespread among architects.

However, such explanations are at best partial. They do not, for example, account for the direction and character of the current outburst of self-criticism. This has shifted from a concern with technical and economic performance, and with quality narrowly conceived as an absence of physical failures, to more fundamental issues. Such books as MacEwen's *Crisis in Architecture* (MacEwen, 1974), Brolin's *The Failure of Modern Architecture* (Brolin, 1976), Blake's *Form Follows Fiasco* (Blake, 1974), Heimsath's *Behavioural Architecture* (Heimsath, 1976) and Sommer's *Tight Spaces* (Sommer, 1974) are all fiercely critical of current theory and practice as they perceive it, though they vary in the degree to which they accept or reject the body of ethical, social and aesthetic doctrines which characterize "Modern Architecture". The extent and radical nature of this criticism suggests that current models of architectural activity have broken down, that they no longer encompass clearly seen and urgently felt needs.

For models, in the sense of analogues which can be constructed and manipulated in advance of actual execution, are essential to self-conscious design. The use of such analogues, or more accurately homomorphs, is in fact what makes self-conscious design self-conscious. Plan and action are separated. The balance between what is part of the plan and therefore self-conscious, and what is part of execution or action and therefore taken for granted, has varied, both historically and according to the nature of the task. For example, detailed consideration of methods of erection forms part of the design both of Brunelleschi's dome for Florence Cathedral (Mainstone, 1977) and of many of Nervi's designs for concrete structures. On the other hand, an historical overview of design reveals a progressive, if slow, development in the power and scope of modelling, though the oldest methods, literal physical models and drawings, continue in extensive use.

Sir Christopher Wren's great model of St. Paul's Cathedral. Literal physical models are perhaps the oldest of the techniques for envisaging and manipulating buildings in advance of construction, and remain important today

We know that Egyptian sculptors used geometrical grids to set out their work (Panofsky, 1955) and we may assume that Egyptian architects did likewise. By classical times the characteristic modular principles described so confusingly by Vitruvius (IV, 3, 3–8) had been developed. And from the mediaeval period we have the remains of drawing on both tracing floors and stones (Harvey, 1950; James, 1972). These were geometrical models; we know also from records and a few surviving examples that physical models were used as well. The general adoption of the Indo-Arabic numeral system made

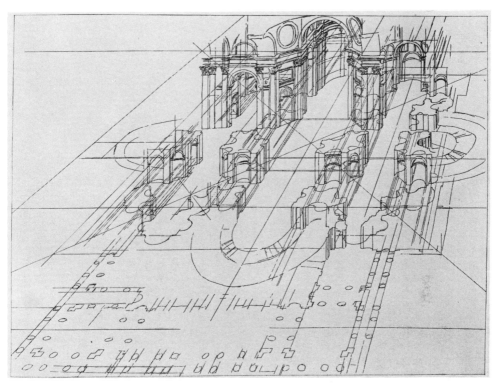

Early perspective of Bramante's design for St. Peter's, Rome. We no longer think of perspective as a "design method", yet it made possible much quicker and more accurate conceptualization of buildings in three dimensions

possible, or at least much more convenient, the scale drawing; and the invention of perspective the quick and relatively accurate conceptualization of buildings in three dimensions. One way of viewing the development of architecture from the Renaissance to the eighteenth century is in terms of the exploitation of the increased power of conception which these new types of model gave to the designer; a development which reaches its limit in the stage designs of Bibiena and the fantastic architecture of Piranesi, where invention is not limited by the cost of construction.

The further development of architects' models of their task was inflected by the rise of the architectural school. The establishment of the Beaux-Arts, with its emphasis on competition winning and on the rapid formulation of concepts which could thereafter be elaborated but not altered in principle, leads directly to the notion of architecture

Stage design by Antonio Galli Bibiena. One way of viewing the development of architecture from the Renaissance to the eighteenth century is in terms of the exploitation of the increased power of conception which the new model, perspective, gave to the designer

as a compositional task in which elements are arranged within a three-dimensional grid. This important change is to be seen effectively complete at the beginning of the nineteenth century in Durand's *Precis* (Durand, 1809). Durand recommends planning by setting out elements on a grid; the facade is developed afterwards according to an appropriate style, and this was the subject of more detailed and

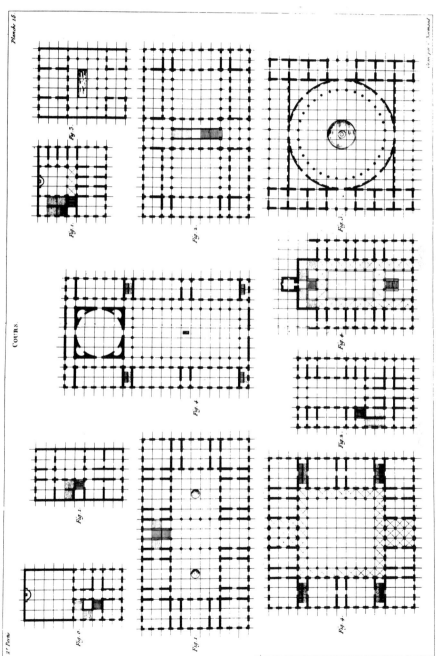

Durand's method of planning with grids, from the *Precis*. The emphasis in the French architecture schools on the rapid formulation of concepts leads directly to the notion of architecture as the compositional task in which elements are assigned within an abstract three-dimensional grid elaborate drawings. The Modern Movement developed one aspect of this tradition, the spatial grid, but progressively discarded the process of elaboration.

This historical development of models or homomorphs is a development of method. The nature and power of the conceptual tools available to the designer determine in no small measure what he can conceive and accomplish. And conversely, the limitations of method will be expressed as limitations of the design. This is as apparent in architectural schools and offices today as it is in the history of architecture. The student or young architect who cannot draw freely or confidently will design within the limits of his powers of representation. He is the victim of "analogue take-over": his tools and models constrain his thinking. This is obvious enough, but the more general point that the architecture of any period is limited by its stock of models and methods has not been generally grasped. The recent revival of interest in architectural drawing has, however, been accompanied by, or perhaps has stimulated, a recognition that the particular drawing styles encouraged by the Modern Movement, the "neutral" draughtmanship of the engineering drawing, and the preference for models over drawings, were themselves part of the attempt to eliminate other kinds of architecture for which other kinds of drawing had been developed, notably the elaborate Beaux-Arts rendering (Stern, 1977).

Drawing, however, is only a limited and partial model for architectural activity. It concentrates attention on appearance, arrangement and the means of construction; generally, on physical relationship. It is a static model, and limited in its capacity for representing dynamic situations; complex social relationships, for example. As long as design was either conventional, as in the Beaux-Arts, or part of a face-to-face interaction between an architect and his individual client, this did not matter. Similarly, while construction remained conventional and the physical environment produced by a given design correspondingly predictable, visual representation was enough. Increasingly from the mid nineteenth century, however, new building types, new materials, and perhaps above all the new mass clientele have undermined these conditions.

The founder of architectural method is Viollet-le-Duc, the great rationalist. While we can find in Viollet-le-Duc the origin of some of those features of academic architectural theory which are now under attack, notably the emphasis on engineering calculation and economy, he raises many of the problems that are still with us. In his tenth discourse, "On method" (Viollet-le-Duc, 1872), he writes that:

"It must needs be confessed that modern architects, surrounded as they are by prejudices and traditions and embarrassed by an historical confusion in respect to their art, are neither inspired by original ideas or guided by definite and well understood principles; a fact the more plainly betrayed the more elaborate and complex are the monuments they are called upon to design and execute."

Without method, he argues:

"With the increase in our material and intellectual wealth we gain practically only embarrassment and confusion; our very abundance is a stumbling block. The more knowledge we acquire, the greater the strength and accuracy of judgement needed to render this knowledge practically available and useful, and the more necessary it is to discriminate and classify according to severe principles."

Method, as he sees it, requires meticulous attention to the "programme of requirements", the selection of an appropriate method of construction, proper regard for the nature of materials, not only practical but expressive, and finally (but only finally):

..."admitting into this expression a principle of unity and harmony, that is to say, a scale, a system of proportion, a method of decoration, appropriate and significant as regards the destination of the edifice... "

His contemporaries, he thought,

"... either unnecessarily sacrificed convenience and disregarded the most judicious use of materials for the sake of an harmonious form, or satisfying all the conditions of their work, and employing their material most judiciously, they have been unable to harmonise the whole so as to produce a unity of expression."

If the problem could be so alarmingly clearly defined, so long ago, and a solution suggested, which, we shall see, is at least congruent with modern attempts to solve the same problems, why are today's criticisms of architecture so closely parallel to those of Viollet-le-Duc? The founders of the Modern Movement were deeply influenced by this theory; how is it that they failed to apply it? There were three reasons. Firstly, Viollet-le-Duc laid the heaviest emphasis on the proper understanding of the means of construction and the use of materials, which he saw as being the greatest failing of his contemporaries, and his emphasis was continued by his disciples. The "programme of requirements" and the *appropriateness* of expression received less emphasis; in fact it came to be thought that the latter problem would wither away if historical styles were abandoned. Secondly, the problems created by abundance — of materials, techniques, and social demands — increased faster than solutions could be developed. Thirdly, and most importantly, method itself did not develop; for while Viollet-le-Duc calls for an appropriate method, and describes what in principle it must achieve, he does not in fact provide it, except to say that we must proceed from the simple to the complex, which unfortunately was a mistake, though in terms of his rationalist background an inevitable one.

Since he wrote, there have been continuing efforts to place architecture on a sounder intellectual and practical foundation. The growth of concern, first with structural theory, then with "building science" and latterly with psychophysics and social science, in architecture schools and to a lesser extent in practice, illustrates this development. These are attempts to expand and make more concrete the architect's model of his task. But they have not been well integrated with the existing model of the design process based on drawing. In the schools and in practice we tend to find a division between the numbers men, the hard-heads, the polytechnists whose calculations somehow never produce a building and the 6B pencil artists, who can generate broad concepts but are often unable or unwilling to adapt them to the calculations of the technicians. Undoubtedly this is partly a matter of personalities; but it also indicates that we have as yet no model of architectural activity which is generally seen to encompass both. The revival of interest in method after the second world war was largely an attempt by the numbers men to do away altogether and finally with the conceptual designers: and it failed. Just why, we shall see later. But it did serve to reveal that mathematics, by itself, was not a sufficient model for architecture any more than drawing, by itself. Just as in Viollet-le-Duc's time, buildings that were ugly but sometimes workable were produced alongside buildings that were unworkable but sometimes beautiful. Yet despite the lack of a method which is generally accepted, teachable, and capable of containing the two approaches, some architects have developed ways of tackling these problems in practice, which achieve both practicality and quality. They have a method; but it is not yet an explicit method.

The much debated crisis of architecture today can thus be seen as a crisis of method. The conflicting voices with which we began call on the one hand for a more humane architecture, for an architecture that is once again decorated and ornamented, for a revival of drawing and a new and more inclusive awareness of architectural quality, and, on the other hand, for a more practical architecture, physically comfortable, free of technical defects, and better adapted to the life and aspirations of its users. This exactly reflects the existing dichotomy of approach, of method: each "side" in the debate is, as it were, demanding more of the same. While this will undoubtedly lead to some improvements, in that a continuing band of pragmatic practitioners will draw more even-handedly on the theories and models of both sides than their proposers do, it will hardly resolve the problems of architecture in any general way. A new account of method is needed, an inclusive account, which will contain the new aesthetics and the new pragmatics, just as they themselves seek to include a wider range of aesthetic possibilities and a wider range of practical conditions.

1.3   Problem solving as a model for architecture

The models for architecture that have been mentioned so far are very narrow. To try to build out from such a limited base to encompass all the material with which, it would appear, architecture should now be concerned, would be a risky undertaking. Here, the opposite method will be adopted: that of working in from a still more general model of activity to the more specific activities of architecture. This broader model is derived from research into problem solving activity in general, and specifically from the work of Newell and Simon (1972), which both incorporates much of what has been said by other writers such as Poincaré and Polya (1945) and goes beyond them in seeking to construct a theoretical psychology of problem solving. Newell and Simon define a problem as follows: "A person is confronted with a *problem* when he wants something and does not know immediately what series of actions he can perform to get it." If we look again at the distinction between self-conscious and unselfconscious design, which, it has been argued, is what distinguishes architecture from building, it can be seen that self-conscious design involves, in Newell and Simon's terms, a problem, whereas building or unselfconscious design does not. Method, which we have been calling the model of the activity, is then the list of actions that must be performed to get from the problem to the solution, the "design" and ultimately the building; the actions themselves are the problem-solving process or the design process.

The idea that problem solving is the distinctive feature of architectural activity is not new. As Reyner Banham put it, in a characteristically sharp attack on the whole notion, "Back from Buckminster Fuller, through Le Corbusier, W.R. Lethaby and deep into the industrial smog of the Nineteenth Century, authoritative architectural voices have insisted that 'A problem well stated is a problem solved', or words to that optimistic effect" (Banham, 1965). Banham's point is that architects have not shown themselves to be universal problem solvers; rather, they are able to do architecture and practically nothing else. Otherwise, "Why is it that this profession of architect, supposedly equipped with a sovereign technique for solving problems, is never invited to solve other professions' difficulties ... " So far from broadening the scope of architectural method, as is optimistically suggested here, Banham considers that the problem solving approach has unduly narrowed and restricted it: "If... the profession had rejected Problem Solving because they perceived its narrowness and lack of humanity, if one single architect had stood up and said 'Problem-solving is a load of horse-shit', then it would have been a profound demonstration that architecture is a humane study." Such criticism deserves to be taken seriously, particularly since it is precisely in the interests of greater humanity that a better approach to method is being advocated.

Part of Banham's criticism is certainly directed against a too narrow and quantitative approach. And another part is directed against architects' inability to see any kind of solution to a problem other than a building. These accusations of narrowness must be borne in mind in considering the detailed account of method given later. The third part of his criticism is directed against the notion that architecture and problem solving are simply interchangeable ideas, that experience or training in the solution of architectural problems fits people for the solution of "problems" in general. To meet this criticism it is necessary to look in more detail at the sense in which the theory of problem solving is or may be applicable to architectural method.

To describe architecture as problem solving is clearly an abstrac-tion. If we take a purely naturalistic or observational view of architecture, that is, if we simply look at what goes on in architectural offices, then much of the work we see being done is not problem solving at all. Indeed, if it were so, no design for a major building would ever be completed, for human beings are not well adapted to continuous directed thought. Much of what actually goes on is mechanical, repetitive, imitative. It may be methodical in the sense of following well-established habits or patterns, methodical in the sense that industrial work that is being carried out according to some optimum pattern established by work study is methodical. But method, in the sense in which we are concerned with it here, is that which gives direction and effect to this mass of routine activity — what makes it into design. It is the small fraction of the total activity which gives it form that is essential, and it is from this point of view that it is worth considering architecture as problem solving.

Not only is problem solving a small part of total architectural activity; there are many kinds of problems. The simple general definition of a problem conceals this variety. There are crossword puzzles and chess problems and the problem of what to have for dinner and the problem of the best way to drive to work and many more. Many of these belong to a large subclass which we can conveniently call *puzzles*: cases in which we know what has to be done, and that it can be done (by definition, so to speak) but not exactly how to do it. Determinate games which are within our information handling capacity, games like noughts and crosses and solitaire are examples of puzzles; determinate games which exceed our capacity, like chess, and indeterminate games like go are full-scale problems. There seem to be cases in which productive activity in the arts and sciences takes on the character of puzzle solving; this is the way many eighteenth century writers saw the arts. It is the way that Kuhn (1962) sees certain periods of scientific activity, and it is possible to represent certain architectural design processes, those which are "quasi-algorithmic", in this way; but generally design problems, of which architectural problems are a subclass, are not puzzles. Design problems are in general distinguished from other problems by the fact that in a design problem we do not know exactly what we are trying to achieve. We may know in general terms: we want a man-powered flying machine, or a hooked rug, or a house for a family of six on a steeply sloping site, but before we can actually achieve this thing our needs and wishes have to be made specific, and once that is done, producing the thing may not be too hard. More generally, following Wade (1977), we can say that design problems are concerned with "closure of the terminal state" or deciding what it is that is to be done, and also whether it *can* be done. In summary, part of a design problem is finding out what the problem is.

Turning back again to the activities which go on in architectural offices, however, it will be apparent that just as much architectural activity is not problem solving of any kind, so much architectural problem solving is not design, at least if the distinction drawn between design and the solution of puzzles is accepted. Much of what architects at present do *does* have the character of puzzle solving, in that the objective is known; it is clear that there is an answer, and the area of work or amount of information involved is quite limited. The sizing of a lintel for a small opening in a masonry wall, or an eaves gutter for a roof, are examples. Again, it is the fact that much of architecture is merely puzzle solving that makes architecture possible in a reasonable time and at a reasonable cost.

While much of the architect's activity is not problem solving, and much of his problem solving is not design, this does not quite answer Banham's criticism of architects, or of the problem-solving approach. To do this it is necessary to introduce some concepts developed by

Newell and Simon (1972): the "task environment" and the "problem space". Their overall map of the problem solving process is described as follows:

> "Proceeding inward from the task environment, there is the problem space, in which problem solving takes place as search; then the methods, which are the means by which search takes place; and finally the production system, which is the programme organisation by which the methods are realised in terms of elementary processes and basic characteristics of the IPS."

IPS is an acronym for "information processing system"; we may substitute "mind".

"Task environment" may be roughly translated as "situation". Newell and Simon argue that it is unnecessary and indeed impossible to describe the task environment itself, the Kantian *Ding an sich*. However, they suggest that there are at least two ways of talking about the task environment which do not involve misleading abstraction. One is to talk about "alternative, isomorphic presentations of the *same* environment. We mean by the structure of the environment precisely the set of invariants that are preserved under translation from any one of the isomorphs to any other." Another "is to construct a hypothetical problem space that is objective only in the sense that all the representations that human subjects in fact use for handling the problem can be embedded as specialisations in this larger space." In their work this hypothetical space is constructed by collecting protocols of problem-solving behaviours, from which problem spaces can be extracted, to the point of diminishing returns. This method is not applicable to architecture, since the task environment of architecture is extremely complex: how complex will be explained in part in Chapter 3.

The "problem space" is the problem-solvers' internal representation of the task environment. The construction of a problem space out of the elements provided by the task environment is the first task of the problem solver. Newell and Simon admit that they have little to say about how this is achieved though in many cases it is clear that it is "ready-made"; that is, an appropriate problem space exists in the long-term memory. It is necessarily, however, an abstracted representation; this follows from the limitations of the short-term memory which will be discussed in more detail in Chapter 5. Different problem solvers may and probably will use different problem spaces, since they will abstract from the task environment in different ways. While the concept of the task environment is perhaps "transparent", the concept of the "problem space" may be less so and a simple example may be helpful. Among the types of problem which Newell and Simon used in their empirical study of problem solving behaviour was "cryptarithmetic", thus:

$$
\begin{array}{rl}
\text{LETS} & + \\
\text{WAVE} & = \\
\hline
\text{LATER} &
\end{array}
$$

where each letter stands for a digit and the sum is arithmetically correct, the problem being to find the numbers represented by the letters. One of their subjects ruminated at length about what *kind* of problem this was: amongst other possibilities, he considered that it might have something to do with the positions of the letters in the alphabet, or the shapes of the letters, or that it might be treated algebraically. Each of these proposals represents a different "problem space".

We are now in a position to answer Banham's criticisms. Each of them has in effect the same content: faulty selection of the problem space from the task environment. The narrowly quantitative approach ignores those elements that *cannot* be quantified; the tendency to see the solution as a building ignores the elements that might suggest that something else would be better. And his more global criticism is based on the asssumption that a "problem solving" approach inevitably involves the selection of those aspects that permit known routine solutions; that is, that problem solving implies the solution of puzzles. But the kind of map of problem solving on which this discussion is based has no such implication; on the contrary, the suggestion is that by better understanding problem solving as a process, and specifically the kinds of problems which architects encounter and their structure, such traps for the unwary will be better avoided. They will never be avoided altogether, for there are strong psychological structures which tend to establish and maintain such thought blocks; but they can be signposted and identified.

1.4 Solving problems

So far we have considered only two elements of Newell and Simon's map of problem solving: the task environment and the problem space. It remains to be seen how the concepts of methods and production systems apply to architectural problem solving, and how the problem space is used in the process. Whether or not the problem-solving effort will be successful depends largely on whether or not the problem space is a "good" representation of the task environment. That is, it must first of all, contain a solution; in the cryptarithmetic example, the problem spaces based on the shapes of the letters and on their position in the alphabet did not contain a solution. In architecture it is possible that even a problem space which *is* a good representation of the task environment may not contain a solution; the task environment may, for example, contain conflicting demands. In this, architectural problems differ from the puzzles studied by Newell and Simon. However, assuming that this first condition is met, it is important in the case of very large problem spaces, such as are regularly encountered in architectural design, that the problem space should contain all the *structural* information which the task environment offers, but no more. "Structure in the problem space is equivalent to redundancy. By virtue of redundancy, information present in one part of the space becomes predictive — at least heuristically — of properties in another part of the space" (Newell and Simon, 1972). If the problem space contains more structure than the task environment, some will be spurious and potentially misleading; how many errors in human affairs, and especially in architecture, have arisen from importing to a problem more structure than the situation or task environment warrants? If, on the other hand, the problem space contains less structure than the task environment, the problem will take longer to solve than it need, since redundancy reduces the effective size of the problem space to be searched. In general, structure helps in selecting a course of action and in evaluating the situation to see whether it is worth going on with the current line or whether a return should be made to some previous position or idea.

Having constructed a problem space the problem solver proceeds to search it for a solution. Newell and Simon identify three basic methods of search: *recognition*, or "knowing the answer"; *generate-and-test*; and *heuristic search*. Recognition might appear trivial but it is the basic procedure of unselfconscious design, and also the most common penultimate stage of more complex design procedures; the problem is reduced to a point at which a known procedure, device, method of construction, or whatever, can be applied to the remaining stages. (We should note that too-rapid reduction or closure of the problem towards a known solution is one of the sources of Banham's criticism of the problem-solving approach.) Generate-and-test involves producing candidates for the role of "solution" and then seeing whether they in fact comply with whatever tests or rules are available for determining whether or not something is a solution. Again, generate-and-test is quite commonly used in architecture, notably in all those cases that are cases of *selection*: where it is known that what is wanted is a classical column or a toilet paper holder, or a side chair with a chromium-plated steel frame, and a number of these things are available from which, on the basis of more or less explicit criteria, we can make a choice. It is also possible for this process to be applied to whole buildings, as in what Broadbent (1973a) calls "iconic" design: a situation in which the available building types are all standardized and the "designer" simply selects the building type appropriate to the task in hand, the task itself being defined in such cases by adaptation to the building type as much as is the building type by adaptation to the task.

Generate-and-test is a good method when the generation and the testing of solutions are both easy and cheap, and the size of the problem space is not very great. But architectural design problem spaces are frequently very large. The order of size can be indicated by a simplified example given by Starr (1963). Starr considers the case of a design decision involving three components, each of which may vary in material, thickness and finish. Component 1 has four possible materials, two possible thicknesses and three possible finishes. Component 2 has four possible materials, three possible thicknesses, and two possible finishes. Component 3 has three possible materials, one possible thickness, and three possible finishes. Assuming that all the materials, thicknesses and finishes of the components are compatible, a comprehensive search of this small, determinate problem space would involve examining $4 \times 2 \times 3 \times 4 \times 3 \times 2 \times 3 \times 1 \times 3$ or 5184 potential solutions. Architectural problem spaces are in many cases not even fully determinate and obviously, even at the level of components, finishes, and so on, involve many more possibilities than have been allowed in this example. Clearly, as Starr argues, we must and do take steps to reduce the number of alternatives actually considered in any complex design problem. We must resort to the third method of search: heuristic search. The essence of heuristic search is to make use of information already obtained to guide the remaining steps of the problem-solving process; the search process is redefined as a search for information which will limit the area of search, ultimately to the point at which generate-and-test or recognition methods become practicable.

All this still leaves open the question of how a problem solver selects a problem space, and here Newell and Simon state that their theory is "tentative and incomplete". However, without attempting a detailed account of these activities, they suggest that they are relatively simple; at any rate, more simple than might be supposed, and largely determined by the task environment: "typical task instructions contain a large amount of information that can be used to define a specific problem space and programme for working on the task — and this information is likely to determine which of various alternative representations a subject will use" (Newell and Simon, 1972).

Method in architecture must concern itself extensively with the question of problem space construction. In general, we start by "defining the problem". A number of initial decisions are taken which eliminate the need to examine a very great number of the possibilities. Thus it is not uncommon for an architectural task to begin with some such statement as "What is required is a 400 bed chest hospital." This proposition may or may not prove to be true on investigation, but assuming that this or some similar statement is found to be true, we can see that it greatly limits the field of study, and that the process involved can be described not merely colloquially but logically as one of definition. The problem is defined as lying in a certain class, hospitals, and the field is further reduced by adding two species, chest and 400-bed. Also implied in this formulation (*pace* Banham) is the inclusion of the whole in the class of buildings. Thus, in the ordinary process of approaching design problems we limit the problem by accepting or assuming certain descriptions of what the problem is, which immensely reduce the size of the problem space, and which carry with them a whole tradition of approaches, attitudes, methods and programmes which give us a great deal of further assistance.

This process is indeed very ordinary, so ordinary that its great practical significance does not attract attention; and insofar as it *has* attracted attention, it has frequently been hostile. Radicals, and particularly radical investigators of design methods, have been inclined to talk and to attempt to construct systems of design as if the acceptance of traditional definitions of problems were a bad thing; but, on the contrary, what is being suggested here is that it is a good and necessary thing, mischievous only if it is uncritical, or an excuse for a general opposition to inquiry or change. These evils will not arise so long as the bases for design are made explicit, so that they can be subjected to critical testing; but this, too, depends on method.

In architectural design, then, it appears at this very preliminary stage of the analysis that Newell and Simon are right in supposing that problem spaces are to a considerable extent ready-made. It will be necessary to consider further just how they are constructed in the first place and how they are transmitted. The next stage, the actual process of search in the problem space, is carried out by methods, programmes or plans. Programmes is the term which Newell and Simon use for the most basic of these: it is a set of rules linking more elementary behaviours or "elementary information processes". Formally a programme or "production system" is a set or hierarchy of conditional statements or *productions* of the form "IF A THEN B" where A is an environmental condition and B an action. In a production system there is no distinction between content and structure, except insofar as the order of production itself carries information. A programme is logically identical with a method or plan. "To paraphrase Polya, a method is simply a plan you use twice" (Newell and Simon 1972). Since the term "method" is used here to include the process of establishing a problem space, and "plan" has other connotations in architectural discourse, the term "programme" will generally be used for this aspect of the problem-solving process.

Once again, we can illustrate the development of programmes by considering it as a process of definition. If we are faced with a genuine problem and not a mere puzzle, we are, at the beginning of our inquiry, in a condition of uncertainty. We are trying to locate an object in a field, and to do this we must seek information. We are playing a game like twenty questions, in which, if we are clever, we can locate a single object amongst a very large number (1,048,576, to be precise). Cleverness in this case is equivalent to economy, to having a sophisticated as opposed to an unsophisticated search strategy; that is, referring back to Starr's example, cleverness is *not* having to consider 5184 possibilities. Now it can be shown — in fact it is a basic proposition of information theory — that the most sophisticated strategy in asking questions is to ask them in such a way as to eliminate exactly half the possibilities each time. A common, if elementary, illustration is the problem of locating by questioning a single chessman on an invisible chessboard. As we can see from Figure 1.1, six

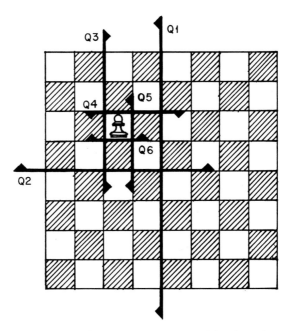

Figure 1.1   Locating a chessman on an invisible chess board

questions are required. Of course, this sophisticated approach is made possible by the fact that the problem space is extremely well structured, or highly redundant, the problem space in this case being the chess board. If we did not know that a chessboard consists of 64 squares in an array 8 × 8, the problem would be much more difficult, since we should "waste" a lot of questions on discovering the shape and structure of the problem space. This example thus serves to illustrate both Newell and Simon's point about the importance of structure in the problem space and the advantage of having a ready-made problem space with which to tackle a problem. The point becomes even more important when we realize that the problem space for architectural design is not two-dimensional, like a chessboard, but must necessarily have a very large number of dimensions, so that it cannot be represented or modelled as a whole in any simple intelligible way. We can also see that this process, or programme, for searching the problem space, in which each question restricts the space remaining to be searched, is a process of definition.

1.5 Plan of this work

The outline of the process of problem solving just given provides the plan for what follows. Chapter 2 deals with knowledge and information, since goals, problem spaces, programmes and tactics all depend on the kind, quality and structure of the knowledge available to the designer. Chapter 3 describes the task environment of architecture, or, more exactly, the professional "extended problem space" within which the problem spaces for particular tasks are constructed. Chapter 4 considers the question of goals in architecture: again the generalized goals of the extended problem space rather than the specific goals of individual designers. Chapter 5 investigates some types or classes of architectural problems and the problem spaces appropriate to them, and on this basis proposes a general structure for architectural problem spaces. And Chapter 6 proceeds to the level of programmes, the more detailed methods of problem solution, and also treats the question of detail design.

Knowledge in architecture

2.1 Introduction

If goals, problem spaces, programmes and tactics all depend on the kind, quality and structure of the knowledge available to the designer, it becomes important to ask, what is this knowledge like? Information has been spoken of rather lightly, as if it were always quite clear what is and what is not information in the context of a given design problem; but this an over-simplification. It is not necessarily at all clear; even if we are sure that what we have is relevant information, it may not be clear how it is to be used; we may know the moves of the chess pieces, but not yet the shape of the board, or vice versa. Different views and approaches to the question, what is going to count as information?, can lead to radically different problem spaces, and certain kinds of view can ensure that the problem space used is not an adequate map of the task environment. It is necessary, therefore, to examine at some length the relation between knowledge and architecture.

2.2 Architecture as craft

Theoretical understanding, throughout human history until very re-cently, has been a slow and tentative addition to practical skill. With the rise of science, this situation has to some extent been reversed in many productive activities, and almost completely reversed in educa-tion. The influence of widespread theory-based education on attitudes to knowledge has been profound. More and more it is taken for granted that skilled people — pilots, surgeons, engineers, architects — do their work largely or wholly by applying thoroughly-worked out scientific theory; that their practice and their available theories are mirror images of one another, or related as the mould and the casting. Such a view has become conventional, and it is supported by the long and arduous courses of predominantly theoretical training which candidates for these and other professions must undergo. Occupations that do not require such a theoretical preparation are regarded as somehow defective, and occupational groups who wish to raise their social status frequently press for an extended period of formal education of an increased theoretical content.

Voices, both authoritative and polemic, have been raised against this tendency, and the de-schooling of society has been proposed (Illich, 1971). Such arguments have not so far proved very effective. Professional organizations regularly complain to the various institutions of higher education that their graduates or diplomates are lacking in practical skills. The educators very reasonably retort that the right place to learn practical skills is in practice. But the real issue is one of orientation and attitude. The newly qualified entrants to the professions are not merely inexperienced; they are unwilling to accept the gap which exists between their painfully acquired knowledge and the problems of day-to-day professional life. (Of course the reverse may also be the case: the practitioners may be out of date and unwilling to accept new theory-based approaches. But that is a separate problem.) For, though many of the professions now draw heavily on stocks of knowledge and techniques which have been generated by scientific research, the mirror-image or mould-and-casting theory of the relationship between theory and practice is largely mistaken. Every profession is still to a great extent a craft, and its practice and progress in most cases depends as much on the growth of these craft elements as on the development of theory. In the more technically advanced professions, research and practice are in a symbiotic relationship, each conferring benefits on the other but nevertheless quite separate, and having their own lives and character. Where the incursion of science into the problems of the profession is historically recent and less fundamental, the link between the two may be tenuous indeed.

Some illustrations may help to bring out the importance of craft skills, even in professions with a high technical and scientific content. As a first example, let us consider commercial airline pilots. Pilots are trained in simulators, and pilots for major airlines constantly refresh their training in the simulator when they are not in the air. These simulators, as we might expect, reproduce the instrumentation and the visual information which the pilot would have in a real aircraft. But they are also constructed, with great trouble and expense, so that the simulated control cabin moves on a system of hydraulic rams, as the real aircraft would move in response to the controls. Proprioceptive feedback is necessary if the whole training experience is to be effective- the pilots still fly "by the seat of their pants", even in modern aircraft with their comprehensive instrumentation. Such "seat of the pants" knowledge is essential in almost every practical activity. Often it is unverbalized: we can say that in these cases the practitioner knows "what to do" but not "what he does".

A further example, this time from medical education, may be helpful. This story was told me by a practitioner of an older generation; but things have, perhaps, not changed so much. A group of graduate students were "walking the wards" with a distinguished physician. They were asked to examine a patient with a lump in the abdomen. Each student poked the lump, examined the case history, asked various questions and so on. After the examinations were complete, the great man asked, "Well, gentlemen, what is it?" Various suggestions were offered and rejected. At last, the knowledge and inspiration of the students exhausted, the answer was given: "That, gentlemen, is an hydatid cyst". There was a pause, and then a voice (no doubt from the rear of the group) was heard to ask "Sir, how do you know?" The answer came without hesitation: "It *feels* like a hydatid cyst." The point here, whether or not the medical detail is right, is that the students were in fact being taught something for which the English language does not provide adequate words: how something *feels*. In the absence of words, and thus of theory, teaching has to be by demonstration; and if the demonstration is ineffective, the only recourse is another demonstration. At that time, at least, this particular piece of medical knowledge was a craft skill; and it is the nature of craft skills that they can only be taught by demonstration.

Architects too possess craft skills of many kinds. A striking example is provided by Figure 2.1, which is a flow chart or algorithm for the process of building approval in the City of Sydney in 1972. This flow chart was first published in the "City of Sydney Strategic Plan" in that year. Despite its very considerable complexity, nobody, until that time, had bothered to work it out formally or write it down. Yet a great many architects had learned to guide their projects through this process as quickly and efficiently as the process itself permitted. To the novice in practice it was an appalling mystery, to the experienced practitioner something done automatically. Yet it is very doubtful if any of the experienced practitioners could have written down the process without much effort and error. (It was finally done by a firm of management consultants.) As Wade (1977) puts it, "most architects have learned problem solving by engaging in it, not by understanding the organisation of the process."

The impact of other kinds of knowledge on architectural design can only be understood against the background of this craft knowledge. It is therefore worthwhile to describe the nature and effects of craft knowledge in somewhat more detail. One of the most important characteristics of craft knowledge, transmission by demonstration, has already been identified. This carries with it an unwillingness, and indeed an inability, to distinguish between different kinds of results achieved; for example, between those aspects of a plan which make for good circulation, and those which make for a certain aesthetic result. We may illustrate this from an early manual of method, "Roriczer on Pinnacles" (Holt, 1947). Roriczer wrote in the fifteenth century, and he provides an algorithm for pinnacle design, which commences: "Would you draw a plan for a pinnacle after the masons art, by regular geometry? Then heave to, and draw a square ..." And he goes on to give a quite elaborate geometric construction, derived ultimately from Plato. But he gives no reasons for adopting this construction rather than another; he makes no attempt to distinguish between what is important for stability and what is important for aesthetic effect; he simply gives a set of rules for securing the desired result, in the manner of a recipe. This kind of "global" approach has often been noted by commentators on the assessment process in architecture schools.

In general, craft knowledge is operative knowledge; knowing how, or "know-how" rather than knowing what. To the extent that it is figurative, i.e. called up before the mind's eye, it is sparsely verbalized; it need not be verbalized at all. Hence the reliance, as we have seen, on demonstration rather than explanation. Insofar as verbal rules are used they are proverbial; formulae used to release stored knowledge rather than the knowledge itself. Thus, in the good old days before the adoption of the metric system, architects used the rule "half the span in inches plus two" to estimate the size of timber joists. The only warrant or excuse for such rules is that, in certain rather limited sets of circumstances, they work. Sturt, in his classic autobiographical description of the craftsman's way of life *The Wheelwright's Shop* (Sturt, 1923), has made the point exactly:

> "The nature of this knowledge should be noted. It was set out in no book. It was not scientific... My own case was typical. I knew that the hind wheels had to be five feet two inches high and the fore-wheels four feet two; that the 'sides' must be cut from the best four-inch heart of oak, and so on. This sort of thing I knew, and in vast detail in the course of time; but I seldom knew why. And that is how most other men knew... the whole body of knowledge was a mystery, a piece of folk knowledge, residing in the folk collectively, but never wholly in any individual."

Craft knowledge thus depends on faith; the mysteries of the craft are what the master knows, and they lead to mysticism. On the one hand everything seems down to earth and practical; but because there is no generalization, no theory, no rigorous investigation, failures, when they occur, whether because the rule of thumb has been applied beyond its proper scope, or through some entirely contingent circumstance, cannot be understood. This element of risk and uncertainty makes the rules of the craft, or the individual's habitual working patterns, not so much a guarantee of success as a sort of magical ritual designed to ward off failure.

Craft knowledge is also poorly structured, or lacking in structure. This is much the same as saying that it is operative knowledge. A feature of all operative thought is that the thinker is a prisoner of the system of behaviour, unable to stand outside it, to take an overview, to make it figurative, and thus to analyse it into its parts and distinguish their systematic connections. (It follows from Godel's theorem that this is true to some extent of all knowledge, but it is especially characteristic of craft knowledge.) The level that will permit this kind of overview is the level of theory; in architecture, the still embryo study of method.

Those who have much experience in architectural practice will no doubt recognize the match between much of everyday architectural activity and the description of craft knowledge offered here. In particular, they will perhaps have noted Sturt's reference to the vast accumulation of detailed knowledge built up over the course of time; the kind of knowledge that leads the experienced architect to know what size and shape a door frame must be: the depth of the rebate for weatherproofing, the thickness of the jamb to take the screws for hinges, the largest sized pieces of the appropriate timber commercially available, the need for a back-ploughing to control shrinkage and its usefulness in preventing water crossing between the two skins of the cavity brick wall by way of the back of the frame, and a dozen other things, many of which are now to be found in manuals and handbooks of practice, but which few of the older generations of practitioners learned in that sort of way. At a somewhat higher level of organization, many offices have solutions to standard problems which are known to "work"; that is, to meet the usually inexplicit but nonetheless real criteria of performance and appearance which that particular group has developed. And individuals may have a style of dealing with whole buildings, composed of all sorts of strange things — preferred geometrical shapes, methods of construction, and details all together. Analysing such sets of assumptions systematically is a great deal of hard work, and contributes nothing to the solution of the immediate pressing problems of practice, whatever its long-term advantages. So it is seldom if ever done.

This unexamined or craft character of much architectural knowledge at all levels produces in architects a defensive and dogmatic attitude. In general the profession's response to studies of method has been a classic example of Schon's "dynamic conservatism" (Schon,

1971). Broadbent (1973a) quotes Eric Lyons, a deservedly admired architect and later president of the RIBA: "Design method, oh, yes. That's where they do all those charts and diagrams instead of designing buildings?" The existing craft-based system actively resists analysis, partly with good reason, because of the effort and time involved, and the limited efficacy of the results so far secured, and partly out of fear based on the mysterious nature of so much architectural knowledge. Wordsworth (1800), writing of the problems of the poet, has precisely expressed the difficulty: "...his own feelings are his stay and support, and, if he set them aside in one instance, he may be induced to repeat this act till his mind shall lose all confidence in itself..." Nevertheless, there is difficulty and embarrassment in the established approach too. Wade (1977) gives the example of a student who, having challenged a group of behavioural scientists as to why designers were not appointed to behavioural science faculties, was asked what the architect had to offer the behavioural scientists. He could only reply, "A way of thinking about things." Similarly challenged, as they sometimes are, as to what the architect has to contribute to society at large, few practitioners could do better.

2.3   Knowledge in architectural discourse

Contemporary architects are not the first to have trouble in explaining what they are about to clients who are men of the word not the eyes. Jonson made fun of Inigo Jones for and through his stock phrases:

> "............................he'll tell you
> It cannot else be feazable, or conduce:
> These are his ruling words." (Jonson, 1633)

But when serious theoretical problems arise, as they have done from time to time in the history of architecture, architects and apologists for architecture have been forced to borrow from the stock of theories obligingly provided by other disciplines. Two such bodies of borrowing are of considerable importance in the development of method, and continue to exercise an influence: rationalism and romanticism. The history of both and their interconnection in architectural discourse is well known and will be reviewed only briefly here.

   Architecture faced its first intellectual crisis since the Renaissance in the late eighteenth century. In the late seventeenth century and well into the eighteenth, writing about architecture runs smoothly between well-defined banks. The existence of the great tradition of classical architecture is taken for granted; dispute centres around questions of the interpretation of the tradition and the scope for originality. The tradition is not treated unhistorically but ahistorically; there is little or no attempt at systematization. Within the tradition architects were quite unselfconsciously eclectic, and they acknowledged nothing outside. True, Perrault sought "...debrouiller l'embarras et la confusion ou les Auteurs Modernes ont laissé la plus grande partie de ce qui appartient aux cinq espèces de Colonnes" (Perrault, 1683), but this seems, at least according to Herrmann (1973), to have been merely rationalizing tidy-mindedness, rather than the product of any sense of history. Colen Campbell is more typical:

> "We must, in Justice, acknowledge very great Obligations to those Restorers of Architecture, which the Fifteenth and Sixteenth Centuries produced in Italy. Bramante, Barbaro, Sansovino, Sangallo, Michel Angelo, Raphael Urbin, Julio Romano, Serglio, Labaco, Scamozzi, and many others, who have greatly help'd to raise this Noble Art from the Ruins of Barbarity: But above all, the great Palladio..." (Campbell, 1717)

Here we notice the eclectic treatment of the tradition, and later in the same passage the condemnation of the continental baroque, as departing too far from the central tendency.

During the early part of the eighteenth century, beginning with the *Dictionnaire Historique et Critique* of Bayle, comparative historical studies made their appearance. The writers of the Enlightenment found the comparative method a valuable tool in criticizing the existing state of society, though at first their method was literary rather than observational. One quite unintended effect of this search for consistency in the records of the past was the calling into question of the classical tradition in architecture. This questioning too was largely literary in its origins and methods; the monuments of architecture outside Italy remained little known. At first the issue was one of historical theory; the received doctrine of the classical tradition was that what was oldest was best (Lovejoy, 1948); Roman architecture was thus superior to, for example, Gothic architecture. It followed that Greek architecture, being older still, was, in its turn, superior to Roman. So, at least, Laugier argues (1753). Even as a theoretical proposition this generated some controversy. When it was followed, in 1758, by the first publication of Greek remains, Le Roy's *Les Ruines des Plus Beaux Monuments de la Grèce*, Piranesi was moved to defend the honour of his country with his *Della Magnificenza ed Architettura de Romani*. The quarrel raged through thirty years and several countries. There is no need to follow its course here. The banks were broken; and the situation was rapidly and increasingly complicated by a growing flood of historical publication. Henceforth, writers on architecture were forced to take up one of two general positions: a purely taxonomic approach, arranging and classifying their material with a growing historical and archaeological sophistication; or an attempt to establish architectural principles of universal validity. In the latter enterprise Laugier was again a pioneer and set a precedent, even for those who rejected his conclusions.

Laugier was not a practitioner, not even an amateur; he was an intellectual, and his views were correspondingly abstract and extreme. He was widely criticized by contemporary professionals for proposing rules that were too restrictive, both aesthetically and in terms of practical construction. But his very extremism, which makes him such a perfect example of architectural rationalism, served also to keep his work alive as an active irritant in the system of architectural thought; fifty years later architectural writers were still seeking to answer him. Laugier was, of course, not only a rationalist; his ideas had many sources. He was a Jesuit priest, steeped in the classical authors and especially in Plato and Aristotle. The rules for architecture which he gives in his *Essai* are, as Herrmann (1962) points out, a paraphrase of Aristotle's rules of poetry; every part must be essential:

> "I should like to convince everybody of a truth which I myself believe absolutely, namely that the parts of an architectural order are the parts of the building itself. They must therefore be applied so that they not only adorn but actually constitute the building. The existence of the building must depend so completely on the union of these parts that not a single one could be taken away without the whole building collapsing."

The idea that the parts of a building should be what they seem was not new; many of his critics accused Laugier of plagiarizing Cordemoy, whose influence he acknowledged. What was new was taking it literally instead of metaphorically: the attempt to find some one fundamental principle "self-evidently so" from which the rest of architecture could be deduced. And Laugier's justification for his first principle, by way of history, was quite new too. As was common at the time, his history was not empirical; it was an imaginary history, an account of what might have happened; what, in a rational universe, *must* have happened. And what must have happened, Laugier thought, was the construction, at the beginning of all construction, of a "primitive hut"; a hut not unlike the bowers and shelters which Laugier may have seen in the countryside: four posts set in the ground at the corners of a square; framing tied to their tops to join them; and a simple thatched gable pitched over all. The orders and the pedimented gable, and of course the roof itself, were thus justified; nothing else was.

Laugier did not invent rationalism as a philosophy; he merely applied it to architecture. Like other major intellectual and cultural movements, the origins of rationalism are not simple. But its classic formulation is due to Descartes, roughly a hundred years before Laugier wrote. Whether or not, as Broadbent (1973a) suggests, Descartes derived his rules of logic from his thoughts about architecture, he is certainly a fundamental source for most subsequent attempts to rationalize or systematize design. His philosophy continues to influence continental, and especially French, thinkers right down to the present, and provides the higher order theory from which the tradition of architectural rationalism begun by Laugier has constantly renewed itself. Descartes' four rules of logic, the basic principles of rationalism, were as follows:

> "The first rule was to accept as true nothing that I did not know to be self evidently so; that is to say, to avoid carefully precipitancy and prejudice, and to apply my judgement to nothing but that which showed itself so clearly and distinctly to my mind that I should never have occasion to doubt it. The second was to divide each difficulty I should examine into as many parts as possible, and as would be required the better to solve it. The third was to conduct my thoughts in an orderly fashion, starting with what was simplest and easiest to know, and rising little by little to the knowledge of the most complex, even supposing an order where there is no natural precedence among the objects of knowledge. The last rule was to make so complete an enumeration of the links in an argument, and to pass them all so carefully under review, that I could be sure I had missed nothing."
> (Descartes, 1637)

There are few modern writers on method in architecture who do much more than follow Descartes' prescription.

Laugier is the father of structural rationalism: the notion that architecture is "nothing but" structure. The trouble with rationalism generally, however, is that it is difficult to justify the selection of the first principle, which takes place by "intuition". Some parts of our knowledge, such as our knowledge of the validity of the syllogism, do depend on intuition; but they survive because there is, empirically, no alternative. Architectural rationalism, however, has never operated at any very elevated epistemological level. There were, and are, plenty of other candidates besides structure for the position of architectural first principle. Thus Durand, the most influential of early nineteenth century architectural writers and teachers, takes Laugier severely to task for having chosen entirely the wrong principle; in *his* opinion the first or governing principle of architecture is economy:

> "The exercise of architectural talent, should therefore be con-fined to the solution of two problems: in a private building to produce the most suitable one possible with the money spe-cified; in a public building, its purpose being stated, to produce the least expensive one." (Durand, 1809)

More sophisticated versions admit of more than one "first principle". Viollet-le-Duc, a pupil of Leclerc, who was himself a pupil of Durand, in a passage already referred to, admits at least two and perhaps three: programme, materials and proportion.

The continuation of rationalism, through Choisy, Perret and Le Corbusier, into the general background aggregation of ideas which makes up the conventional wisdom of modern architecture, has been documented by Banham (1960). Large and constructive as its in-fluence has been, the rationalist tradition has become an obstruction to the development of architectural method, and this in two ways: first, by encouraging the belief that design must proceed in accordance with *a priori* principles, rather than principles sought in the design situation or task environment; and second by supporting the notion that the selection of principles can be a matter of individual taste, and is not itself subject to criticism, that it is enough if the principle appears clear and distinct to the designer. The ill-effects of the latter belief have been compounded by the influence on architecture of a separate or at least separable tradition in modern ideas: the tradition of romanticism.

Rationalism was first taken over into architectural discourse as a response to the challenge of history, as a way of making sense of the intolerable diversity which faced architects when the classical tradi-tion began to be undermined. On the European continent and especially in France, rationalism also proved sufficiently flexible and adaptable to meet the gradual onset of industrialization: new materials and new planning problems were, in the main, absorbed into the practice of architecture by rationalist architects. In England indus-trialization progressed more rapidly, and the rising power of the middle classes posed a greater problem for architecture. Cartesian rationalism had little prestige amongst English thinkers, for whom the most sophisticated model of knowledge was the empiricism of Bacon and Newton. In attempting to explain themselves to the new patronage of self-made men and political committees, with standards based not on the old cultivated taste or respect for it, but on the ledger and the machine shop, architects were fortunate in having the unwitting assistance of men better trained in the handling of words: the English romantic poets.

The romantic movement is historically extraordinarily complicated. It is less a coherent set of ideas than a diffuse and inconsistent set of reactions to the emergent forces of science and of centralized government. In one branch it begins with Rousseau, in another with the English tradition of gardening. However, it is not necessary to analyse this complex ferment in depth in order to bring out the ideas that had the most immediate and lasting effects on architectural method. The essential doctrine is the doctrine of artistic inspiration, a new kind of truth inherently individual and essentially anti-scientific. This doctrine was formulated in the early years of the nineteenth century by a small group of writers whose names, at least, are still taught to most schoolchildren in the English-speaking world: Wordsworth, Coleridge, Keats, Shelley, Byron. Even before architecture, serious literature had had to confront the mass audience, and, by and large, cared very little for what it saw.

"For a multitude of causes, unknown to former times, are now acting with a combined force to blunt the discriminating powers of the mind, and, unfitting it for all voluntary exertion, to reduce it to a state of almost savage torpor. The most effective of these causes are the great national events which are daily taking place, and the increasing accumulation of men in cities, where the uniformity of their occupations produces a craving for extraordinary incident, which the rapid communication of intelligence hourly gratifies."   (Wordsworth, 1800)

This vigorous dissatisfaction with "the public" was accompanied by a defensive reaction against the market, against commerce, against industry, and against science. Defensive, because these things were felt as forces acting in conjunction to subordinate literature to the market with its "frantic novels, sickly and stupid German tragedies, and deluges of idle and extravagant stories in verse." A reaction, in that new and extravagant claims were made for the status of literature and "the arts" generally. Art for the first time ceased to mean skill in any kind of making, and came to mean a limited class of production only; creative, original, organic, become words of praise to oppose to imitative, mechanical; liberty was opposed to rule (Williams, 1958). Most significant for our present purpose is the emergence of the claim to a special kind of knowledge and a special kind of truth, imaginative truth, which is the special prerogative of the poet or genius; genius in its modern sense is another word coined at this time. Again, an often quoted passage from the same source summarizes the whole complex of ideas as well as it can be done:

> "Aristotle, I have been told, has said, that Poetry is the most philosophic of all writing; it is so: its object is truth, not individual and local, but general, and operative; not standing upon external testimony, but carried alive into the heart by passion; truth which is its own testimony... The Poet writes under one restriction only, namely, the necessity of giving immediate pleasure to a human being possessed of that information which may be expected from him, not as a lawyer, a physician, a mariner, an astronomer, or a natural philosopher, but as a Man... To this knowledge which all men carry about with them, and to these sympathies in which, without any discipline other than that of our daily life, we are fitted to take delight, the Poet principally directs his attention..."
>
> (Wordsworth, 1800)

Like the rationalist tradition, romanticism has conferred many benefits on architecture; it is the mainspring, or perhaps one should say the vital force, of the Arts and Crafts Movement, of Ruskin and Morris; especially it has contributed to individual freedom of expression and to concern with the process of production. On method, however, its influence has been stultifying. For, while it is possible for the theory of genius and individual inspiration as a source of knowledge which is not in its nature subject to any kind of criticism to reach a sort of accommodation with rationalism, in that intuition can apply to the "concept" and rationalism to the details, it is not possible to establish any similar compromise between romanticism, in this limited sense, and the serious empirical study of problem-solving procedures in architecture.

It is, however, hard to say, in the present state of the art, which is the more obstructive to progress in architecture: rationalism, which provides a veneer of observation and careful thinking on bases which are profoundly irrational; or the belief in inspired conceptual design, basing itself on knowledge revealed to genius and superior to ordinary processes of investigation. Yet these ideas are deeply embedded in the architectural consciousness; and in default of any better (that is, any more truthlike and more telling) explanation of what architects are about, will continue to be used. As things stand today, the only alternative source of theory is in the philosophy of science, which is itself in a state of some turmoil.

2.4 Scientific knowledge and architecture

In the last two sections, traditional or craft knowledge has been criticized as too narrowly empirical for many of the purposes of architecture; and the rationalist and romantic traditions have been criticized as too abstract and *a priori*. These observations are not especially original. Many thoughtful architects have concluded that some better kind of knowledge was necessary to leaven the architectural lump; and, taking the example of engineering, have inferred that the kind of knowledge required is scientific knowledge. After all, until very recently science has, despite romantic resistance, enjoyed great prestige; and in principle it seemed that architecture should not separate itself from such a major force of the times. The writings of the pioneers of modern architecture often display a curious amalgam of rationalism, romanticism, and appeals to the new science; for example, Le Corbusier (1923), Gropius (1935) and Moholy (1928). The level of scientific understanding displayed is generally that of the intelligent layman; that is, rather low. Science thus came to occupy a curious position in the architectural pantheon: admired and misunderstood, welcomed as a saviour and yet rejected as a potential tyrant.

The growth, after the second world war, of building science, and its influence on architectural education, has not changed the situation as much as might be expected. Architects now acquire a much better knowledge of certain aspects of the behaviour of structures, materials, and environmental physics; but their concern with these matters is practical, not theoretical. They know, and their teachers know, that in their later career they will have little need to perform the detailed calculations, let alone recall or understand the theory on which they are based. The metatheory, the philosophy of science, is altogether outside their circle of interest and is not taught; and reasonably enough, since it is not taught to many science students. Thus the view of science held by architects in general continues to be that of the "educated layman" who is not specifically educated in science. This may be an acceptable state of affairs while the impact of science on architecture is confined to certain enclaves, or areas of specialist advice. However, insofar as architecture can or should be completely transformed by adopting scientific knowledge and scientific method in their entirety, architects must come to understand what science is about at a much more profound level. The questions, how is scientific knowledge different from or better than other kinds of knowledge? and, how like or unlike is architectural activity to scientific activity? become central ones for method.

To start with it may be helpful to look at some rather common or conventional views of what science is. The first of these is often associated with the name of Sir Francis Bacon, and it is called the inductive view of science. Bacon was not himself a scientist, but one of the first great popularizers of science. And the feature of science, or natural philosophy, upon which he fixed as distinguishing it from other branches of philosophy was the making of observations and experiments. There was no room for hypothesis or theory in Bacon's view of the growth of science; knowledge grew by the collection of observations. And this view was accepted by many eminent scientists after Bacon, and seems to have been widely attributed also to Newton, on the basis of the celebrated phrase which occurs at the end of the *Principia*: "Et hypotheses non fingo." Theory was supposed to emerge from this collection of observations by a logical process. And as the logical process of obtaining many instances from a single proposition is called deduction, so the logical process of obtaining a single general theory from the observation of many instances was called induction.

Now even this rather general beginning to the subject of scientific knowledge introduces subjects which are hotly contested by a numerous society of specialists. What Bacon and Newton did or did not think on various questions related to science is a matter of concern and dispute for the historians of science. And to go further into these matters raises more and more technical philosophical issues, on which an architect is not well-qualified to write. The result is all too likely to be yet another layman's view, no better than the lay views it seeks to replace. Nevertheless, these issues have an important bearing on method in architecture. And the bridge between architecture and philosophy is not likely to be begun from the philosopher's end. So what will be undertaken here is a lay account of some specific ideas in the field, and an indication of their relevance to architecture and their influence on later and more specifically architectural arguments, but with the qualification that this account has no pretensions to authority or rigour.

The problem of induction is closely related to the problems of architectural method; for as we shall see later, a conventional view of method in architecture is that it is or should be inductive. But induction in science turns out to have serious difficulties. Some of these difficulties were pointed out as early as the eighteenth century by Hume in his *Treatise on Human Nature* in the form of two principles:

"That there is nothing in any object, consider'd in itself, which can afford us a reason for drawing a conclusion beyond it."

and

"That even after the observation of the frequent or constant conjunction of objects, we have no reason to draw any inference concerning any object beyond those of which we have had experience..." (Hume, 1739–1740)

In other words, deduction works because the conclusions say no more than the premises say; but in induction the conclusion *does* say more than the premises say, and how is this to be justified? Despite numerous attempts, this problem remained for long unsolved; at least Russell regarded it as unsolved when he wrote his *History of Western Philosophy* (Russell, 1946). Popper considers himself to have solved this problem (Popper, 1963) though he has not so much solved it as dissolved it; that is, he has proposed a view of science in which induction does not appear to be required. In so doing he deprived scientific knowledge of any claim to logical necessity, and substituted the ideas of well-tested knowledge and truthlikeness.

Popper's proposed solution to the problem of induction depends on the proposition that all knowledge is impregnated with theory. That is, there is no such thing as "pure" observation or "mere" sense data. Observations are made and data gathered on the basis of some belief or theory in terms of which those observations or data will be useful or significant. So the collection of data does not produce the theory: the theory was there beforehand in the mind of the scientist. This, however, raises two other issues. First, where do the theories come from? And second, what are the observations for? The first of these questions is the easier to answer, at least in a preliminary way. Theories spring from previous theories, from likely stories, from myths or conjectures; they are products of the creative power of the human mind, aided by human society which has learnt to conserve and transmit such products. Popper is not so much concerned with the psychology of theory production as with its logic, and this has led to some misunderstandings with other historians and philosophers of science (Lakatos and Musgrave, 1970). His point is not that scientists may not sometimes be led to formulate new theories by brooding over an accumulation of observations, but that the observations must have been accumulated on the basis of some theory, which they turn out not to fit too well, and that the new theory is logically *independent* of the data.

What then is the connection between the data and the theory? What *are* the observations for? The obvious, because traditional, answer is that they serve to confirm the theory. This Popper denies. On the contrary, he considers that the purpose of collecting observations is to attempt to falsify the theory; theories that are allowed to survive and become part of the body of science are not those which have been "confirmed" but those that have survived the most rigorous tests so far devised for them. Confirmatory instances, or supporting evidence can be found for theories which are both specious and useless (e.g. von Danniken, 1967). Science on the other hand consists of well-tested knowledge. Amongst the tests may be mentioned the test of consistency with other well-tested theories, so that science, though certainly not completely internally consistent, and less consistent that many *a priori* theories, is more consistent than, for example, craft knowledge. Science cannot be completely internally consistent because it is not "true" in the sense that all doubt about its propositions has been for ever eliminated; it is a picture of the world, a portrait which is constantly being redrawn to a better likeness of the original, which becomes more and more "truthlike", to use Popper's term, but never *becomes* the original. "More truthlike" here is *not* equivalent to "more probable". The arguments are too technical to be detailed here, (but see Popper, (1963), p. 228 ff.)

However, the foregoing account is too simple, even for a layman's essay. It amounts to what has become known as "naïve falsification theory". An unwarrantable distinction is drawn between observational propositions (data, observations) and theoretical propositions (theories, conjectures, intuitions). Observational propositions are already theory impregnated (Lakatos, 1970). Nor are they themselves "proved"; propositions can only be derived in logic from other propositions, never from observation. And finally it can be shown that there are important scientific theories that cannot be disproved by a finite number of observations. These difficulties, and others, are partly overcome by "sophisticated falsificationism" in which...

> "A specific theory T is *falsified* if and only if another theory T' has been proposed with the following characteristics: (1) T' has excess empirical content over T: that is, it predicts *novel* facts, that is, facts improbable in the light of, or even forbidden, by T: (2) T' explains the previous success of T, that is, all the unrefuted content of T is included (within the limits of observational error) in the content of T': and (3) some of the excess content of T' is corroborated." (Lakatos, 1970)

In this more sophisticated statement the issue of what is fact and what is theory becomes a methodological decision: the comparison of competing theories will include comparison and testing of the theories which go along with their "facts".

If we look at scientific activity and scientific knowledge in the light of Popper's solution of the problem of induction, then there are some suggestive analogies with design, but also some significant differences. A number of theories of design have taken an inductive view of the design process (see Chapter 5); that is, they have proposed that what the designer does or should do is to gather facts about the proposed building, and then either by an intuitive leap or by a logical process (such as some kind of mathematical model) integrate these facts into a design. Now clearly this is the same logically as the problem of induction in science, in that the mere collection of facts is supposed to generate another kind of entity with more structure, a design; so that we can say with some confidence that this model of design is a false one, although a design is not exactly the same as a scientific theory. And Popper's approach suggests a new kind of model: design must commence with some theory or theories as to what the proposed building is to be and proceed by the gathering of information to test those theories and adapt them to form new and better theories. Here, however, the analogy is somewhat cruder and the differences between science and design are more important. For design must end in a unique solution, a *final* "theory", whereas it is the nature of science in Popper's view to be progressive, to generate alternative theories and to replace existing ones. Of course one might consider the individual building or design as corresponding to an individual theory, and a series of buildings or designs, within the work of a particular firm or historical period, as corresponding to the general progress of science. Eberhard Zeidler, architect of the McMaster Hospital, in an unpublished lecture delivered at Royal North Shore Hospital Sydney in 1976, used Popper's model PI-TT-EE-P2 in which PI is an initial problem, TT a tentative theory and EE attempted error elimination, concluding in a new problem P2, in describing the development of his ideas through a series of hospital designs. Let us, however, confine ourselves for the present to the development of an individual design.

Then, assuming that the designer must start with a theory T as to the nature of the building, what will be the characteristics of a new hypothesis or theory T1 such that it will be "better"? How does design progress? The criteria for a better scientific theory given previously are at least suggestive. They are, first, excess empirical content; a better scientific theory predicts novel facts. In what sense, if any, can a new design predict? Clearly it makes predictions about the form of the final building and its interactions with the behaviour of its users; and these may indeed be novel, in the sense that the passage from Lakatos suggests, that is, forbidden by, or not accommodated by, the initial model T1. The second condition, that of including everything envisaged by T1 that has not been refuted, is clearly also desirable in the case of an improved design, though in practice this condition is sometimes not met. The final criterion, that some at least of the new predictions must be corroborated, is also relevant; for the varied or more detailed proposals will generate a demand for further or more detailed information, which will permit their predictions to be tested and either corroborated or falsified.

If this description of the progress of design seems elementary and obvious, it should be noted that it excludes not just one but two commonly held notions of the way in which design should proceed: the pure inductive theory and the pure conceptual theory. Both of these will be discussed and criticized at greater length later. At least two other issues of importance are raised. First, how does design terminate? For it is not clear on this account that there would ever be a point at which the current design Tn should or could not be replaced by still another Tn+1. This is indeed a very difficult question, and an extended answer will be attempted in Chapter 5. However, a partial answer is that in design the process usually reaches a point at which no new design can be devised which represents an improvement on Tn either in the direction of increased empirical content, or in the direction of eliminating anomalies; this still leaves the problem of deciding between competing "equal" theories or designs. In practice, of course, the process is often terminated arbitrarily by limitations of cost and time.

Secondly, our attention has been drawn to the theory-laden nature of "facts". This is of the utmost importance in practical design. There is a constant temptation to seek, in the process of design, for some point of security; and the practical man finds this in the "facts". This recalls Russell's observation that the practical man is the man who has no idea what to do in practice. For the "facts" of design are of very varying quality, and many of them turn out to be largely *a priori* theories, with little or no empirical content. And just as the improvement of theories in science may involve alternately regarding one proposition or group of propositions as a "theory" and therefore subject to testing and improvement, or as "fact" and therefore part of the given background, so the development and conclusion of a design process turns out to involve a similar alternation and mutual adaptation between what is given or desired and what is proposed or designed.

This discussion has departed considerably from the view which most architects would hold of science as a useful source of facts and generalizations. And it is true that building science and building research are a source of much harder, better tested or more "truthlike" propositions than many of the other sources on which architecture relies for its "facts". But firstly, without some understanding of the ground rules of science, such "facts" are likely to be treated either with undue scepticism or an equally dangerous dogmatism. And secondly, the constant accumulation of "facts" without some theory or method by which to organize them, may do as much harm as good. It is interesting in this context to note the relative failure of the lexical approach to making sense of architectural information, exemplified by the Ci/Sfb system of classification. This approach relies on the establishment of an *a priori* "reasonable" organization of the material; but since it is not based on any design method its rationality conflicts with its use; anomalies abound; users have to memorize the system, which adds to their load of trivial information; and no very marked improvement in the success of designs has resulted. Again, to make use of facts we must have a theory. As Hillier and Jones (1977) put it:

"The architect today is at the centre of an extraordinary proliferation of literature and documentation. He has endless "information" available to him had he the time to read it all, but little to guide him as to when he might need a particular piece of it... Simply increasing the amount of information available to the designer does not necessarily increase his effective knowledge. It may diminish it."

Earlier, the question of where theories or notional designs come from was passed over rather lightly. This is not likely to be satisfactory to architects. In the conventional wisdom of architecture "creativity" is highly valued; and it would seem that it is just in the generation of ideas, concepts or notional designs that creativity would be important. It is certainly a question on which method should have something to say, and to this subject the next section will be addressed.

2.5 Creativity

"It must of necessity be that even works of Genius, like every other effect, as they must have their cause, must likewise have their rules." (Reynolds, 1769–1790)

Where then do preliminary designs, notional theories, and so on come from? If, as was previously suggested, they are to be seen as adaptations or developments of earlier theories or designs, how did these, in their turn, come into being? At some point the regress through previous theories must terminate, or so it would seem. Popper's answer is that:

"Every animal is born with expectations or anticipations, which could be framed as hypotheses; a kind of hypothetical knowledge ... This inborn knowledge, these inborn expectations, will, if disappointed, create *our first problems*; and the ensuing growth of our knowledge may therefore be described as consisting throughout of corrections and modifications of previous knowledge." (Popper, 1972)

On this hypothesis the series does not terminate: it extends back into the process of biological evolution.

"Just like theories, organs and their functions are tentative adaptations to the world we live in" (Popper, 1972)

Such a view goes directly against a long established and indeed long dominant body of psychological theory: the theory that all our knowledge, including any theory, is derived from experience. Modern psychology may be said to begin with John Locke's attack on the notion of innate ideas. In his *Essay Concerning Human Understanding* Locke wrote:

> "Let us then suppose the mind to be, as we say, white paper, void of all characters, without any ideas; how comes it to be furnished? Whence comes it by that vast store, which the busy and boundless fancy of man has painted on it with almost endless variety? Whence has it all the materials of reason and knowledge? To this I answer in one word, from experience; in that all our knowledge is founded, and from that it ultimately derives itself." (Locke, 1690)

This was a brilliant and enormously fruitful conjecture; it continues to be influential right down to the present day, through the behaviourist school of psychology.

Nevertheless, like other successful theories, the "white paper" theory of mind has generated problems which it does not seem adequate to solve. Interactionist theories, which hold that minds have dispositions and characters of their own and that knowledge and theory result from the interaction of these dispositions and characters with the objects of experience, originated with Kant and have gained support from a number of directions in recent times. Popper maintains such a view on essentially logical grounds. But in psychology too the Gestalt school generated a body of observations best accounted for by the interactive hypothesis (Koffka, 1935), and Piaget in his studies of child development has emphasized the interaction of internal and external factors in concept formation. More recently, Chomsky and his school in linguistics (Chomsky, 1965) and Newell and Simon in the empirical study of problem solving have argued for this kind of view.

These fundamental theoretical issues may not seem directly relevant to architectural method. Yet one of the objectives of method must be to de-mystify design; and if induction is excluded, the ultimate origin of designs becomes mysterious, so long as it is held that not only all knowledge, but all structure, comes from experience. But if we do not need to, and cannot, drive a wedge between theory and observation, then this difficulty disappears. Instead of having to hypothesize somewhere a "black box" creative process which is not only inaccessible but inexplicable, our attention is directed to the use and modification of traditions, of existing bodies of ideas, theories, and designs in the culture, and also to the development of personal styles and even the notes, sketches and other more transient statements of interim theories or designs in the process of development.

An overview of this process of cultural change is provided by Murdoch (1956). He distinguishes four types of innovation: *variation, invention, tentation* and *cultural borrowing*. Making use of this taxonomy it is possible to group and classify innovations according to the process or processes that produced them; and some of these processes turn out to present little difficulty. Each requires therefore to be discussed at some length.

Variation is the modification of an existing system or type either as a result of changing circumstances or because the random variations of the processes of production or maintenance throw up some particular example which is recognized to be an improvement — a successful mutation, to use a biological analogy. Variation is characteristically slow and evolutionary; Alexander (1964) has singled it out as the type of "unselfconscious" design. In the context of modern technology, variation is often referred to as "extrapolation"; that is, doing the same thing as before only a little bigger, or smaller, or whatever the relevant dimension of change may be. Examples can readily be found in the development of cars, aircraft, steel and concrete structures, and in other technical aspects of building. Much change in architectural aesthetics is also variation and it is this that enables us to speak of the "development" of individual or historic "styles". Innovation by variation is a fully intelligible "glass box" process.

Equally familiar and transparent is the process of *cultural borrowing*. Ideas from another part of the world, another historic period, or even another part of the same culture are taken over and applied to the solution of some problem — even if the problem is only meeting the demand for novelty. The spread of Gothic or Renaissance architecture or in our own period of the Modern Movement on the one hand, and on the other the revivals of past styles which marked much of the nineteenth century and which have again become fashionable in the mid twentieth century are examples, of which every architect will be aware. Similarly, the imitation of the life styles of the famous or wealthy by the less fortunate is an example of cultural borrowing. And the contemporary interest in "primitive architecture" as a source of solutions to current architectural problems is yet another example. In fact our age is probably more catholic in its borrowing, and certainly better equipped for it, than any preceding one.

The type of innovation that Murdock calls *invention* is not transparent, though it can be understood after the fact. Invention "involves the transfer of elements of habitual behaviour from one situational context to another" (Murdock, 1956). Putting it another way, a problem in one field or frame of reference is "just seen" as having an analogue in another field or frame of reference, where a method of solution is known. The difference between this process and *cultural borrowing* is that in the latter the frame of reference, the form of the problem, is the same in the two cultures. In the case of invention, a jump, an "intuition", is required to bring the two frames of reference together. Thus Newton's initial insight in his solution of the problem of the orbit of the moon involved "just seeing" that a satellite might be a limiting case of the behaviour of projectiles, a field which he understood as a result of his studies of gunnery. Well-known anecdotes from the history of science and technology that are similar in their general character are the story of Watt and the kettle, and Fleming's serendipitous discovery of penicillin. In architecture a classic example is Frank Lloyd Wright's synthesis of two separate traditions of planning, the English free plan and the Beaux-Arts axial plan in his prairie houses. Broadbent (1973a) has discussed other examples of invention in architecture under the name of "analogic" design.

Finally, there is *tentation*, or trial and error. This is the method of last resort. Where motivation is high and the problem urgent, people "will ordinarily try out first a number of variations and reconstructions of existing habitual responses, but if all these fail they will resort to 'random behaviour' in the course of which they may accidentally hit upon some novel response which solves the problem.... Crises are particularly conducive to tentation" (Murdock, 1956). Famous examples of successful trial-and-error solutions of problems are Daguerre's development of photographic emulsion and Edison's filament bulb. Trial-and-error solution of complex and ill-defined problems is unlikely to be successful; at best it is time consuming and costly. However, like variation and cultural borrowing, trial and error is transparent.

Having gone so far, it is evident that a great deal of change in architecture, and the origins of many theories and designs, can be described in terms of processes that are commonplace and transparent: variation, cultural borrowing and tentation. Nevertheless, invention, the type of innovation that most fully deserves the connotations of the word "creative" and which certainly has a place in the development of architecture (though perhaps a smaller place than is commonly imagined), remains obscure. It has been suggested, however, that we can understand it after the event, and this suggestion now requires some justification, by way of an excursion into psychology.

As has been remarked earlier, our notion of creativity has a relatively short history, and is part of the radical change in ideas that took place at the end of the eighteenth century and the beginning of the nineteenth, which we call the romantic movement. Amongst the leaders in this change, it was Coleridge who contributed most to our understanding of creativity. He gave a great deal of thought to the psychology of the subject, and he anticipates in many ways modern opinions on the operation of the mind. He distinguishes three categories or classes of mental function: the primary imagination, the secondary imagination, and the fancy. The primary imagination is the human mind's contribution to our ordinary experience of the world — an idea which Coleridge derived in part from his reading of Kant. "The Primary Imagination I hold to be the living Power and prime Agent of all human Perception ..." (Coleridge, 1817). For Coleridge, as for many modern psychologists, experience is a construct: "Into the simplest seeming 'datum' a constructing, forming activity from the mind has entered" (Richards, 1934). The primary imagination is creative, but it is not what we ordinarily mean when we speak of creativity; it is the normal or fundamental mode of mental life.

The fancy is also creative, but in a mechanical way.

> "Fancy ... has no other counters to play with, but fixities and definites. The Fancy is indeed no other than a mode of Memory emancipated from the order of time and space; while it is blended with, and modified by, that empirical phenomenon of the will which we express by the word Choice." (Coleridge, 1817)

Fancy, in fact operates much in the way in which computers at present operate, sorting and re-examining concepts without being able to change them. Variation and cultural borrowing are activities of the fancy. We may compare it to a student of the Beaux-Arts "composing" — that is, assembling — "elements of architecture" — doors, windows, staircases, columns and the like — to produce a design.

The Secondary Imagination "is identical with the primary in the *kind* of its operation. It dissolves, diffuses, dissipates, in order to recreate, or where this process is indeed impossible yet at all events it struggles to idealise and unify" (Coleridge, 1817). The secondary imagination gives us the great innovations, the achievements which are universally recognized as creative, though it is not confined to them, and may operate in trivial matters as well. (Equally, for Coleridge, the fancy may be an important element, though not sole agent, in great creative work.) Where the fancy reassembles existing concepts, the secondary imagination creates new concepts: it enlarges our vision of the world.

The clearest modern account of the operation of the secondary imagination is that of Schon (1963). Schon argues that the basic process involved is the perception or intuition of analogies, which he calls "the displacement of concepts": some existing concept is used as a metaphor for handling the new situation. This is distinct from the mechanical transfer of a technique unchanged from one situation to another: the existing concept is transformed in a poetic way. Schon's argument is amply illustrated by historical examples of the adaptation or extension of words and concepts to meet new problems and situations, and by descriptions of innovations with which he was personally concerned during his association with the Arthur D. Little "think-tank". A striking feature of Schon's "displacement of concepts" is the economy with which it describes innovations at all levels from the most trivial development of slang to the most profound works of science and art.

Closely similar to Schon's displacement of concepts are Koestler's "bisociation" (Koestler, 1964) and Ehrenzweig's "dedifferentiation" (Ehrenzweig, 1967), though their accounts are confused by the introduction of psychoanalytical schemata. What they have in common with Coleridge and Schon is the belief that imagination depends on the ability to relax the rigidity of our concepts, to render them, temporarily at least, not watertight but permeable, and thus to allow them to take in, or be stretched to cover, new material.

These are theoretical/historical approaches. Other approaches have come from psychology proper. Guilford (1957) and Getzels and Jackson (1962) have proposed two new types or categories of mental ability, "convergent" and "divergent" thinking. There is by no means universal agreement as to the usefulness of these categories — they have, for example, been severely criticized by Kuhn (1964) and Gardner (1973) — but they have attracted interest and exercized some influence. Zangwill (1966) has summarized their main features as follows:

> "In... convergent thinking, the aim is to discover the one right answer to the problem set. It is highly directed, essentially logical thinking of the kind required in science and mathematics. It is also the kind required for the solution of most intelligence tests. In divergent thinking on the other hand, the aim is to produce a large number of possible answers, none of which is necessarily more correct than the others though some may be more original. Such thinking is marked by its variety and fertility rather than by its logical precision."

It is at least tempting to connect convergent and divergent thinking with the primary and secondary imagination, respectively. Further, Hudson (1962) has suggested on the basis of a variety of evidence that "the converger... achieves a sense of security by restricting himself to a relatively narrow range of impersonal, technical topics." Convergers, on this view, would be reluctant to tolerate the relaxation and ambiguity essential to the displacement of concepts.

Other insights into creativity are provided by a variety of practical techniques which have been developed for aiding innovation. A useful general discussion of these techniques has been provided by Broadbent (1966) and a detailed review of several by Jones (1970a). Three of the best known are brainstorming, morphological analysis and synectics. Much publicity has also been given to de Bono's "lateral thinking", but his method does not in principle extend the earlier ideas, though it differs in detail.

Osborn's "brainstorming" (Osborn, 1963) is a group activity. Both the composition of the group and the conditions under which it works are important to the success of the method. The members should include some people not directly connected with the problem, and should be of differing backgrounds and experience. (We may compare Beer's (1966) description of the desiderata for an operations research team.) They throw out ideas in a permissive atmosphere, without criticism or attempts to synthesize. The ideas are recorded and subsequently independently assessed.

Morphological analysis is a device for forcing the overlapping of frames of reference. It involves setting up a matrix in which one dimension consists of the necessary actions or parts "in principle" and the other consists of the techniques or devices that can be used to achieve these actions. New combinations of actions and techniques can then be extracted from the matrix (Zwicky, 1967). Gregory (1969) and Grant (1977a, b) have given clear descriptions of the method and related it to the architectural context.

Synectics is a system devised by the Invention Research Group at Harvard, under the chairmanship of Gordon. It aims at changing the frame of reference within which a problem is considered by using one of three types of analogy: *personal* analogy by which the designer identifies himself with the system being designed; *direct* analogy by which the problem is compared with known facts or methods in another branch of art, science or technology; and *symbolic* analogy which is purely poetic and based on similarity of subjective affective responses to the problem in hand and to some other activity (Gordon, 1961). The close relation between the views of Gordon and Schon is not coincidental, since they were associated at the Arthur D. Little organization, and both acknowledge the benefit of mutual discussion of the field.

It is clear that all these systems are devices for forcibly breaking out of the conventional frame of reference, in the interest of innovation. Zwicky produces the overlapping of concepts mechanically; Osborn and Gordon use the interaction of people with different backgrounds and frames of reference to produce the same effect. The processes of the imagination, which for Coleridge are internal, are here externalized. However, their operation is still not mechanical; what these techniques do or strive to do is to establish situations favourable to creative intuitions. The problem space of the individuals involved is extended or a different problem space is substituted.

The purpose of this long excursion has been to show that the origins of theories, or designs, or the preliminary hypotheses or notions which enable designs to be begun, are not metaphysical. In many cases they are not even mysterious: we have seen that some of the most important are transparent. Even the processes involved in invention must be seen as normal activities of the great majority of human minds, and even of animal minds (Kohler, 1925); activities that can be stimulated and made more effective by quite simple techniques. We cannot in biological or neurological detail say how any of these processes are mediated, nor can we predict their outcome, but we can describe in principle what they do. Confusion and mysticism are generated by the use of words such as "creative" and "intuitive" both to indicate differing degrees of achievement and also to imply a difference in *kind* of achievement. Most of what has been said so far deals with differences in kind; we must now turn to differences of degree, concentrating on the process of invention.

Invention of a sort is involved even in daily physical acts which we perform without the necessity of conscious thought. As Jones (1970a) puts it:

> "The apparently simple action of writing, and the even simpler action of reaching for a pencil without looking for it, are just as inexplicable as is the composing of a symphony, perhaps more so. (Nobody has yet programmed a computer to produce outputs that are anywhere near as 'intelligent' as bodily movement, but we seem to be in sight of composing music automatically.)"

We can and constantly do adapt our bodily movements to new situations. Far more than mere variation is involved here. Similarly, speakers of any given language constantly produce sentences they have never spoken before, a productive feat so remarkable that Chomsky proposed a radical revision of current language theory to account for it. Perceiving the "necessary" truth of the elementary syllogism — all A are B, all B are C, therefore all A are C — requires, so students of logic used to be taught, an act of intuition, though a simple one; nevertheless there are those who cannot manage it. Understanding the calculus seems to require a greater intuitive leap; but the leap is not so great as Newton and Leibniz made in conceiving it. There is a continuum connecting these achievements, a continuum which extends from "ordinary" activity through productivity in a particular or limited field, through inventiveness, in the sense in which we speak of an "inventor" to the peaks of human thought and art.

To flesh out this brief discussion of differences in degree within productive activity, it may be worthwhile painting a sort of composite portrait of the great innovator, the man of genius, with special reference to architectural examples. There is of course an extensive literature, from Vasari and Samuel Smiles to the more recent writers to whom reference has already been made. Here it is only necessary to give an impression, to establish a non-mystical image of the causes and the rules of the works of genius, the point being to suggest that while method certainly cannot guarantee great work it need not inhibit it; and that, conversely, the existence of genius is not evidence that method should be dismissed from consideration. In this sketch of genius we may take for granted exceptional intelligence or "general ability" and unusual persistence and determination. But these traits must have a point of application; that is, a problem. The degree of achievement is estimated after the event in large part by the difficulty and importance of the problem solved. To find such problems usually requires a deep knowledge and experience of some field which is in itself a difficult one; in the arts and architecture, it also requires knowledge and experience of the medium (Gardner, 1973). But besides this the genius often has an unusually *wide* range of experience, sometimes as a result of happy accidents, but often deliberately sought, either in his own field, or in related fields, or in fields apparently unrelated. Thus Michelangelo was a sculptor before he was an architect, and one aspect of his achievement is the substitution of a sculptural conception of architecture for a painterly one; Wright had his only formal training in engineering and worked by choice for two leading architects whose styles were radically opposed, Silsbee and Sullivan; Le Corbusier worked for the most radical architects of three countries, travelled widely and was active as a painter and sculptor as well as in architecture. The genius, in fact, is often distinguished not only by native ability and deep knowledge, but also by having a view of the problem which transcends the "normal" professional view, an "extended problem space" which is unusually rich and varied.

From the point of view of knowledge in architecture and architectural method, then, we are not absolutely compelled to postulate a special kind of knowledge, lying forever beyond the domain of method, in order to account for the generation of preliminary ideas, even novel ideas, even ideas that history later judges to be great. And since we are not absolutely required to do so, it may be productive to set aside, at least for the moment, prejudices about creativity and approach the attempt to give an empirical account of method with an open mind.

2.6   Knowledge in architectural practice

Most of the information that architects use in designing is not as well
tested as scientific knowledge, nor as poorly tested as romantic
inspiration, nor as difficult to achieve as creative insight. It depends to
a very large extent on various kinds of consensus, and on authority
based on presumed skill and on experience. This is sometimes true
even in cases in which it might at first sight appear that decisions are
well based on facts that have been tested to the level required in the
physical sciences. Let us consider the case of the sizing of a steel
beam. An architect might undertake this himself, but he is more likely
to get a structural engineer to do it for him, and he is unlikely to check
the result, unless it appears wildly contrary to his previous experience.
Thus he is relying on authority: on the engineer's professional claim to
skill in this particular area. The engineer in turn, in this simple case,
may make some elementary calculations or more likely refer to
published load tables, on whose authority he relies. In doing so, the
engineer is, first of all, accepting the analogy between his manipulation of mathematical symbols and some future events in the real world;
that is, he is accepting that the equation system he uses, or the one
which was used to generate his tables, is in fact a reliable model of
certain physical systems. Thus far he is making use of well-tested
theories; many systematic observations of the behaviour of steel beams
under load have been made. However, he is also relying on the
general consensus that the quality of steel as a material is subject to
very little variation, a consensus which is supported by some evidence
in the form of regular factory sampling and testing, but which depends
on a combination of practical experience and statistical analysis and
has a somewhat higher probability of error. In determining what the
loads on the beam are likely to be the engineer is making use of much
shakier statistical evidence about the ways in which people customarily use buildings of various kinds, and particularly about the weights
and distribution of the objects that they put in them. He also makes
assumptions, again based on relatively limited evidence, about wind
strengths, the probability of earthquakes, and a great many other
contingencies. Had we taken a column in a multistorey building rather
than a simple beam as our example, we might include still shakier
assumptions about the probabilities that the maximum likely load on
an average section of floor will not be uniformly applied over all floors
of the building. Finally, in deciding what factor of safety or load factor
to allow, the engineer is relying entirely on a consensus, albeit in
recent years a world-wide consensus, among structural engineers as to
what is reasonable; that is, on the balance between cost and the risk of
collapse that is acceptable. The risk currently adopted is very low; but
there is a vocal minority who argue for an even lower probability.

Without labouring the point further, it can be seen that this apparently simple, routine, science-based decision is in fact only possible because of a very complex and far-reaching consensus, in part empirically based but embodying many assumptions; a consensus which has first evolved historically by agreement among experts and subsequently been given legal or quasi-legal authority in building codes, national standards, or the codes of practice of professional institutions.

All this is not intended to undermine confidence in the advice of structural engineers, but to bring out a point about practical activities in general: that they depend on a mix of information of varying quality. Much of the information that architects are compelled to use is of far poorer quality than the advice of structural engineers, which is highly reliable. As an example, let us take anthropometric information. Handbooks and tables are available which indicate the range of such important human dimensions as eye height, maximum reach, head height when standing, and so on. Many designers make use of these tables in deciding window heights, the height and width of storage shelves, benches, door handles and other potentially critical building dimensions. On the whole designers who make use of this kind of information do better than those who merely guess or rely on measuring themselves or their secretary. Nevertheless anthropometric data are often used with insufficient awareness of the methods used to arrive at the figures they contain. To be reliable, they must be based on measurements of a very large sample of the population. The process of taking such measurements is skilled and laborious and therefore costly, so that in the main they have been made by the military, using recruits: that is, young healthy adults. The most commonly used tables are in fact based on data collected by the US armed forces. Making use of them for design purposes thus makes the assumption that the population designed for is reasonably like the population of recruits to the US armed forces. In designing, let us say, a general hospital in Australia this assumption will lead to a certain amount of error. Many of the user population will be sick, some will be old, some visitors will be children. However, the error may be tolerable in terms of the percentage of people inconvenienced. In designing such a hospital for a south-east Asian country, on the other hand, or a specialized facility for children or the old, the error would probably not be tolerable: the physical dimensions of these populations would be substantially different, and different specialized tables would have to be sought out. We have here a case of information that is moderately reliable, but of limited application; its successful use involves extrapolation and judgement. Other similar examples could be drawn from meteorological information, from the site investigation of subsoil conditions, and from standards established for lighting, thermal and acoustic comfort.

A superficially similar, but in reality very different, case is provided by standard data on room layouts. Many sets of "design standards" are available which provide layouts for rooms of many types, giving furniture dimensions, circulation clearances, and overall room sizes. Here, as Rapoport and Watson (1968) argue, a further level of assumption is involved. The way in which rooms are used varies considerably amongst social groups; for example, the spacing of furniture depends in an important way on the accepted interaction distances between people, a point which they support by comparing Indian with western layouts, but which is equally relevant to countries, such as Australia, where there is a high proportion of migrants. Such standards layouts are seldom based on actual observation in any case, and where observations have been made there are considerable departures from the designer's predictions (Edwards, 1974) which may be evidence of a further, class-determined difference in attitudes and habits. Old people who have moved to smaller "labour-saving" premises often "overcrowd" them with furniture for sentimental reasons (Heath, 1967) so that there may be age differences as well. Thus these "standard" layouts, which are quantitative and by implication well tested, turn out to be derived from *a priori* assumptions and are either not well tested or not tested at all; in fact, a typical case of rationalist thinking. We must, however, distinguish this from yet another case, that of the organization which has through trial and error in many different cases developed standard designs and layouts of equipment; for example, the standard layouts for tellers' work areas used by most Australian banks.

The performance of building materials, and particularly their long-term performance, has been and remains largely a matter of craft knowledge, that is, of consensus among professionals. This is not to disregard the rapid increase in the number of standards and codes of practice, with their accompanying methods of testing quality, which has taken place in recent years, or the growth of materials science generally. But in the case of standards and codes we must note that they are themselves in effect the record of a consensus reached by a committee representative of the industry; that in many cases the basic research and theory available to such committees is inadequate or inconsistent; and that their output represents a compromise between what designers and researchers would like to have and what the producers and craftsmen feel able and willing to provide. Building materials research is often limited in its value by difficulties of extrapolation from the laboratory to the field; accelerated weathering tests and wear resistance tests on flooring materials are notorious in this respect. Available materials may not have been tested, or the tests may have been carried out in-house or in other countries, so that their reliability is suspect as well as the fundamental theory on which they are based. Failures continue to occur which are not predictable either from experience or from the literature. In general, the use of building materials and the conditions which they impose on the designer depend on a complex mass of assumptions about the characteristics of the material, but also and more importantly about the similarity of any particular batch to the general class and quality of material, and about the similarity of conditions of use. Thus a series of failures of brickwork occurred in New South Wales during the brick shortages of the 1950s and 1960s. The bricks were exactly as they had always been, *except* that they were being delivered and built in hot from the kiln; as they re-hydrated they "grew", causing destructive distortion of the sur-rounding building fabric. The failure of the opaque glass panels in some "curtain wall" facades was caused by the inclusion in the glass manufacture of tiny impurities. These are examples in which the assumption of similarity of the material was falsified. Another example will serve to illustrate the failure of the assumption of the similarity of conditions. A parquet floor was installed in an air-conditioned build-ing; the timber was properly kiln dried and reconditioned to the moisture content appropriate to the conditions which the air-conditioning system was designed to maintain; however, in use the building manager turned the air conditioning off during the weekends, with the result that the timber absorbed moisture from the uncon-ditioned air, expanded, and formed an undulating surface which was visually interesting but difficult and dangerous to walk over.

The point of this argument is not to denigrate the contributions of building science to architecture. It is, rather, to make clear that at any given time the knowledge available to the professional is a complex amalgam of many different kinds and qualities of theory and observa-tion. There is a percentage of applied science in the full sense: well-tested generalizations of clear applicability. There are areas where an attempt has been made to apply scientific method, but the link between theory and practice is tenuous. There is some reliance on authority, whether scientific authority or that of experienced persons of various kinds. There are untested theories and *a priori* assumptions, often developed by reasoning of considerable ingenuity. There is a considerable reliance on professional consensus. And, informing or selecting from all these, there is the experience of the individual practitioner or group of practitioners.

Every design decision by an architect thus carries with it, usually implicitly rather than explicitly, a decision or a series of decisions as to what is going to count as knowledge. That is, he has to distinguish between what is "given" and what is part of the problem. The unreflective moralistic response to this is that he should not treat anything as "given". But this is clearly impossible. The impossibility is nicely illustrated by Eberhard (1970) in his story "The Warning of the Doorknob". In this parable Eberhard pictures himself commissioning the design of a new doorknob for his office; after some time the designer returns; he is concerned as to whether a doorknob is the best way of opening and closing a door. Then he begins to worry about whether a door is the best way of controlling privacy. Then he sees that this is connected with having four walls around the office. "Finally, our physical designer comes back and he says with a very serious face, 'Mr. Eberhard, we have to decide whether capitalistic democracy is the best way to organise our country before I can *possibly* attack your problem.'" And Eberhard also paints the alternative picture, in which the designer successively becomes concerned with ergonomics, metal working, metallurgy, and finally atomic physics.

The boundary problem is real and unavoidable. It is, as the Eberhard fable implies, not removed by doing "more research"; in fact the same problem is held by some to arise in scientific research itself (Lakatos, 1970). But the economics of cost and time will in most cases prevent any significant research, other than, perhaps, literature research or consultations with authorities, being done at all. We shall see that for a similar reason comparatively little of any given project is "new design"; not only background knowledge but whole elements have to be taken for granted if design is to proceed at a reasonable cost. We must note too that this would be true in a socialist or an anarchist as opposed to a capitalist state; even if the constraint of cost is removed there remains, as Bell (1973) has argued, the irreducible constraint of time. The decision as to where to draw the line in a given case must rest with the professional, or at best with the design team; its only guarantee is that the people concerned should be well educated, and where necessary re-educated, experienced, and in the legal sense "reasonable men".

Chapter 3

The task environment of architecture

3.1 Introduction

The architect's view of a particular design, his "problem space" for that task, is not newly created in each particular case. He brings to each such situation his previous experience; and it is this, it has been suggested, which enables him, in a reasonable time, to construct a "problem space" from the task environment of a particular problem. His task environment is wider than that provided by the immediate task. This conveys benefits; it also has risks; it may lead him to choose a wrong problem space for that problem. This chapter will seek to identify some major elements which go to make up the professional world view, the total task environment, of the architect in practice. In doing so, it will also attempt to describe them. Such an attempt is doomed to failure for a number of reasons. Firstly, as was pointed out previously, it is not possible to describe any task environment completely. Secondly, individuals and tasks differ, and a description that is apt for one situation may not be apt for another. For example, a doctrinaire socialist might make a selection of elements radically different from that offered here, or describe some of the same elements in different ways. And thirdly, each element is a broad field, requiring for its proper explanation specialized knowledge; and some are under-researched and ill-understood. From the point of view of method, however, it is the existence of _some kind_ of world view that has to be established and borne in mind. Strictly, it is not a task environment that is described, but an augmented problem space, one which takes in some at least of those matters that are usually factored out in attempts to discuss method in architecture. What follows, then, is suggestive or typical rather than comprehensive or precise: a first sketch of an ecology of architecture.

3.2   Aspects of the social macroenvironment of architecture

The task environment of architecture increasingly includes wider
segments of the total society. Not only is the situation in which the
architect designs for an individual client, on a site isolated from and
having little impact on other buildings, increasingly rare; but both the
professional and social value systems are changing so that it is no
longer considered to be by any means sufficient for the architect to
satisfy the legal owner of the building he designs; he is also expected
to have concern for the users of the building and for an increasingly
far-ranging class of effects, or possible effects of the building on society
at large and even on the world. This problem, it will be suggested, is
by no means unique to architecture. It is reasonable, then, to begin
any account of the task environment of architecture by attempting to
identify, however broadly and tentatively, main features and problems
of modern societies, and in particular modern Western "post-
industrial" societies. Three such features which have been singled out
by a number of writers on contemporary affairs, and which seem to
have special significance for architecture, are the growth of bureaucracy, the incidence of change, and the formation of a counter-culture.

The importance of bureaucracy and its tendency to growth in
modern societies is notorious. Parkinson's Law (Parkinson, 1957) is
generally admitted to be too true to be funny. But besides the internal
growth dynamics of the bureaucracy, there has been a long-term trend
towards increasing demand for public services, which carry with them
increased public administration. Recent estimates of the size of the
not-for-profit sector of the economy *in the United States* suggest that
over 30% of all employment is now provided by or depends on
federal, state or local government, schools, hospitals and charitable
bodies — all essentially bureaucratic organizations (Ginzberg, 1976).
In Australia, according to the 1971 census, 19.88% of the population
were employed in the census categories of communication, public
administration and defence, electricity, gas and water, and community services, i.e. in the not-for-profit sector, and a further 6.93% in
finance, insurance, real estate and business services, so that roughly
26% of the then employed population can be taken to be part of the
bureaucracy. If we look at the corresponding figures for type of
occupation, they suggest an even higher proportion: 32.75% of the
employed population were classified in the three categories of professional, technical and related workers, administrative, executive and
managerial workers, and clerical workers (Australian Bureau of Statistics, 1975). By no means all of these were employed in government or
in the not-for-profit sector; but as Galbraith (1967) has argued,
bureaucracy is just as significant a feature of modern business as it is of

modern government, and the two are, to a considerable degree, interdependent.

The bureaucracy has not only increased in extent; its power has grown, and continues to grow. In the political field, Lord Crowther-Hunt has given an impressive account of the relative helplessness of Ministers vis-à-vis the organizations that are supposed to serve them (Crowther-Hunt, 1976). There is no reason to suppose that the situation in Australia, the United States, or in any other developed country is essentially different. Again, Galbraith (1967) has pointed out that managerial control of the large corporation is equally independent of its nominal owners, and in the special context of the United States he has sought to demonstrate the interpenetration, in terms of agreed goals, mutual accommodation and the like, of the corporate and government experts and administrators: the "technostructure".

It is not, however, the extent and power of the bureaucracy that are important in relation to architectural method. It is, rather, the character of bureaucracy, its ideals and its operation as a system, and their pervasive influence, which must be taken into account. Weber, in his pioneering analysis, described the structural traits of the bureaucracy as "a permanent organisation involving co-operation among many individuals, each of whom performs a specialised function" (Aron, 1967). It is hierarchically organized and essentially impersonal; and its main type of action is "Zweckrational" action, or rational action in relation to a goal. Modern bureaucracies are distinguished from those of the ancient world, or from that of the Roman Catholic Church, by their reliance on science (in the limited and defective sense of quantifiable and allegedly neutral data); they thus correspond to Galbraith's technostructure. They have not in general adopted the self-critical ideals of science. The bureaucratic personality is primarily concerned with security, not criticism, and the bureaucrat may become "psychologically incapable of dealing with anything that is *not* quantifiable" (Berger and Berger, 1972). There is a close analogy with military organization and with the organization of industry under the influence of the kind of work study pioneered by Taylor and Gilbreth (Emery *et al.*, 1974) and an emphasis on performance and achievement and criteria of efficiency based on least cost (Bell, 1973). The hierarchical and impersonal nature of the organization promotes and is maintained by a love of rules and regulations which serve to maintain the organization and to provide a basis for consistent, and therefore "rational", action. Traditionally, such regulations were justified by reference to authority, but today they are more often given some scientific or pseudo-scientific support. By a process known as goal displacement the regulations and procedures, the means of bureaucracy, tend to be substituted for the ends for which the organization was originally created (Berelson and Steiner, 1964); "guidelines" becomes "standards" and then "rules".

Architecture has been deeply influenced by these ideals: rationality, impersonality, performance in terms of the quantifiable values of cost and time. A survey commissioned by the NSW Chapter of the Royal Australian Institute of Architects in 1977 found among corporate, institutional and governmental clients and potential clients one general criticism of the performance of architects: inability to guarantee the final cost and completion time of the buildings they design. The bureaucracy as client seeks to enforce its ideals on the architect and indeed on the world, since in the nature of things cost and time on large projects cannot be guaranteed by architects, who have no control over them after their design is complete, and indeed can only be very problematically assured by anybody else. The adoption, to some extent unconscious, of ideals of rationality and impersonality is the very point that has provoked some of the most bitter and most justified lay criticism of modern architecture; the public "can, and do, reject even well proportioned and skillfully designed buildings or environments that have a rotten social content" (MacEwen, 1974); in this case the rotten social content is the implication that the individual is subordinate to an *a priori* system and to the calculus of cost-effectiveness.

Bureaucracy also affects architecture in a more direct way through the proliferation of regulations. Not the smallest design can be carried out without prolonged exchanges between the designer and bureaucracies of local government and the public utilities. Woodford, Williams and Hill (1976), in what we may hope will be a seminal work, have discussed the value of standards for the external residential environment. Their report "rejects the widely held notion that standards are intrinsically beneficial, and argues that wrong ideas about standards lead to wrong uses that may actually damage the environment." They go on to say, "We are too ready to take the easy way round a difficult problem, to seize upon a number without appraising and judging for ourselves, to regard the meeting of a standard as the most important test of quality." While the scope of their material is limited, the application of their conclusion is much wider. It points to a disease which runs right through the contemporary practice of architecture, an industrial disease produced by working in a bureaucratic society: concern for the rule and indifference to the result.

Finally, and perhaps worst of all, the practice of architecture may itself be bureaucratized. Public architectural offices and many large private offices "provide an 'ecology' ... that is not merely unsympathetic to architecture, but in many cases positively hostile to it"

(MacEwen, 1974). The office as part of the designer's task environment is the subject of a later section; here it may be noted that bureaucracy is a stimulus to method in the narrow sense of routine or quantifiable procedures, and that fear of bureaucratization is an enemy of method. But, as we shall see, method itself, pursued as a scientific inquiry and not *a priori*, turns out to provide its own criticism of bureaucracy.

The incidence of change has a double stress: both the incidence and the change are important. The actual rate at which people's daily lives are changing may or may not be greater than in, say, 1840; but information about change, information of all kinds indeed, is vastly more available. Bell (1973) gives some terrifying statistics on the growth of telephones, mail sent, radio and television sets and stations in the United States. Emery and his collaborators (1974) have described the effect of these and similar changes in other countries forcefully: "The change that has taken place in intra-species communication is a greater mutation than if man had grown a second head." At the same time, change itself has become institutionalized. In becoming dependent on science, bureaucracy has welcomed an enemy within its gates, for science, even when the attempt is made to reduce it to a mere source of data, is liable at any time to lead to a more critical approach. The strategy of "dynamic conservatism", the systematic self-defence of institutions against disruptive change (Schon, 1971), is increasingly undermined as professional values which favour the acceptance of change conflict with the values natural to the institution.

The consequence of this widespread sense of change is a corresponding sense of instability. It is argued by many writers that "Western" society is undergoing yet another metamorphosis; the new is straining at the dying shell of the old. Schon (1971) writes of a move "beyond the stable state", Emery and his collaborators of a change from the "disturbed reactive environment" to the "turbulent field". Bell (1973) and Kahn and Wiener (1967) discuss the "post industrial society"; and Galbraith (1977) has chosen to entitle his Reith lectures *"The Age of Uncertainty"*. The "turbulent field" model, first proposed by Emery and Trist (1965), is useful in analysing certain kinds of design problem, and will therefore be described in more detail.

Emery and Trist identify four types of causal texture in the environment. Only two of these need be discussed here; the third, the disturbed reactive environment, and the fourth, the emerging turbulent environment. The disturbed reactive environment is an environment in which organizations are competing, for markets, resources or clients or some combination of these, but in which these organizations are not yet so large or so widespread that their actions are seen as affecting society as a whole. There is a stable background, which can be presumed for planning purposes to persist independently of the organizations' actions. It is suggested that this type of social environment is characteristic of the industrialized countries between 1895 and 1967, approximately. With improvements in communications and advances in engineering making for economies of scale, the disturbed reactive environment has been subject to waves of rapid growth in organizational size; there have been three such waves at approximately thirty-year intervals, in 1895–1900, in 1927–1930, and in 1967–1969. The last wave has, according to this analysis, produced the turbulent field environment.

Three trends contribute to this emergence. They are the growth in the size of organizations, whose actions have effects, both intended and unintended, on wider and wider areas of society; the increasing interconnectedness and interdependence of the parts of the society, which allow such effects to be transmitted ever more rapidly to remote and unpredictable sectors; and, as we have already noted, reliance on science-based knowledge and technical improvement which creates a continuous undercurrent of change. Emery and his collaborators summarize the combined effects as follows:

> "For organisations these trends mean a gross increase in their area of *relevant uncertainty*. The consequences which flow from their actions lead off in ways that become increasingly unpredictable; they do not necessarily fall off with distance, but may at any point be amplified beyond all expectations; similarly, lines of action that are strongly pursued may find themselves attenuated by emergent field forces."

Instability, and its accompaniment of unpredictability, are peculiarly difficult for architecture to cope with, since the design and construction of major buildings is itself an extended process, requiring short- to medium-term predictions of the future, and the building when completed has to have a lifetime, and thus a predictable use, proportionate to the expense involved.

The counter-culture, or adversary culture, is not, in any of its essentials, new. This cannot be too strongly emphasized, since it is characteristic of this movement to claim that its doctrines are new and radical. It is the logical extension of the Romantic Movement into the post-industrial world. Romanticism itself can best be understood as a rejection of the values of the eighteenth century enlightenment. In particular, it sought to substitute the value of emotion for that reason, the value of the individual for that of the wider society, the value of originality for that of social consensus, and the value of liberty for that of order. There is, as already discussed, a conscious rejection of science and of industry: Snow's "two cultures" have their origins here. Certain key words appear or take on their modern usage at that time: artist, genius, creative, original (Williams, 1958). There is, inherent in this complex of ideas, a tendency to extremism, as Russell has argued (Russell, 1946). Nevertheless, since romanticism by definition lacks the self-critical apparatus of science, it is compatible with a deep conservatism; most of the literary and the artistic establishments, as well as the young and innovative, hold fundamentally Romantic views.

The transition to the post-industrial state has intensified this traditional body of reaction. Bell (1973) speaks of "a widening disjunction between the social structure (the economy, technology, and occupational system) and the culture (the symbolic expression of meanings) as against the Marxist supposition that "a single organising institution... frames the entire society"; though he refers to a period of a hundred years, rather than approximately two hundred as suggested here. The contemporary versions are given form and direction by the need to reduce complexity, and thus differ in detail from the original reaction against the excessive claims of rationality. However, older features have not been lost, but have been attracted to new ideas and strategies.

Three main defensive strategies are identified by Schon (1971), and a rather similar set is proposed by Emery and his collaborators (1974). Schon's "dynamic conservatism" makes use, first, of selective inattention — ignoring an innovation as far as possible; secondly of containment or isolation of the innovation, leading in the extreme to compartmentalization of the organization; and thirdly, co-option, or the minimal, perhaps only nominal and superficial adoption of the innovation by the organization. The division proposed by Emery and his collaborators is intended to apply more widely and can be seen to contain Schon's as a subset. Thus they write in terms of the reduction of choices by three "passive maladaptive" strategies: dissociation, segmentation, and superficiality. Dissociation involves the denial of the value of others, or of innovation. It is equivalent to Schon's selective inattention; for example, the wholesale rejection of science and technology, or flat refusal to be concerned with the problems of poor countries. Segmentation consists in the intensification and exaggeration of social divisions, thus excluding concern with groups other than the "in-group". This corresponds to Schon's "containment" or "compartmentalization" and is exemplified by women's liberation movements, or by "union bashing" conservative political groups. Superficiality reduces the level of involvement in the ends pursued; its analogue is Schon's co-option or least change; innumerable examples are provided by the treatment of serious topics by the press, television and radio, and by the general hedonism, prodigality and compulsive search for play of the counter-culture.

These tendencies, as the choice of examples was intended to indicate, cut across conventional notions of radicalism/conservatism, and are profoundly inimical to the production of good architecture, which requires commitment over long time periods, collaboration, and a clear understanding of the forces at work in a given situation. We shall see that similar maladaptive strategies may be adopted for coping with complexity *within* the process of design.

Such a brief account of complex and wide-ranging social forces, based on only a limited number of available theoretical accounts, may itself be subject to a charge of superficiality. The intention here, however, is not to develop new theories of society, or even to evaluate those that already exist, but to show by selected examples how a picture of the wider social environment can interact with the designer's picture of his task. This might have been accomplished in a different way, for example by historical analysis of the writings of leading architects of the immediate past. But returning to the point made earlier, no picture of the task environment can be complete. The task environment described in this and the succeeding sections of this chapter is really an augmented problem space, which may help to bring out and clarify features of the more specialized problem spaces whose description is the main objective of this account of method.

3.3   The industrial environment of architecture

Architecture is a part of the building industry. This is often asserted, but seldom seriously considered, least of all by architects. Books on the building industry are, in general, written by economists and management consultants, rather than architects. The tradition by which the architect sees himself as, in general, on the side of "the client" and opposed to "the builder", or at best acting as a quasi-arbitrator between the interests of these parties, no doubt accounts, in large part at least, for this curious neglect. Involvement or identification with building is unprofessional. Recently the severe world-wide decline in building, deliberately brought about, in many cases, by government action, has to some extent convinced architects that they have much in common with the contractors, subcontractors, suppliers and workers who make up the rest of the directly employed building labour force. From the point of view of method, it is the strengths and weaknesses of the industry in terms of its productive capacity that are important, since these impose limitations on what can be produced, and thus on what can be designed with reasonable hope of execution. But the productive capacity of the industry in turn depends on its broader nature, and on its position in the economy as a whole.

In developed economies the construction industry is responsible for a large proportion of the gross national product. The form in which the statistics are published, and for that matter collected, often makes it difficult to distinguish between building construction and other capital works, such as roads, bridges and dams. Stone (1976) suggests that at that time about one-sixth of the national income in America was devoted to building, and that the figure in the United Kingdom was approximately one eighth. In Australia in 1971–1972 the value of new buildings completed, government and private, was $2991m. or approximately one twelfth of the gross national product. Completion figures are not a reliable indicator of the on-going level of activity, but they will serve to indicate the general scale of the industry.

The demand for buildings is inherently liable to large fluctuations, which, coupled with the size of the industry, contribute to economic instability. In general, buildings have a long life, and the replacement rate is low. The industry, for reasons to be discussed, is diffuse and inflexible, so that local demands have on the whole to be met by local resources. Changes in the rate of family formation, the decision to provide new forms of welfare, or changes in the location or kind of employment of the population thus produce disproportionately large changes in the demand for building. Handler (1970) gives the following example. Assume a community with 1000 dwellings, with 50 year lives, all occupied, 2% of which have to be replaced each year; and assume that 30 new families join the community. Then the annual construction rate will jump from 20 to 50 dwellings, an increase of 150%. The following year this particular immigration is over; demand drops back to 20 new dwellings, a fall of 60%. This is of course a simplified model; demands for various kinds of facilities are not in phase and there is some levelling out as a result. Further, the building stock is not usually fully occupied. And there is the possibility of accepting reduced standards, or adopting various devices of management to make fuller use of the existing stock. These last points lead to further instability, since if building prices rise, new building can usually be deferred, and this in turn can lead to a disproportionate fall in demand (Stone, 1976).

The deliberate actions of governments accentuate this inherent instability. The possibility of deferring construction, the large size of the industry, and its generally poor organization and consequent political ineffectiveness, make the control of construction an attractive means of economic regulation. Government construction itself amounts to about one quarter of total construction in Australia (Australian Bureau of Statistics, 1975); in the United Kingdom to as much as one half. Government can also control construction to a large extent by manipulation of interest rates and bank reserves, which affects the profitability of private construction, and the availability of capital. Thus government, in seeking to control inflation, can "squeeze" the building industry both directly and indirectly and quite rapidly. It may also attempt to use the industry to stimulate the economy in times of depression, but because of the relatively long lead times for construction this does not have such a rapid or such a predictable effect. Even where designs are being held ready for execution, the cash-flow curve for major projects is quite flat at the beginning, while tenders are being called and evaluated, builders are establishing themselves on site, and excavation and site works are being carried out. Stone (1976) is generally critical, not so much of government intervention in the industry as such, as of some of the more academic assumptions on which it is often based. Whether or not such criticisms are justified, it is the case that government action has tended to increase, rather than reduce, the instability of the industry.

The "boom and bust" character of the industry has a number of adverse effects on the quality of construction, which in turn influence and form part of the task environment for design. The following discussion relates specifically to the Australian building industry, but it has, no doubt, its parallels elsewhere. Since builders have little control over the market, they are reluctant to commit themselves to heavy fixed costs; building firms are notoriously under-capitalized. Mechanization of the industry has taken place, but not by way of large permanent capital equipment. Heavy equipment such as cranes and bulldozers is very generally leased; where this is not so, it is usual to recover the whole cost of the plant on the job for which it is first purchased. There has been widespread and increasing use of small power tools, such as drills, saws, power fixing devices, and the like, which are low in capital cost and give a high return in increased production. And there has been a tendency to transfer operations from the site to the factories of material suppliers and subcontractors; as with the leasing of plant, this spreads the capital investment as widely as possible over the industry. Lack of capital investment contributes to rigidity of construction costs and prices (Handler, 1970). There is thus a catch-22 situation: instability in the industry prevents reliable volume production, and this in turn prevents economies of scale and mechanization, so that building costs rise disproportionately to costs in other parts of the economy, and the industry continues to be unstable.

The effects of instability on the labour force are equally serious and equally involve a catch 22. It is just as difficult for builders to employ labour on a permanent basis as it is for them to invest heavily in capital equipment (Hutton, 1970). A minimum of skilled labour is in fact permanently employed; but the bulk of the labour is transient. The generally unpleasant and dangerous conditions of work on the building site, and the uncertainty of employment lead to a constant drain of skilled labour out of the industry into more permanent employment in other industries. The apprenticeship system does not provide an adequate rate of replacement (Hutton, 1970) and the craft unions are understandably reluctant to reduce their members' security still further by permitting other methods of training, for example through technical colleges alone. In times of peak demand, therefore, skilled labour is at a premium; builders are forced to compete in over-award payments, and labour turnover is high (Crichton, 1966). Substitution of processes which can be carried out by unskilled or semi-skilled labour, or off-site work is encouraged. Similar considerations apply to skilled supervisory personnel (Hutton, 1970); large construction firms have increasingly substituted professional staff, such as engineers, for the traditional craft-trained supervisors. All of this tends to increase the insecurity of skilled labour, and provides a further stimulus to the practice of subcontracting. At the same time the dependence of the industry on a large body of unskilled labour, without job commitment of any kind, and organized into large and militant unions in itself increases instability through strike action for both economic and political ends.

It is a commonplace that the traditional builder has largely given way to the entrepreneurial contractor who employs subcontractors to carry out the greater part of the work. Again, according to Hutton, between 60% and 70% of total costs to building contractors may consist in payments to subcontractors. Construction has become "basically the installation of factory-made parts plus the 'manufacture' of parts on the site by sub-contractors under the supervision of a contractor" (Handler, 1970). The subcontractor provides skilled labour, much of the capital equipment, and also, though detailed figures are difficult to obtain, notoriously much of the capital by way of credit, whether voluntarily or under duress. The subcontracting system increases unpredictability of performance in two ways. Firstly, it greatly increases the complexity of site organization and promotes unexpected delays. Bromilow (1969) has argued that the greatest single contribution to the efficiency of the building industry would be the elimination of delay due to lack of co-ordination, and this means predominantly lack of co-ordination of subcontractors. Attempts to promote better organization, however, have frequently resulted in strike action by unions, who are as it were notified in advance of the best times to press their claims. And secondly, the actual execution of the work is placed at two removes from the architect; main contractors who have a record of competence may be selected, but they will be guided in their selection of subcontractors by administrative factors and the availability of credit, at least as much by skill. The current form of building contract agreed by the Royal Australian Institute of Architects and the Master Builders Federation of Australia imposes extremely onerous, not to say penal, responsibilities on the architect who attempts to exercise more than a minimum of influence in this area. As a result, the quality of the work is unpredictable; for however sound the specification, no amount of inspection can ensure that the result is substantially better than the workmen concerned are willing and able to carry out (Heath, 1974a). This is also, of course, an effect of the continuing decline in the supply of skilled labour. Finally, the multitude of subcontractors contributes to the diffuseness of the industry and its lack of political organization, which in turn encourages ill-conceived tampering by governments.

Building materials can be broadly divided into structural materials, those of which the building carcass is actually composed, and finishing materials. In general the former are used in very large quantities and have to be correspondingly very cheap, so that they consist of minimally processed mineral and forest products. They also tend to be massive, not only because of their origins, but also because the density of the component materials contributes substantially to the thermal, acoustic and fire performance of buildings. Thus transport costs place rigid limitations on sources of supply. In a country such as Australia, where urban centres are far apart, this is a major cause of inflexibility in the substitution of sources of material supply. In more densely populated countries the significance of transport costs may be less, but it is still true that the possibilities of substitution are limited. Finishing materials, on the other hand, are used in much smaller quantities, are more highly processed and expensive, and are often transported for great distances, especially where water transport is available. There is in fact an international market in such materials. Timber products occupy an intermediate position; many countries, including Australia, depend heavily on imported timber.

The reliability and availability of materials varies considerably. The question of reliability has been discussed already. Availability of finishing materials, particularly those for which there is a national or international market, is relatively predictable, though specific shapes, colours, finishes and so on may disappear without warning, and firms may amalgamate or cease operations between the completion of design and the moment when the material must be ordered for installation in the building under construction. The supply of structural materials is less predictable. Like the rest of the industry, the producers of these materials are affected by the boom-and-bust cycle, and their markets are more limited than those of the producers of finishing materials. Their production is thus aimed at the average level of demand; and in times of boom particular types of brick, cement or timber, or even all bricks, cement and timber of good construction grades, may suddenly cease to be available. Quarries and claypits are not renewable resources, and forestry planning has often been inadequate (Hutton, 1970), so that the most convenient and suitable supplies become exhausted, and may be difficult to replace. This difficulty has been increased in recent years by the growing concern for the environment, which has often focussed on supply sources of building materials because, in their nature, they must be near major population centres or otherwise highly accessible.

The low capitalization of the building industry and its lack of organization discourage effective innovation. In Australia, as in Britain, public expenditure on building research is about 0.04% of the value of building work (Kennedy, 1970) and there is little or no industry-funded research; in the US, Kennedy suggests, industry-funded research is more substantial. Nor is there great incentive for on-the-job innovation; such innovation, as Kennedy rightly argues, must usually begin with the design, and here the risks are high and the returns are low. As he says: "If a novel design requires that new machinery be bought or new working procedures developed... then the contractors are likely to respond with higher, not lower bids." When this is taken together with the risks of failure inherent in technical innovation, it is understanable that cautious and experienced architects will propose such innovations only to meet some overriding need of the client, and then only if the client understands and accepts the risk. In general, changes in building technology take place only because the established methods have become completely impossible. Insofar as change is evident, it is in the area of supply of finishing materials, where more technically advanced producers tend to seek new markets, or a share of old ones; and here the difficulties of testing have produced, on the whole, a sad record.

Given the factors making for instability and unpredictability, it is hardly surprising that the industry is notoriously unable to meet the bureaucratic requirement of performance in terms of time and cost. Boom demand leads inevitably to hyperinflationary movements in the cost of materials and labour, which compound variations in the general rate of inflation, in themselves largely unpredictable. Construction time is equally affected by shortage of labour and materials, and also by industrial action of various kinds, by the difficulties of organizing subcontractors, and by such external factors as changes in building regulations and, as Bromilow has pointed out in his analysis of the time performance of the industry (Bromilow, 1969), especially by the actions of building owners in proposing variations to work that is under way.

All of this must be taken into account in considering the behaviour of another significant element of the industry, the private investor. Criticism of the influence of "developers" and of private building investors generally has been well-nigh universal, harsh, and largely justified by results. Yet the risks of investing in building are such that only a very high rate of return indeed could induce any reasonable entrepreneur to invest in this, rather than some other industry. It is indeed for this reason that government is easily able, by manipulating the interest rate, to drive the private investor from the market. In these circumstances, it is odd that investors have (historically speaking) so regularly proved inept at assessing the demand for buildings. The recent world-wide boom in office construction, for example, sparked by a genuine demand originating with changes in the structure of the work-force and post-war shortages, ended in a condition of over-supply which was often grotesque. This failing of the entrepreneurial psychology does not, however, seem to be confined to building, since similar conditions of over-supply appear in other industries, such as the electrical goods industry. In building over-supply does not even, for the reasons discussed, lead to a significant drop in price per unit, or in the main to any improvement in quality.

As an element of the architect's task environment, the building industry contributes heavily to uncertainty. In the technical aspects of his work, the reasonable architect is necessarily conservative. Paradoxically, as we shall see, this conservatism makes design itself easier; but the residual anxiety makes heavy demands, and the inevitable failures of prediction contribute to the poor reputation of architects as a group. Conservatism also conflicts with some of the values of the profession; and it is to the structure and values of the profession and their often unacknowledged influence on method that we shall now turn.

3.4   The professional environment

In our context, "the professional environment" might be taken to refer to the professions generally, or to the group of professions especially associated with architects in the building industry: civil, structural, mechanical, and other specialist engineers, and quantity surveyors, where that profession exists. The intention here is somewhat narrower: it is the architectural profession, its recruitment, education, formal organization, literature, and self-image, which is meant. Every architect in practice defines himself and his work to some extent against this background, accepting or rejecting parts of it according to his attitudes and experience. It helps him to form his problem spaces, just as his awareness of the capacities of the building industry does; but it extends beyond any particular design task.

It is convenient to begin with the formal organizations which represent the profession: professional institutes and related organizations. Here we may take note of Mant's (1975) distinction between professionalism as legitimization, and technical professionalism. Legitimization includes the attempt to secure monopolistic or sole right to act in a defined area of expertise, or alleged expertise (Wilensky, 1964). This aspect of the professions generally has been severely criticized in recent years, and architecture has not escaped its share of criticism, though in fact architects have been less successful than other established professions in protecting themselves by legal means. While legitimization is, naturally, a recurrent concern of professional organizations, it is not of much concern for the practice of design, or for method. It is the concern of professional organizations with technical professionalism, and the values and objectives that the official representatives and prestigious members of the profession publish and promote which to a greater or lesser degree influence design.

The major analysis of the ideology of the architectural profession has been carried out by Lipman (1970, 1976). His work relates specifically to the United Kingdom, but it is indicative of more general attitudes. Drawing on interviews, on inaugural addresses by successive presidents of the RIBA, on RIBA annual conference reports, and the series of "Architect's Approach to Architecture" lectures which are a continuing feature of the *RIBA Journal*, he has identified a number of "socially oriented service objectives" of the profession, and formed estimates of their importance in terms of frequency of mention. By far the greatest number of references in his tables (Lipman, 1976) are to "social engineering orientations", mainly concerned with designing and planning to meet what are conceived to be broad needs of society (570 references). Next are "professionalism orientations" (266 references), over half of which (158 references) refer to the need to "increase efficiency and ability of architectural service". Next are "aesthetic orientations" (254 references) with which may be grouped "social symbolism orientations", so that taken together these refer-

ences are in fact more numerous than those to "professionalism". Next
are "serviceability orientations", or references to "architectural functionalism"; but there is a large residual category consisting of 142
references to the design of man's physical surroundings in accordance
with his needs, and 184 references to basing architectural design
decisions on the needs of man. In general, the picture is of an
overwhelming concern with "user requirements" (the subject of
Lipman's discussion in the paper from which these figures are taken),
at a variety of levels, from broad planning to detailed design, a
concern which incorporates a strong commitment to aesthetic values.
Canter (1970) similarly demonstrates a belief on the part of architects
they they should be "client centred". This general picture is partly
confirmed but also qualified by Mackinnon's (1961) study of the
personalities of American architects recognized by their peers as being
"creative". These men ranked aesthetic and theoretical values most
highly, above social, political, religious and economic values. This
result tells us a great deal not only about the limited sample of the
American profession actually studied, but about that professional
group as a whole. It is clear that these men were selected as "creative"
by their peer group *because* of their aesthetic values, and that it was
their achievements in the *art* of architecture that caused them to be
known and respected. We should also note the relatively low valua-
tion of user needs in the process of making awards for architectural
merit. Lee (1971) cites studies by Perin (1970) and Hassid (1964)
which show in Perin's words "that the basis of judgement did not
include any such category"; that it *did* include an aesthetic category is
obvious. These anomalies are perhaps partly explained by Gutman's
recent studies (Gutman, 1981) which identify three *competing* role
models amongst American architects: an architect as *professional*, the
architect-artist and architecture as a *service industry*.

It is, perhaps, no news to be told that at least until recently the
majority of modern architects have espoused a group of doctrines
which may be loosely identified as "functionalism", or that they attach
a primary value to aesthetics. Functionalist theory has a history
reaching back over two hundred years, which has been thoroughly
studied (De Zurko, 1957; Banham, 1960). It represents the long
struggle of architectural practice to come to terms with the emerging
mass society, and to adapt to the bureaucratic values of long-term
planning, efficiency, quantifiability and so on. It is not surprising that
its two main periods of doctrinal development and application were in
Germany and Scandinavia after the first world war, and in Britain after
the second. It is certainly the only current candidate for a body of
general theory in architecture. Aesthetic orientation, on the other
hand, has a connection with architecture which extends back into

prehistory; though this is to some extent specious, since the way in which we ordinarily distinguish architecture from mere buildings, in periods that precede the organization of an architectural profession, is by the qualities of size and prominence, and evident concern with aesthetic quality. But what is important to notice here, though it is obvious enough, is that these long-established and self-evident sets of values are in conflict.

The conflict between "functionalism", with its implications of conformity to bureaucratic norms and acceptance of overall social planning, on the one hand, and the humanistic and specifically aesthetic values which architects also espouse has not been ignored. It was awareness of this conflict which led Gropius to propose his doctrine of "psychological functionalism" (Gropius, 1956). There has nevertheless been a continuing rift in the profession between the romantics and the rationalists, between the soft-hearted and the hard-headed, expressed, for example, in the repressed but never extinguished tradition of expressionism (Sharp, 1966), in the division between "organic architecture" and the influence of the Bauhaus in America, and more recently by the various proponents of autonomous housing, ecological architecture, participatory design, "post-modernism", and so on as against "big architecture". In fact, so far from successfully bridging the "two cultures" as Snow hoped (Snow, 1956), architecture has incorporated the split between the culture and the means of production: incorporated it as a division within the profession, within office organization, and within the attitudes and methods of individual architects. These divisions have been exacerbated because, while "functionalism" has progressed in the sense that more aspects of architecture have been quantified and subjected to the constraints of cost and return, and thus made acceptable in terms of the ethos which the most numerous and powerful clients — governments, institutions, and large businesses — understand and support, there has been no comparable progress in aesthetic theory. Architects' explanations of what they are about have thus more and more been in terms of function, user requirements, social dynamics, and the like, and less and less in terms of aesthetic qualities, which play such a large (if not dominant), but imperfectly articulated part in their own desires and purposes. Dishonesty feeds on dishonesty, and having been trapped by an inadequate and contradictory belief system into deceiving others, architects also deceive themselves. Serious and extended discussion of aesthetics, as opposed to vague references, is socially unacceptable, not only among architectural psychologists (Heath, 1974c), but among the profession at large. There is an urgent need for the resolution of this underlying conflict, for a new view of the designer's task, a method which does not divide the world in that kind of way. The fish is not in the bottle; but designers have to learn that it is not. At present, new recruits to the architectural profession are taught, to some extent by precept but much more forcibly by example, that the fish is very tightly englobed.

Like other kinds of education, architectural education conveys values as extensively, and perhaps more effectively than, practical knowledge, productive ability, or the habit of critical thought. The schools conserve and transmit the values of the profession, and in most countries are closely monitored by professional committees concerned with the setting of educational standards, to ensure that they do not depart too far from the conventional wisdom. Of course they are also largely responsible for changes in the profession, which originate both from proposals of the professional organizations themselves, intended to adapt future members to real, imagined or anticipated changes in the conditions of practice, and also within the body of academic opinion, which has become increasingly independent, and has developed attitudes and aims which are often quite at variance with those of the practitioners (Markus, 1975). To clarify the functions of the schools, and the way in which they serve to create and limit the task environment of their graduates, it is necessary briefly to review the history of architectural education. Unfortunately there does not appear to be any general historical study of architectural education as distinct from accounts of the development of particular schools, and since research on this topic is beyond the scope of the present work, the account given here will necessarily be impressionistic.

Studio instruction is still central to architectural education. That is, students spend much of their period of study working on tasks that are supposed to be analogues of the tasks which they will face in practice, with the advice and assistance of qualified and more or less experienced architects. This system is almost two hundred and fifty years old. It has its origins in the competitions for the Prix de Rome, first organized after the formation of the French Academy in the early eighteenth century. These competitions were conducted under examination conditions of some rigour. The "programme" or statement of conditions of the problem was set in advance and unalterable, and there was naturally an emphasis on speed of decision and skill in presentation. With the establishment of formal architectural schools, the Beaux-Arts and the Polytechnique, education was divided into two: formal lectures, largely in history, then the new and exciting research subject, and studio work in one of a number of private "ateliers", run by practitioners, which aimed still at teaching the student to succeed in the official competitions and ultimately the Prix de Rome. The detailed and accurate historical, or more precisely archaeological, knowledge and the powerful, if highly abstracted, planning techniques (Van Zanten, 1976, 1977) which evolved from this system were the envy of other countries, and towards the end of the century the educational methods of the Beaux-Arts were widely copied in new architecture schools in England, America, and indeed wherever schools were founded (MacLeod, 1971).

The only alternative model for formal architectural education developed before the second world war was that of the Bauhaus. It differed from the Beaux-Arts system in a number of significant ways. History was discarded, or all but discarded (Gropius, 1956). Attention was focused on contemporary problems. The concept of designing for human needs, of "functionalism" was introduced, and, as far as the very limited knowledge of the time permitted, pursued. Abstract geometrical design replaced the traditional "elements of architecture", and students were given a special introductory course, the famous "vorkurs", in its principles; simple geometrical forms were considered to constitute the "machine aesthetic". Students were required to go through a craft course, involving not only designing but making, before being admitted to the final course in architecture. These were truly revolutionary changes; so revolutionary that they received little practical acceptance anywhere else until the late 1940s. One thing that did not change, however, was the studio system of instruction.

After the second world war, elements of this system invaded or were grafted on to the by now traditional school system in many parts of the world. The need to attend to contemporary problems had become self-evident; the spirit of the times favoured public service and the attempt to meet the needs and aspirations of a mass society (Jackson, 1970). Teachers imbued with the ideas and ideals of the Modern Movement increasingly found their way into the schools. "Modern" architecture became accepted as a style, and fairly quickly became the only style. In some schools the "vorkurs" was imitated. History teaching declined, or became unpopular. But the notion of craft training and practical work which had provided the concrete element in Bauhaus training was too difficult to assimilate into the existing system. Studio training continued, with more "realistic" programmes, in the sense that they more often dealt with contemporary problems and were more detailed.

This wave of innovation had hardly been assimilated before it was overtaken by another. Progress in science had made to a considerable extent a reality of what for the Bauhaus had been only a dream or ideal: the placing of many aspects of architecture on a scientific basis. "Building science" and "building research" came first, "environmental studies" and "social science" soon after. Since there were no architects adequately equipped to teach these new subjects, architecture schools were invaded by teachers and researchers trained in other fields. This began in the early sixties (Broadbent,1973b); it is still under way. The response of the traditional system all too precisely illustrated the maladaptive strategies of dissociation, denying the importance of the new disciplines, segmentation, or dividing the school firmly into two camps and forcing the students to take sides; and superficiality, or accepting the changes verbally without allowing them to affect in the least the established patterns of studio instruction. And where the schools displayed dynamic conservatism, practitioners not infrequently displayed conservatism pure and simple (Broadbent, 1975).

The tensions created by the existence, in the same school, of teachers and researchers with powerful, well-organized bodies of knowledge, and others whose teaching methods were essentially at the craft level, have proved very difficult to endure. This partly accounts for the premature adoption by some teachers and some schools, of "first-generation" design methods (see Chapter 5). It was hoped that these methods, derived from operational research, from developments in computer analysis, and from system theory in its more primitive forms, would resolve the conflict. Unfortunately, as we shall see, the methods were inherently inadequate to the problems. Traditional studio design, therefore, did better as a teaching method than the new methods; existing prejudices have been reinforced, and the wounds in the educational system remain untreated.

With this, admittedly inadequate, background, let us return to studio instruction, which still remains central to the system in default of anything better. Wade (1977) has advanced a spirited and affectionate defence of the studio. Whilst emphasizing the need for the school to "bring a great deal more information and method to the student than it has been bringing" he argues that the student learns a great deal that is worthwhile, in four areas.

> "First, the design student learns a great deal about the problem solving process. He learns design in the same way that some people have supposedly learned to swim — by being thrown into the water... certainly not a painless way to learn, but having learned, there is much that the designer knows."

He learns, too, according to Wade, about the influence of personality and time on design solutions. He learns about co-operative problem solving. And he learns "what architecture is about. He is initiated into the architectural profession. He learns what questions the profession is willing to address and what questions it is willing to answer"; in other words, he begins to acquire the extended problem space which this chapter seeks to explore.

There are some criticisms which may be made of Wade's arguments. The first concerns the admitted painfulness of the studio teaching system; a failing that has been noticed by many writers on assessment of studio work. Pain is not good for people; it frequently produces avoidance of risk, with a corresponding damping of confident productive activity; yet productive activity is supposed to be encouraged by the studio system. The second criticism concerns the influence of time on design solutions; and here, it may be argued, what the student learns is simply wrong, because the studio design problem is a poor, indeed a disastrously bad, analogue of the practice situation. The design of a private house requires about a man-year of effort. The design of a major building such as a hospital requires in the order of ten man-years of effort by the architects alone, ignoring client's representatives and consultants who make vital contributions. These figures contrast with the periods of from ten to twenty *weeks* commonly allowed for the studio design problem. And the student has many other commitments; he is at best working half time. True, the times given for design in practice include the time taken to produce working drawings, and this might be held to be unfair; the schematic design or sketch plan is produced in much less time, and this, it may be said, is all that can or need be expected from students. But schematic design in practice is usually undertaken or closely directed by experienced architects who know, by virtue of their experience, how to avoid building in pitfalls which later detailed design and documentation will reveal, invalidating the design. Students by definition do not know these things; and if their designs are to be made in any sense realistic they have to find them out by study; so that in fact the student should take much *longer* to complete the same design, even to the schematic level, than an experienced team of practitioners should take to do the whole job. In theory, the studio masters advise the students, but there is not enough time for that either. There are many students and few teachers. The students are all working on different designs which present the teacher with different problems. The teachers may not in fact have much practical experience; or if they have they may not have formulated it systematically.

So what the student learns in the design studio is still in the main what he learned in the nineteenth century: some methods of generating plans, some aesthetic standards, and some ways of connecting the two. These are indeed fundamental skills. In the best schools, every effort is also made to reproduce the client relationship; but again, time is against such realism. But what the student does *not* learn is to test these ideas against available methods of construction, or against the increasingly varied and complex information provided by the scientific disciplines. In fact, he often learns to avoid doing this, and to conceal the evasion skillfully; for if he attempts it, he will fail to deliver his work on time. He is in fact systematically trained in methods which will lead to failure in practice: in careless thinking and misrepresentation. And it is much harder to unlearn things than to learn them. Even if it is accepted that it is the task of firms in practice to teach practical matters to new graduates, their task is made very much harder by the system as it exists.

Much the same can be said of the design process itself. Despite the best efforts of the best schools, *interaction* with the client, the users, and the host of "others" who make up the working environment of design is never more than inadequately simulated. And here early practical experience is of little help; for the young graduate's contacts with the world outside the office are usually severely limited, and there is little incentive for this to change.

It would be good to be able to conclude this discussion with a simple, inexpensive and practical scheme for improving the schools of architecture. But despite many earnest and highly intelligent endeavours, there have been no striking successes. It does seem, however, that the lack of a demonstrably workable, teachable method, is somewhere near the heart of the problem. Without such a method theoretical disciplines remain unrelated to productive activity, practice cannot feed back into theory and teaching — depressingly enough, when experienced practitioners teach, they fall back on the methods by which they themselves were taught — and the schools cannot progress.

3.5   The office environment

Architects work in a diversity of social settings. The most obvious dimension along which work settings vary is that of size. Some work as sole practitioners, sometimes literally by themselves, sometimes employing a secretary and perhaps a draftsman. At the other extreme, there are large public and private offices which may employ as many as a thousand people. But size alone is not a sufficient indicator of the quality of the working environment, though there are certain rough correlations. The methods and habits of work of the individual or the group will be influenced by two main factors: the type of organization or social structure; and the back-up facilities provided. The RIBA study *The Architect and his Office* (Smith et al., 1962) found that a majority of those offices which "performed best" on a number of indices were intermediate in size, between, say, eleven and thirty: large enough to afford reasonable back-up facilities, but small enough to avoid acute problems of organization. Each of these aspects requires some discussion; of the two, the social structure is by far the more important, while the question of back-up facilities can be treated quite briefly.

Throughout the design process the architects working on a given design have constantly to obtain and transmit information. Information has to be obtained from the client, and also, it is to be hoped, from the users, from a variety of authorities, from other consultants, from materials suppliers, and from technical advisory bodies. These flows are not one way; to obtain information one always has to give information, so transmission is also involved. Further, there will be internal records of information obtained and decisions made, which must be stored so that they are not forgotten and can be retrieved when needed, and must also be transmitted amongst those within the organization who are involved directly or indirectly. Some information is needed constantly for reference: acts and regulations, standards, data on commonly used materials and fittings. All of this is a roundabout and complicated way of saying that the life of the working designer is made much easier if he has the support of a competent secretarial and filing service and a good library, preferably with a competent librarian. Very small offices find it difficult to afford these things, and this in effect is what *The Architect and his Office* says. The more laborious proper research, communication, and record keeping are, the less likely they are to be done. And while these are the mere mechanics of method, they are, nonetheless, essential.

Turning now from back-up facilities to the social structure of the office, we can first distinguish two styles of work organization: bureaucratic, or "line", organization, and team, or "batch", organization. The terms "line" and "batch" are derived from the comparable types of work organization in manufacturing industry. In "line" organization there is in principle a clear distinction of the parts of the task, which are carried out by different individuals or groups, as in a production line. Thus we find offices in which the partners or directors are responsible for all client contacts; there is a design group who do all the designing; there is a drawing office under a chief draftsman in which these designs are converted into working documents; and there are field supervisors who are responsible for the interpretation of the documents on site, for quality control, and so on. There may be other separate departments for specification writing, and for the preparation of presentation drawings or models. This is a characteristically bureaucratic system; the staff in each department have clearly defined responsibilities, they are interchangeable and replaceable, there is a hierarchy and there are supervisory mechanisms; each person is employed at a task in which he is skilled or qualified.

Despite its apparent rationality, this system, which is common in large public and private offices, though perhaps less common than it used to be, has serious deficiencies. Even an assembly line does not really operate in the way in which it is nominally "supposed" to operate (Beer, 1966). And there is a fundamental difference between the passing of an object down an assembly line on the one hand and the passing on of the body of information and decisions which constitute a design on the other. In the latter case there are massive information losses each time the task is passed from one group to the next (Schein, 1965). Such losses are inevitable, partly because it is impossible to record *everything* (and impossible to retrieve it if it were recorded), but also because such an organization leads to segmentation, an "us and them" mentality, which in turn creates a reluctance to communicate. There may also be an excessive reliance on written or documented communication rather than face-to-face discussion, which again produces severe information losses. Not only is the forward transmission likely to be defective; feedback of experience and understanding from the executed work to the next design is even less effective. Some of the criticisms of very large offices to be found in *The Architect and his Office* can no doubt be attributed to this pattern of organization. Nevertheless, it can be effective where the nature of the work is simple and repetitive, though it must be said that this condition is seldom if ever fulfilled in an architectural office.

The "batch" system of team organization places the whole responsibility for the development, documentation, and implementation of a design with a team or group who carry out each stage of the work. There will be division of the work among members of the team on the basis of experience, special skills and so forth, but it will be less hard and fast than in a line system. The batch system may be adopted by either small or large offices. Information loss is reduced, though this depends to some extent on the style of leadership and the organization of the team, as discussed hereafter. Nevertheless, the system is not without its difficulties, which arise mainly from the fluctuating workload over the long period of design and construction. During the early stages of design, progress is usually slow, and little labour is required, though there may be flurries of activity associated with particular stages. Then there is a relatively short period of intensive work in preparing the construction documents, which may require the efforts of five times as many people; and finally there is, again, a less intensive demand during construction. Obviously it is not economically possible for everyone who is involved in the documentation stage to work on the job throughout. In practice only a key group can carry right through; and this too has its disadvantages, for these people will be required to spend months and even years of their lives on the one project, and are likely to become bored and discouraged, and even, in extreme cases, to change jobs rather than continue. Teamwork is thus by no means a panacea; but it is better suited to complex problems than the bureaucratic type of organization.

Within a team type of organization, a variety of communication patterns is possible. These patterns have been extensively studied, both in experimental conditions and "on the job"; they recur in many kinds of organized activity. Two are especially important for architecture: the centralized pattern, and the network pattern. In the centralized pattern, the team leader acts as the link between the members of the team and between the team and the task environment. Indeed his position in the centre of the information flow would *make* him the leader, whatever his formal title. His information load will be heavy at best, but while it remains within his capacity, he is likely to be satisfied with his job. Whether or not the other members are satisfied will depend on their personalities, and on the personality and ability of the team leader. This kind of communication pattern cannot cope well with situations in which the information load is inherently high, though it can be "stretched" by creating a hierarchy, on the bureaucratic model, with "middle management" or "non-commissioned officers" inserted between the team leader and the other members to screen out a percentage of the information load. With careful initial selection of leader and middle management this system can work well, and some of the most admired architectural offices are organized on this pattern, as *The Architect and his Office* makes clear. However, each additional step in the chain, as previously observed, increases the risk of information loss and error. This communication pattern is suited only to an autocratic style of leadership.

The network pattern permits, in fact encourages, direct communications between all members of the team, and may also permit multiple communication with the outside world. Each member is able to feel some responsibility for the whole of the work. General satisfaction is likely to be higher. This pattern may be less efficient than centralized organization for the simpler tasks, but comes into its own as the task grows more complex. It does have a limiting size, roughly the size of a "face-to-face" group for discussion. About twelve is a good working number, twenty represents a limit. After that some kind of segmentation has to be introduced, or communication once again becomes ineffective. However, networks can be overlapped, in a "matrix" type of organization which can cope with tasks of great complexity. A communication system of the network type properly requires a democratic style of leadership. It can be strongly argued that a network organization is the one best suited to architectural practice. As Emery and Trist (1960) contend: "The only justification for a rigid division of labour is a technology which demands specialised non-substitute skills, and which is, moreover, sufficiently superior, as a technology, to offset the losses due to rigidity." The demands of technology in the architectural work situation are at present negligible.

Reference has been made to styles of leadership. The distinction between authoritarian, democratic and laissez-faire styles and their effect on group work was studied intensively by Lewin, Lippitt and

White of the University of Iowa, using groups of small children (White and Lippit, 1968). Brown (1954) sees these results as applicable to industrial work situations; and they seem equally applicable to the work of architectural offices. Authoritarian leaders make all policy decisions themselves, and also dictate tactics, reserving the overall plan, so that the group members are largely uncertain as to what happens next. (This pattern of reservation of information is highly characteristic of authoritarian leadership and tends to spread through the organization.) The leader prefers to deal with group members individually, rather than acting as a member of the group. The group is thus "leader-centred". Democratic leadership on the other hand encourages group discussion of policies, and formulation of the overall work plan. The leader acts as a technical adviser to the group, and acts as a group member. Activity is "group-centred". Laissez-faire leadership allows complete freedom for group or individual decision; the leader is completely reactive and non-participative.

Unsurprisingly, laissez-faire leadership is almost completely ineffective. Frustration tends to be high, output low. Autocratic leadership is better in some respects, provided that the leader can maintain control, so that the group does not organize against him; output may be high, though frustration is also likely to be high. Finally democratic leadership, provided that it is effective and does not degenerate into laissez-faire, can maintain both high output and low frustration. Since it promotes the sharing of information, through a network-type organization, it would appear to be the preferable style for dealing with complex problems. The qualification is important: "If the task is straightforward and requires little interpersonal co-operation, there is no compelling reason to believe that 'co-operative' groups should have an advantage over individuals or 'competitive' groups" (Golembiewski, 1962). This does not contradict the previously quoted opinion of Emery and Trist; it re-affirms that task and type of organization must match each other. And finally, we should note the point made by Schein (1965), that leadership is a function, rather than a trait of an individual or a formal position.

It has been implied in what has been said previously that some groups, thanks to their leadership and pattern of organization, are more effective than others. Likert (1961) synthesized research from a wide range of sources to produce a profile of the highly effective work group. This group is taken to be part of a larger organization, and each member, therefore, will be a member of other groups. The group will be "small"; the larger the group, the harder it is to make it highly effective. Each member of the group will be skilled in his role. The group will be established, and experienced in working together. They will be relaxed in their relationship, mutually loyal, and with a corresponding confidence in each other. Their goals and values will be shared, and the most important values will be the most generally accepted. Goals will be set high enough to stimulate, but not so high as to create anxiety. Members will be highly motivated to achieve these shared goals, and will feel a mutual responsibility for achieving them. The atmosphere of the group will be supportive and problem-centred; differences of opinion and criticism will not be seen as personal, but as contributing to the solution of common problems and the achievement of common goals. The group will attempt to help each member to develop, encouraging him to "achieve the impossible" and protecting him from feelings of failure or rejection. While administrative rules for mutual convenience will be accepted, new approaches will be encouraged and rewarded. Communication will be full and frank; there will be strong motivation to communicate and to receive communication; individuals will seek to influence each other and will accept influence from others. The group will influence the leader and communicate to him all the available information, including unpalatable information, by group processes, in a way which would not be possible for individuals. The group will be flexible and adaptable, but because it has well-established goals and values will not change lightly. Members of the highly effective group will make decisions confidently because they thoroughly understand the context in which the decision is to be made. And lastly, the leader's position will be based on evident ability, such that, even in an unstructured situation, he would be the natural leader of the group. In all this, Likert notes, the central principle is that of supportive relationship. Of course, the fact that a group is effective does not guarantee that it works for the "general good"; that depends on the goals and values which the group adopts. However, it is quite likely that such a group will have altruistic values and pursue contructive goals.

So far we have looked inward, at the internal structure of the office. But the organizational environment of architecture includes other groups: clients, users and consultants. Clients and users form part of the specific task environment, which will be treated in more detail later. Consultants, however, are part of the immediate working environment of the architect. Yet they are not normally working with him in the same office; and even in the case of those large public and private offices which provide a range of engineering and surveying services in addition to architectural services, these groups are usually organized independently and may be physically remote, if not in a different building. It is difficult to arrange matters otherwise. The amount of work done by any one of the consultants on a given project is much less than that done by the architects, in terms of man-hours, so that to keep a group of engineers or quantity surveyors gainfully employed it is necessary that they should work on several different designs in the time required by an architectural team for one. Separate organization and somewhat separate location follow. This separateness is emphasized by differences of background and interest; the values and goals of consultant work groups will differ from those of architects, and mutually suspicious and competitive attitudes may, and not infrequently do, result. Even in organizations that officially combine two or more of the various disciplines under the one umbrella, it is not uncommon to find a complete split, even amounting to mutual hostility, between them. Yet it is essential to the work of design that these divisions should be overcome. The effectiveness of an architectural work group, and thus its value as a task environment for those working within it, will depend heavily on the extent to which its members can accept their collaborators from other disciplines as honorary members of the group. This requires that both sides should be concerned with each other's problems, goals, and values, and perhaps also that they should have rather more technical knowlege of them than is usual. It also requires that they should work together over a long period, perhaps over many projects, and establish the habits of mutual support and communication needed for such an extension of the work group. The proper atmosphere must be created in the first place by the leaders of the two organizations. Just as the leader is important in creating a supportive atmosphere within the group, it is his task to create a mutually supportive relationship between groups working on the same task.

This section has sought to depict four aspects of the general architectural task environment. The general organization, dynamics and values of society at large, the specific economic and industrial structure of the building industry, the values of the architectural profession, and the organization of architectural offices, make up a field of forces which influence the processes of design quite apart from the specific circumstances in which any particular building is conceived. Whether intuitively and as part of their inexplicit professional knowledge, or through some more or less developed theory, architects respond to these forces. The attempt to objectify method must refer back, from time to time and in greater or lesser degree, to judgements and decisions arising from this environment. For, unless we can specify our decisions and their sources, a significant part of what we do remains covert and inexplicit, not subject to critical discussion.

Goals in architecture

4.1 Introduction

Problem solving aims at some goal. What is the goal of architecture? It is not simply the erection of a building. From the point of view of the client and the users the building is, at least in most cases, a means not an end; it is constructed in connection with some on-going activities of theirs. It is the building-in-service, what the economists would call the stream of utility which flows from the building, which they want; and this must also be a major goal of the architect. But what will those activities be, and how do they relate to an as yet non-existent physical setting? Will they change over the life of the building or even over the period of its design, and how can the building be designed to cope with such changes? Who is to decide these questions, and what is the role of the architect in the decisions? Human activities are not merely mechanical, they have dimensions of emotion, affect, value, and how are these things to be expressed? This chapter will examine each of these four issues: the issue of utility, the issue of change, the issue of designing for others, and the issue of symbolism and value, or aesthetics.

4.2 Goals of utility

The concepts of utility that have had most influence on contemporary architects derive from the "functionalist" group of ideas and theories, and more especially from the rationalist wing of functionalism. They are gradually being replaced by more sophisticated views, deriving in the main from sources outside architecture. The process of change, however, is a slow and painful one. The older ideas are well established in the literature and the conventional wisdom, and are, if perhaps only by virtue of familiarity, relatively simple; the new are inherently more complex, and require a certain background of knowledge and theory which is still not everywhere available, even at the "leading edge" of theoretical change, in the schools. Rationalism, as we have seen, is in its origins a doctrine of the late seventeenth and the eighteenth century, and its concept of knowledge is mechanistic and atomistic; in the eighteenth century it was seriously believed, in some circles, that human life and society could be reproduced by properly constructed automata, that is, by clockwork machines, without any random elements.

The development of bureaucracy, of industry, and of militarization have encouraged the view of life as a set of separable, precisely specifiable functions; these are rationalist views, and rationalism in architecture, it has been argued in the last chapter, to a large extent reflects these broader social tendencies. The characteristic modern statements of need in architecture are in terms of "the minimum for existence" (*Existenzminimum*), which it was assumed can be determined by reason and observation, and which will define the tasks of design. Thus Gropius (1956) writes of "...man's biological and sociological life processes" generating "...a practical programme for realising the minimum dwelling". As Lipman (1976) points out, the Parker-Morris report (Ministry for Housing and Local Government, 1961), which established standards for the British housing programme, speaks in almost identical terms. The concern of the pioneers of modern architecture with standards, prototypes (*objets types*) and minima is both understandable and humane in an industrial economy of poverty and shortage; in the post-industrial society it strikes a sour note. Further, since the means of conducting effective "biological and sociological" research into life processes had not then been developed, and given the generally rationalist temper of their thought, it was inevitable that they should determine their standards *a priori*, in the form of axioms. The early CIAM reports are peppered with propositions derived in this sort of way. This established an unfortunate precedent, which has by no means been forgotten. Architects are still inclined to consider themselves entitled, not merely compelled, to make such assumptions about other people's behaviour and needs and then to design on the basis of their assumptions.

This economizing, minimizing attitude, accompanied as it has been by an undue readiness to "know best", has fuelled a reaction against attempts to give precision to concepts of utility; especially where such attitudes have been incorporated, not only into the designs of individual architects, but into the policies of government agencies and even into law. We see this reaction on the one hand in the attack on "architectural determinism" launched by Daley at the Portsmouth conference on design methods (Daley, 1969); and on the other in the preoccupation with user participation in design which distinguishes some American theorists. Thus Mann and Bender (1972) attack the whole concept of standards and performance specifications. Mann contends that "needs" change over time; that they depend on the social context and specifically technology; in general "people are different"; it makes more sense to speak of user "intentions" or "aspirations", which in turn brings out the possibility of conflict and the need for trade-offs. "The legitimate but disastrous quest for hard 'objective' criteria carries with it the temptation to concentrate upon variables which can readily be measured and to neglect those which do not lend themselves to easy quantification and verification." Mann argues that the only way of resolving these difficulties is to involve the user in the design process, by way of a bargaining, argumentative process. He rejects as "false" choices between "pre-established" alternatives, such, presumably, as those of a market.

This kind of argument brings out what Lipman (1976) describes as the diffuse and ambiguous nature of the concept of need. Indeed, the whole area of "man – environment studies" as it is often called is littered with theoretical and methodological stumbling blocks and pitfalls. Two other concepts that require attention are the concept of function, and the "man – environment paradigm" as Hillier and Lea-man (1973) call it. In the case of "function" we must first notice the relational character of the word. Being functional is not a quality of objects or buildings; it is a relation between the object, a user, and the user's purposes. It is seldom the case that purposes are so precisely specifiable that only one object can satisfy them. Thus, when Richard III, or at least the dramatic character of that name, offered his kingdom for a horse, what he had in mind was swift and relatively safe escape; had he known of them, he would no doubt have settled for a motor bicycle, a hot-air balloon, or a Centurion tank. Conversely, still fewer objects are so limited by their original design and construction that only one use for them is possible; as witness those creativity tests which ask for as many unusual uses as possible for a brick or a can of peaches. The most one can extract from an object, as Pye (1964) has made clear, is its "principle of operation", and even that depends on understanding the cultural context in which it was used; archaeologic-al collections contain many objects whose original use is unknown or merely guessed at. All this applies equally to buildings. In general, the relationship between human activity and buildings is rather loose; it has what Rapoport (1969) describes as "low criticality". There are cases, for example work stations of various kinds, in which the interaction between the person and the physical setting is of fairly high "criticality", but that is because the situation has been deliberately designed in that way, with a tight man–machine feedback loop. The more common situation has been analysed by Cowan (1964): most human "activities" can be housed in rooms of under 18.5 square metres; a large proportion in rooms around 14 square metres; and the actual use to which rooms are put may depend on the name on the door more than upon anything else. Some uses are precluded if specialized equipment is not provided; and there is a range of criticality. Thus the more specific the activity and the more specialized equipment it demands, the more critical the size and shape of the space and the layout of equipment tends to be. A squash court, which is an integral part of the game of squash, has its shape absolutely fixed by conventions. Kitchens and bathrooms can be of many different shapes, but the minimum areas and layouts are "determined" by the need to house certain equipment, conventionally demanded and commercially available; and similar considerations can enable other room types to be "logically" designed (Eastman, 1970; Heimsath, 1977). The limits of human vision and hearing may impose physical restrictions on rooms where human interaction is important, like theatres and court rooms. In general, however, it is the attempt to provide the *minimum* of space which makes shape and layout critical; thus the connection between *minima* and *standards* is not a chance one.

Turning from the size and shape of the space to the environmental conditions, we find a similar lack of specificity. Total darkness, noise at painful levels, heat sufficient to produce sweating or cold sufficient to produce shivering, or lack of oxygen, can make the performance of many tasks impossible or very difficult. Yet people do adapt to and work even in such "intolerable" conditions. Thus it is not surprising to find that suitably motivated groups maintain their performance on certain academic tasks in very "disturbing" environments (Hovey, 1928) or under widely varying noise conditions (Clarke, 1969), although there may be "psychic costs" (Glasss and Singer, 1973). Generally, as conditions improve, performance improves, as for example in Weston's study of reading performance (Hopkinson, 1963). However, there is no specific ideal lighting level for a specific task. In the case of the thermal environment it has recently been shown that some variability over a range is to be preferred to a specific constant temperature (Thorne and Purcell, 1976) and the same may well be true of other environmental conditions. "Function" like "need" is a non-specific relation, at least in the areas with which architecture largely deals.

These flaws in the ideas of function and need may be discouraging, but they do not present any great conceptual difficulty. The criticisms of the man–environment paradigm, like Daley's criticisms of "architectural determinism", lead straight into the thorny thickets of epistemology. Hillier and Leaman (1973) see the attempt to draw a clear distinction betwen "man" and "environment" as part of the system of nineteenth century scientific ideas: "...the organism as machine-system operating in an environment with which it is dynamically related by 'causal' connections." It is, they contend, a fusion of three lines of thought: "...the organism–environment concept in biology; the subject–object interdependence in Kant; and the resultant concept of man as the object of science..." They propose as an alternative to this mechanical, spatial and quantifiable paradigm, the substitution of "logical space for spatial space". On the analogy of the structuralist approaches to language and behaviour which they associate with the theories of Chomsky and Levi-Strauss, they call for a structuralist approach to environmental studies. Such an approach would accept that people do not simply react to their environment; they construct their world, test their construct against experience, and modify it *and* the world. There is a close relation between this and recent attempts to apply Kelly's theory of personal constructs, originally developed for psychiatric purposes, to environmental studies (Stringer, 1974). There are analogies with Popper's idea of science and other human mental achievements having an existence that is neither subjective (internal) or objective (an empirical entity subject to measurement). And there is also an analogy with the concept of the problem space, which is central to the present argument. Since this is not a work on epistemology, these analogies will not be examined critically here. It is necessary, however, to raise some issues which may serve to fit these philosophical arguments into the practical activities with which method is concerned.

First of all, does it never make sense to consider interactions of people and things in purely mechanical terms? The answer to this must be no; any physiotherapist treating a "slipped disc" will make this point abundantly clear to the sufferer. It may not make sense to regard the human animal as a ghost in a machine, but we ignore the mechanical aspects of the human body at our peril. They represent limits that should not be overstepped, but not standards at which we should aim. Much the same can be said of anthropometric and psychophysical data; though even at this level, as Rapoport and Watson (1968) argue, cultural variables, that is the way people construe or construct the environment, make their appearance. As we move into more complex situations, the constructed component becomes more and more important. "Hawthorne effects" occur at the simplest level of work study. Yet we cannot say that the empirical study of working patterns is worthless, or that it produces no beneficial results; but interpretation and generalization become more difficult. In general, the practical use of environment psychology is greatest where we are willing and able to settle for less and be specific. This can be extended to the application of other human science disciplines to environmental studies. We can obtain a great deal of useful information. Its nature as information is to indicate, not what ought to be done, but what is likely to fail; it serves to limit our solution space. It does not tell us what the problem is, but what the answer cannot be.

If it is inadequate to look at "people and building" as a mechanical system, yet occasionally necessary to look at people as machines, it is clear that it is more often necessary to look at buildings as machines, or in deference to the sensibilities of structural engineers, as tools. Canter, in an important paper on the theory of function in architecture (Canter, 1970), has resolved the issues in a clear and constructive way. He starts from the proposition that the distinction between people and their environments is an arbitrary one. People do indeed construct their world and seek to maintain their constructs or where necessary to adapt them; this is a dynamic process. Buildings then act as tools which inhibit some stimuli from reaching their users and facilitate others. They may also act to filter stimuli; and they present stimuli, i.e. they convey meaning and value. Examples of stimuli that may be inhibited are rain and wind; light and sound may be filtered; various kinds of social activity may be facilitated. What needs to be facilitated, inhibited, filtered or conveyed in any given case depends on the context, on the frames of reference of the users.

This immediately begs the question: How do we know what the users' frames of reference are? They include expectations, ambitions, aspirations, beliefs and so on, as Mann and Bender (1972) argue. But is it true, as they contend, that these things can only, or best, be determined by an argumentative, interactive approach, by actually involving the users directly in the design process? The idea has obvious appeal. For one thing, as they say, it serves to bring out the fact that frames of reference conflict, as between individuals and groups; and, as they do *not* say, that individuals' frames of reference are not self-consistent. On the other hand, there are serious practical difficulties, which they acknowledge; problems of logistics and co-ordination, of cost and time, especially if, as they suggest, the approach is adopted on a project-by-project basis. The method they propose is the Issue Based Information System (IBIS) which has been developed by Rittel and others. The object of this system is to draw a fairly sharp line between criteria for a solution to a problem, including the weighting of the criteria, which are to be established by the users in debate, and the instrumental questions of how the objectives are to be achieved, measurement, verification, and the development and manipulation of models.

Mann and Bender have in mind, as their choice of examples makes clear, very broad problems, such as those of town planning, though they refer also to industrialized systems for building. It would seem that what they are trying to achieve for these communal decisions is the same kind of mutual understanding of issues that is achieved when a good architect works with his clients for a private house. There, too, if the architect is wise he will encourage husband, wife and children to discuss what they hope for in their home. And there, too, conflicts and issues will emerge, and with luck be resolved; though anecdotally one might comment that there seem to be few endeavours more stimulating to divorce than the construction of a new house. Most of the problems with which architecture deals, however, are intermediate in scale. The time and money available for design are less than in the case of planning or major systems design; but the time that must be devoted to purely technical issues is greater than in the design of an individual house. For the sake of the argument one might concede that these purely economic problems can be overcome. But the more serious difficulty is that for many buildings or complexes of buildings the user population is less identifiable than for either the city or the house. The future users of a housing project, a rental office building, a school, are not identifiable as individuals; and they also change more rapidly and less predictably than the inhabitants of a neighbourhood or a city. There are other cases — a hospital, a corporation headquarters, a factory — where identification, at least as a group, is possible. But often we are forced to rely on representatives; some sample of people selected with greater or less care as a model of the future population of the building. And representation in this sense does not really satisfy the ethical standards set up by Mann and Bender.

There are even more fundamental objections to the proposal, at least insofar as it applies to architecture. The first of these is to the assumption that a sharp line can be drawn between the ends and the means; that, in effect, the professional can be "on tap but not on top", and has nothing to contribute, or should contribute nothing, to the formation of goals. For in practice, in order to give weighting to various goals, we have to know how difficult it is to achieve them. The knowledge of means, for example, of what the building industry can currently achieve, is important in constructing a problem space small enough to be searched successfully for a solution. Conversely, the professional's knowledge of what might be possible, the range of options of which he can conceive, may be wider in some respects than that of the user. In fact, this distinction is just like the man–environment paradigm. To apply an interactive or argumentative procedure in architecture involves educating both sides, as is very well brought out in Weber's (1973) paper on the participatory design of a housing complex, which deals largely with the highly ingenious and sophisticated methods developed by the professionals to educate their user/clients and enable them to debate and decide the issues effectively. Such care and clarity of method undoubtedly contributes greatly to a better match between professional and user problem spaces. Yet however careful the communication process is, it will not be complete. Partly this is, as Seagrim (1968) argues, because no set of representations of a proposed physical environment can possibly include all the information the real environment will contain, and architects have, or should have, more skill in interpreting and extending representations towards reality. But, more generally, the professional will always, for reasons which the earlier discussion should have made abundantly clear, have knowledge that he does not and often *cannot* communicate to the user. If he is committed to serving the users of his buildings, and also the belief that in doing so he must remain neutral — a mere source of technical and instrumental data — this leads to the ethical problem of manipulation, the fear of unintentionally influencing the design; this is the problem of designing for others.

The second objection is equally serious. It concerns the possibility of achieving an agreed weighting of objectives. Here, at the most abstract level, we encounter the Condorcet paradox. As a simple example, let us consider three groups of voters, A, B, and C, who are assessing three possible situations x, y, z; and let us suppose that the outcome is as follows:

WEIGHTING	A	B	C
1	x	z	y
2	y	x	z
3	z	y	x

Then it is clear from inspection that there is no one of the outcomes which is preferred by a majority of voters. Attempts to resolve this paradox have produced an extensive literature, but according to Bell (1973) no solution has been forthcoming. Jones (1970a) rejects the whole process of ranking and weighting on the grounds that only data that are measurable on a ratio or interval scale are subject to transitive arithmetical operations. He gives the example of an individual choosing between cars; he has decided that speed is the most important factor, economy the next most important, and colour is his last criterion. But suppose that the available cars are (a) speedy but not economical or of the right colour, or (b) economical but slow and of the wrong colour, or (c) the right colour but slow and expensive; then the economical car may be chosen. The relationships are not transitive when the ranking process differs from the choosing process. This may be one reason why Mann and Bender (1972) reject the situation of choice between predetermined alternatives; but choices may be predetermined by states of nature just as much as by manufacturer's ranges.

In practice, however, people do succeed in making decisions with multiple criteria. It is at least worthwhile inspecting each situation to see whether the difficulties outlined in fact arise. The force of the argument is that we should not place too much reliance on mathematical treatment of such decisions. But as Jones admits, people frequently use such methods without disaster ensuing. The reason for this is suggested in a thoughtful paper by Grant (1974). After reviewing a number of theories and practices of decision making, he accepts the general line of criticism proposed by Jones, but suggests that the attempt to weight criteria is part of an educational process for the designer, taking it that the designer may include the users or their representatives; and secondly, that weighting will take place in any case in an unexamined and possibly still more fallacious way if such methods are not attempted.

According to this argument, we should substitute for the kind of easy but dubious resolution offered by, for example, cost–benefit analysis, the notion of an education process for designers. Lee (1971) provides an illustration:

> "In our society we have costed the objective of good health, for example, very high indeed and authority (through Parker-Morris) has taken power to insist that people in local authority houses will have *two* loos. If they had full 'freedom of choice' many of them might choose to have one loo and a garage."

Methods of exploring (not determining) such questions have been developed: for instance, the "Home Improvement Game" devised by the Division of Building Research of the CSIRO (Brealey, 1972) and the work of Eisemon (1975). Exactly similar considerations apply to the process of building appraisal; this process of feed-back, as Markus (1970) has argued, educates both architects and the client and user groups.

In summary, a theory of goals in architecture must take account of what Lipman (1976) calls the uneven rationality of the knowledge possible to designers. The picture of design as a mechanical process, like finding and putting together the pieces of a jigsaw, must be replaced by a process more complex and subtle, but nevertheless far from wholly arbitrary or intuitive. For neither the structure nor the "pieces" are given; they have to be constructed. Yet they are not constructed in a vacuum, but in a physical and social world, which excludes some possibilities and opens up others. In this process the goals, the functions, the needs, cannot be clearly distinguished from the design itself; the design process is a series of decisions as to what the goals are. Sometimes in areas of good social consensus, the process may be comparatively easy; the goals may appear clear. But this occasional clarity, fortunate though it is, deceives us if we suppose that that is the nature of design. More often goals will conflict, and there is, again, no simple mechanical way of resolving such conflicts. Design processes must be able to deal with conflicting goals.

4.3   Designing for change

Change — continuing, major, and, viewed in the light of history, rapid — is, it has been suggested, a feature of modern societies that has a primary influence on the broad world view of architects, as of many other people. But it also often forms part of the goal system of architecture. The period of social and technical change is now shorter, often considerably shorter, than the life of buildings. In Sydney, cinemas built in the thirties have been converted to bowling alleys and then again to supermarkets, and still more recently into a more modern generation of cinemas. The Building Performance Research Unit's report on St. Michael's Academy Kilwinning (Markus, 1970) observes:

> "The 'box' classroom is already anathema to the most advanced educationists because it inhibits transition from teaching to learning-based curricula and the breakdown of traditional subject patterns... This is an average school, and the average school is a dinosaur, doomed because it cannot adapt itself to change."

Again:

> "Even in four years this school has undergone important changes. What will happen during the remaining fifty-six years of its planned life is anyone's guess; but no one can doubt that if the rate of change is maintained, or accelerated, a series of crises will occur any one of which may be serious enough to limit the life of the building to a far shorter period."

The study notes three kinds of change which had already taken place: improvizations, building change, and building extension. Improvization included such minor, inexpensive and impermanent changes as the removal of doors in corridors to facilitate circulation, changes in the use of rooms, improvized blackout screens, notices taped to walls. A space intended for the delivery of school milk was first enclosed for security reasons — a building change; and then, when free delivery of milk ceased as a result of a change in official policy, converted to a store — an improvization. A bus-turning area, a garage, a grounds-man's store and an electrical transformer substation had been added — rather minor examples of building extension. How familiar this pattern is! But perhaps the most striking comment to emerge from this study, from the point of view of rate of change, was made not by the study team, but by an educationalist commenting on their work. In rejecting certain of their conclusions about the use of space in the school, he remarked:

> "It is unfortunate... that the appraisal has been carried out on a generation of school design *already outdated*, and apparently without an awareness that its relevance to *modern* design is not at once obvious." (Sharp, 1970; emphasis added)

Not merely outdated, but irrelevant, after four years; the educational system is indeed an area of rapid change.

Handler (1970), summarizing his own research on the obsolescence of schools, identifies two main kinds of change which limit the useful life of buildings: changes in physical condition, and functional change. Both are important, but we are here concerned with the latter. Functional changes can be further divided into environmental changes in the surroundings, obsolescence of the site, technical obsolescence, service system obsolescence, and misfit between the activities and the fabric, which Handler, since he is discussing schools, calls "educational obsolescence". Each of these types of functional change influences many types of buildings besides schools. Examples of environmental change that can render buildings obsolete are increases in noise level, arising for instance from new jet aircraft flight paths, or changes in the amount and kind of passing traffic, due to new road construction or the redirection of traffic through formerly quiet roads, resulting in accidents, noise and pollution (Appleyard and Lintell, 1972). A site may become obsolete if standards change; many old hospital sites are now obsolete because of insufficient parking space. Locational obsolescence occurs when the character of the surrounding population changes; in Sydney, the movement of new families to outer suburbs has rendered many churches, hospitals and schools in the inner city obsolete. Service system obsolescence occurs when the mechanical, electrical and communication systems provided no longer meet current standards; office buildings erected in Sydney between the wars have had to be demolished because it was impossible to provide the telephone and power services required for modern business communications and office equipment, let alone install air conditioning or modern fire detection and prevention systems. Misfit between the activities and the fabric is exemplified in the discussion of the appraisal of St. Michael's Academy. A striking recent example is the decline in the use of cafeterias in government offices which has resulted from the introduction of "flexitime"; given the choice many workers prefer a sandwich at their desk or even to skip lunch altogether so that they can leave work earlier in the evening. And we should include in this category those cases in which technical or social changes render a whole category of buildings obsolete, as in the decline of the cinema already mentioned, the elimination of the tuberculosis hospital, or the dramatic drop in demand for residential mental hospitals brought about by improvements in psychopharmacology.

This account of the causes of obsolescence is of some assistance in predicting, not the changes that will affect the life of a given building, but the likelihood, rate, and degree of such changes. It makes possible a "sensitivity analysis" which will indicate the need for investment to mitigate the effects of change. Thus, if a proposed building houses activities that are especially sensitive to environmental factors, in the sense outlined previously, that make intensive use of the surrounding site area, that are highly dependent on characteristics of the population served which are known to fluctuate, such as average age, or on good access, that require intensive and modern services, and which are the subject of much social concern and conflict and/or are highly valued, then we are entitled to conclude that the building is extremely sensitive to change. Hospitals and airports meet most of these conditions; so do some types of university building and some factories. Other buildings can be arranged on a descending scale of sensitivity; though, as will be argued later, it is important to look at each case on its merits, and not to assume that a given "building type" will always have the same character.

We may go further, and attempt to predict the likelihood, rate and degree of each of these types of change in the context of a given project. This is more hazardous than predicting the overall sensitivity of a project to change. In neither case can we place very great reliance on the results. Yet we may be able to do better than we should do if we simply disregard the possibility of making such an investigation. There has been a great deal of work done in recent years on the forecasting of technical and social change, and some of the results show promise. Bell (1973) discusses extrapolative forecasting, intuitive forecasting, forecasting by means of matrices and contexts, and the study of diffusion times. A kind of extrapolation that is relevant to architectural problems is the logistic or S curve. Its application depends on the assumption that where there is some kind of growth which seems to be exponential, like the growth in business communications previously referred to, this cannot in its nature be indefinitely continued; it must reach a point at which it will slow or even diminish; this is the top of the S. The steeper the curve, the more the short-term change, but the sooner the point of contraflexure will be reached. Intuitive forecasting by the "Delphi" technique is probably the only method that is regularly, if unsystematically, used in architecture. It involves asking a number of people, identified as expert, what changes they expect, and examining the areas of agreement and disagreement through confrontation and debate. There has also been some small influence on architecture, through its presentation at conferences on design method, of Zwicky's morphological charting, which is a matrix method (see section 2.5). Finally, we have the study of diffusion times, the rates at which discoveries with technological possibilities are exploited. Historically, the time required for the recognition of the commercial possibilities of new discoveries has dropped over a period of approximately seventy years from thirty to nine years; the time required for implementation of this perception has, however, dropped by only about two years, from seven years to five (Bell, 1973). What is difficult here is not so much predicting the commercial availability of some newly discovered technical process, but predicting the social impact that it will have. People were slow to become conscious of the radical changes implied by the cheap motor car, or by television.

The point of seeking to predict and characterize changes, so far as architectural method is concerned, is to attempt to avoid or mitigate their effects on buildings, particularly the costs of premature obsolescence. So far very little work indeed has been done on this problem. Much more attention has been given by architects to devising methods of coping with change in physical terms when it does occur. Yet all the strategies so far devised have high costs associated with them. It therefore seems important to be able to make some kind of informed guess as to their likely effectiveness.

Now, what strategies for coping with change are available? One, adaptation, has already been identified; minor and temporary changes, easily reversed, may be made. But this is not strictly a design strategy. There are three design strategies in current use: designing for flexibility; the long-life loose-fit concept, to which "low energy" is now often added; and scrapping. Each has, or has had, enthusiastic advocates. Each is often misunderstood, and often misapplied. Each has, however, its uses in some circumstances.

Flexibility is itself a somewhat flexible concept. The structure, the services, the envelope, and the internal partitions may each be made more or less adaptable to a variety of future contingencies. The extreme case, in which all of these elements are capable of being altered fairly rapidly and through a fairly wide range, is represented by

Price's "Fun Palace" project. This project has not been realized, and proposals to embody some of its more extreme features in the Centre Pompidou by Piano and Rogers were apparently abandoned in the course of detail design. The nearest realized equivalents are the more elaborately mechanized theatre stages, and the cost is extremely high. Without a drastic change in technology, it is doubtful whether environments of this degree of flexibility will ever be cheaper than the alternative of providing a number of more specialized spaces, or scrapping and replacing, for non-theatrical situations.

In general, flexibility of structure can be created by either over- or under-provision. Over-provision involves designing for, say, twice the

Centre Pompidou Paris, by Piano and Rogers. An extreme example of design for physical adaptability, though the finished building does not go so far in this respect as the original proposal

anticipated live load, sizing columns for additional floors, and the like. The cost of over-provision is not excessive; assuming that structural cost will be of the order of 15% of the total building cost or less, a substantial increase in the live load can be secured for perhaps 20% of the structural cost, or 3% of the total budget. By under-provision is meant the increase of spans and reduction in the number of supports so that the supporting members will not interfere with future changes in layout. This is a much more costly approach, since the size and therefore the cost of the horizontal members increases directly with the load but in proportion to the square of the span. Halving the number of supports can double the cost of the structure.

What we may call the typical case of flexibility is the one in which internal partitions, some services, and perhaps the envelope of the building are designed to be altered with moderate ease and rapidity. This demands that the building design be modular, so that dismounted elements can be fitted into their new locations, and so that service points in proportion to the estimated demand will be available in the new arrangement. Such systems have been fully worked out only for office buildings and for some system-built schools. They are intrinsically costly, because for the system to work there must be over-provision. No space in a modular building can ever be of minimum size, unless fortuitously this happens to be a modular size; otherwise all dimensions have to be the next modular size above the minimum, and the modules have to be fairly large for economy in erection and dismounting. In rental office buildings the costs are passed to the customer; in other types of building the costs may not be so easy to absorb. Similarly, there has to be over-provision of lighting and power points, and of other service outlets if real flexibility is to be achieved. There are also some environmental limitations. Partitions that can be readily moved have to be light and thin, which means that their acoustic quality is poor. This can be made acceptable in office buildings, where by and large it is speech privacy that is wanted, by deliberately raising the ambient noise level; but in school or university buildings, for example, where lecturing with amplification, or the showing of films or playing of music may be normal activities, it is not tolerable. Finally, the cost of demolishing and re-erecting "demountable" partitions may actually be higher than that of demolishing a brick wall and erecting a new one, though it is less messy. There are of course many more technical aspects of flexible and modular construction which cannot be discussed here. The point is that it is not applicable to all situations, and so far works well in just one building type, the office building.

Attempts have been made to adapt the kind of flexible arrangements developed for office buildings to other building types, but they have not been notably successful. Special efforts have been made in the case of hospitals. Here the problem is complicated by the very high level of servicing required, particularly soil and waste plumbing. In office buildings, plumbing is usually concentrated in limited non-flexible areas: a "service core". In hospitals this will not do. The problem posed by soil and waste plumbing is that ideally it should go straight down, since it is gravity-borne. Where it has to be diverted sideways, the pipes are usually required to be laid to a considerable fall. Thus to conceal them in the ceiling space, which is usually desired for reasons of appearance, ease of cleaning, and so on, requires that the ceiling space be very deep. The idea of enlarging the ceiling space so that it is big enough not only for plumbing falls but also for maintenance men to move about in, and to permit the use of very deep horizontal structure, giving structural flexibility, was first applied at Greenwich Hospital in London. This has become known as the "interstitial floor". It has since been used on a much larger scale at the McMaster Hospital in Canada, by Zeidler and associates (Zeidler, 1974). Without entering into any discussion of the technical advantages and disadvantages, it is obvious that flexibility is being purchased at a very high price indeed in these buildings.

Flexibility, then, is easy to provide where the quality of the environment required is not too rigorously specified, where the level of servicing is low, where, it follows from this, the changes in the nature of the use of space are not very great. If these conditions are met, and frequent changes are expected, flexibility is the obvious design approach. As we move away from these conditions, the premium paid for flexibility increases; and if we find that we are in fact building an additional floor of the building for each floor of usable space provided, as in the "interstitial floor" concept, then it may be more rational to look at other solutions.

The long-life loose-fit concept stems from the work of Cowan previously referred to (Cowan, 1964; Cowan and Nicholson, 1964/5). If the majority of activities can be carried on in rooms of a certain rather limited range of sizes, why not simply provide rather more such rooms than appear to be needed immediately, and rely on adaptation? There is over-provision, but quite possibly no more than is required to make a modular system work, and the costs of over-providing structure and designing for demountability are avoided. There are two difficulties. One is that in certain uses the range of sizes required may be greater than Cowan's research indicates; his range of variation of most used room sizes is only about 30%, whereas Sharp in his comments on the Building Performance Research Units study already discussed suggests a range of working areas/pupil in schools of 500%. This does not invalidate the loose-fit concept; it does point to the need for further research, and specific research in each case. The other difficulty is, again, the provision of services, and here the possibilities are exactly the same as in the case of "flexible" designs. Again it is doubtful whether an economic solution can be found for the building in which there is a high provision of plumbing services which cannot be concentrated in a limited area.

Scrapping might be thought not to be a design solution at all, but rather the failure of design. This is not so, if it is recognized from the beginning that the life of the building is limited. Design can take into account ease of demolition, and re-use of demolished materials and equipment. Where a building is needed now, but is subject to many or all of the factors making for early obsolescence, designing for scrapping is the obvious solution. This proposal will no doubt recall the innumerable "temporary" buildings which have proved far more permanent than their more elaborately designed and constructed fellows. However, these long-lived temporary buildings seldom meet the conditions set up here; they are, precisely, loose-fit adaptable space, so that new uses keep being found for them as others decline. It is the highly serviced, single purpose, socially sensitive building that should be designed for scrapping.

It should be recognized, too, that these three strategies are not mutually exclusive. Investigation will often reveal that some parts of a proposed building are more sensitive to change than others. Thus a hospital, for example, might be designed with its operating theatres and laboratories scrappable, its wards long-life loose fit, and its administrative spaces flexible. Again, whether or not such an approach is feasible can only be determined by study of the individual case.

In summary, we can neither afford to exclude the possibility, and even probability, of change from method, nor can we avoid the problems of design by attempting to construct buildings so flexible that nothing need be decided in advance. Both solutions are, at present at least, too expensive. But again, this depends on the present state of technology. Even quite minor changes in technology, such as a change from gravity to powered sewerage disposal systems, might make a very substantial difference. For the present, however, architectural method must include the assessment of sensitivity to change, the prediction of likely changes, and the selection of strategies to cope with change. All of these areas, but especially the first two, are at present under-researched.

4.4   Designing for others

The purposes or goals served by particular buildings are, almost always, those of a number of people or groups of people. There are, indeed, cases where designer, owner and user are all the same person, but this is unusual. More often the designer is not the same person as the owner or client; and the owner or client is usually not the only user and may not be a user at all. Further, "the designer" is in fact commonly a group of professionals drawn from various disciplines; "the owner or client" may be a company or some other kind of large organization; and the users may be subdivided into many groups whose interests and activities differ. All of these people, designer or designers, owners or clients, and users as groups or individuals, may have their own separate or separable interests and purposes in relation to the building.

These different groups and their different purposes and goals create both practical and ethical problems for the architect. The practical problems arise because their goals may conflict. For example, the policies of the administration or even of the cleaning staff of an institution may conflict with and in practice frustrate arrangements made for another group of users, the "inmates" (Ittelson, Proshansky and Rivlin, 1970). The notorious failure of the Pruitt-Igoe housing scheme, as compared with the survival, at least, of many other very similar developments, may have been due as much to the policy of the housing authority that controlled it as to the design (Yancey, 1971). Such conflicts cannot be entirely avoided, but they can to some considerable extent be contained by appropriate design methods; just how will be considered in a later chapter. It is the ethical problems that the task of designing for others creates for the architect which will be considered in this section.

Here we must distinguish between the persuasive and biasing effects of governments, large corporations and other elements of the "planning system" as described by Galbraith (1967) and those of individual professionals or groups of like-minded professionals. The planning system may employ professionals, as advocates or researchers, but the goals are then those of the institution and not those of the professional. It is the question of the behaviour of professionals, and specifically of those who mean well, rather than the contrary, which will be taken up here. It is not more important than the political issues; it may not be *as* important; but it seems that the manipulative efforts of the planning system are beginning to be widely understood, and effective, if difficult and heroic measures for combating them are being developed (Francis, 1975). They are therefore not a problem so much for theory as for action. The situation of the professional designer, on the other hand, is the subject of much confused thinking.

The kind of ethical anxiety to which designing for others can give rise has been well summarized by Churchman (1976) when he asks: "Is it immoral for one man to decide what is good for another and to influence decision makers to make 'appropriate' changes?" In Churchman's case this anxiety springs from the clash between what he treats as two moral imperatives: the prudential or utilitarian morality which he takes, in general correctly, to be the moral position of designers and planners, and the extreme individualism which is so widespread in modern thinking and derives from the Romantic Movement. Churchman defines his individualism by way of a quotation from Kant: "So act, as to treat humanity, whether in your own person or that of another, in every case as an end withal, never as a means only." Churchman does not attempt any synthesis of this conflict; he concludes that the individualistic, ateleological morality is an enemy of planning, of prudential morality, though an enemy which should be respected and loved. Indeed, no resolution of this conflict is possible so long as one takes the view that society is *radically* divided into individuals on the one hand and social movements on the other.

Radical individualism of this kind leads to an equally comprehensive ethical relativism. An absolute value is placed on the wants, needs, demands and so on of individuals. Further, and as a consequence of this, the definition of what is good is taken to be just what people want, need and demand. If one person decides for another, therefore, he is imposing his view of goodness in a deceptive or tyrannical way. Designers, insofar as they decide for others — and design can be represented as largely if not wholly the making of decisions — are, on this view, in a morally untenable position.

It is easy to show that this account of the ethics of designing is a totally confused one. If it were true that all wants, needs, demands and so on, all interests in fact, are equal, then there would be no reason to prefer those of any one group or individual before those of any other. There would, therefore, be no reason why the architect should not have his way as much as anyone else, if he could get it.

This conclusion would not be acceptable to many architects, and presumably not to anyone at all who is not an architect. We see the professional as having a responsibility to those who pay for and those who use the buildings he designs which transcends his own interests. This view of the role of the professional has little to do with any higher-order theories of goodness or individualism; it is simply the way in which our kind of society has defined the profession of architecture and the other professions.

An architect or designer, as an advice-giving professional, has expressly or implicitly made certain promises to the clients and users for whom he designs. These promises include an undertaking to discover what their interests are and then to endeavour to serve them. This of course includes placing the interests of clients and users above his own, if their interests conflict with his. Further, although this is less generally understood and accepted, where the interests of the client conflict with those of the users, or the interests of one group of users conflict with those of another group, the designer's professional duty is to try to minimize the destructive effects of such conflicts. Insofar as an architect breaks these largely implicit promises, he is quite likely to suffer penalties, either at law or in terms of professional reputation. Designers are quite right to be anxious about their responsibilities, but wrong to define those responsibilities in terms of currently fashionable individualistic and relativistic views.

This anxiety about exercising undue influence, or being "manipulative" as it is sometimes phrased, seems to affect most deeply those who have made the most strenuous efforts to avoid and overcome any such tendency. Thus, towards the end of a paper which discusses a very carefully worked out system for improving communication and participation between designers and users in the design of houses, Weber (1975) observes:

> "Designers, as anyone else, structure their activity according to how they perceive reality. Thus in the processing and managing of information for deliberative dwelling design — developing of a language for discourse — designers become regulators. Not only do they control the criteria for the selection of those parts of reality which are to be represented, but also define the process of selection and representation. Even when trying to be impartial, designers cannot help manipulate information which is biased by their perception of reality and which may not be shared by lay participants in a design process."

The architect is here represented as *reluctantly* but *inevitably* imposing his ideas on others. Other writers agree as to the inevitability, but discount the reluctance; Rittel and Webber (1974), for example, see the "expert" as *necessarily* "also a player in a political game seeking to promote his private vision of goodness over others".

As accounts of the ethical goals of architecture, these positions are clearly quite unsatisfactory. All possible human relationships are reduced to a single model: one of selfish advantage seeking or "manipulation" in which one person or group wickedly pursues secret goals at the expense of another. This reduction conceals rather than explains. In this view, we would say that the mother "manipulates" her baby into behaviour she wants by giving or withholding contact and attention, while conversely the baby "manipulates" the mother by crying, smiling, kicking, and other behaviour which serves to attract and hold her attention. We "manipulate" our neighbour in the restaurant by asking him to pass the salt; and he "manipulates" us by using this trifling service as an excuse for opening a conversation.

Now, while it is clearly true that activities and interests sometimes conflict, and that people sometimes seek to gain their ends by deception, it is simply not true that it is impossible to act disinterestedly, or that designers, if they pursue their interests at the expense of the interests of those designed for, will not be called to account; or, finally, that designers cannot make the interests of those designed for their own.

Consider first the question of disinterested advice or action. In contemporary societies the concept of distributive justice, of fair action or "referee-like behaviour", as Moore and Anderson put it, develops quite early in life (Moore and Anderson, 1969; Rosen, 1980). If we have a concept of what it is to act fairly, then it is possible to act fairly; the notion that "disinterested" judgement is impossible must be rejected. The "expert" is not *necessarily* seeking to promote his *private* vision of goodness. He may, of course, in fact be acting politically; or he may be employed as an advocate of some group or interest, in which case the "vision" he is seeking to promote is neither necessarily his nor necessarily private; or he may be incompetent so that he *appears* to act in this sort of way when in fact he is seeking to act with equity; but the critical point is that he is not *compelled* to act in that way. Indeed if injustice, inequity and manipulation were inevitable, the concept of justice or equity could never have arisen, and we should certainly not regard injustice as immoral. This whole confusion has arisen because the correct perception that people, including designers, have interests and biases, both conscious and unconscious, has been combined with the false belief that such interests and biases cannot be either declared by their holder or quite clearly perceived by other people; especially is this likely to be the case if the interests and biases of a designer conflict with those of clients or users, and there is some opportunity for debate and discussion.

This brings us to the question of what, in fact, happens if designers act in ways that are contrary to the interests of clients or users in some significant way. Here we commonly find competitive or contradictory goals being pursued quite openly, not covertly or privately; and we also observe that the designer is often, perhaps more often than not, the loser, in the sense that, whatever goals are achieved, they are not his. To take an example from recent years in the planning field, there was a clash between the authority charged with the task of reconstructing the city of Darwin after its destruction by cyclone and the people of the city or, at least, some of their representatives. This clash was perfectly clear in terms of differing goals: the planners wanted a replanned (new) Darwin; the residents wanted a reconstructed (improved old) Darwin. In the event, the planners lost. More strictly architectural examples of the frustration of designers' objectives by other groups have already been given earlier in this section. It is seldom the case that the architect who disregards significant interests in the design situation is not called to some kind of accounting.

Architects, then, can in fact consider impartially conflicts between their own interests and those of others in a given situation. Insofar as they fail to do so, either deliberately or as the result of unconscious bias, they are very likely to be subjected to criticism, in the form of the rejection of their designs or of the completed buildings. In practice, so far from seeking to bias outcomes or impose their own solutions, architects not infrequently become deeply attached to the interests and activities of the prospective users of their buildings, and go to great lengths to try and ensure that they are achieved; since, however, the interests and activities of the users themselves conflict, this may also have some biasing effects.

Insofar as we do not regard the intelligence and probity of individuals as a sufficient guarantee of the impartiality of their actions, we have to rely on group processes: specifically, on the process of public, rule-governed, refereed debate in which experts acts expressly as advocates for each of the interests concerned; in fact, on the procedure of the courts. How this kind of procedure can be made relevant to the smaller-scale problems of architecture will be discussed in a later chapter. Here it is sufficient to note that in many countries the courts have developed great experience and skill and very effective procedures for ensuring adequacy of debate. They are, like other human institutions, subject to various deficiencies, both local and temporary and also more traditional and general, such as cost, delay and so on. Nevertheless, where the courts have been entrusted with the resolution of issues in architecture and planning they have often been notably successful. Instances which come to mind are the development of daylighting and smoke abatement laws in England, which led both to improved empirical methods of test and to environmental improvement; in New South Wales, the establishment of urban plot ratio codes; and the American case of Texas Eastern v. Wildlife Preserves as reported by Sax (1970). In these cases the disinterested judgement of complex questions did lead to improvement, though not of course to a state of affairs that was in any sense perfect.

Thus far it has been argued that the charge against the planner or architect of immorality, of "seeking to promote his private view of goodness over others", while it may often be true, is not *necessarily* true. There are problems, but they are problems that can be overcome. It is now necessary to look a little more closely at the design process, and to bring out those features that not only cause this criticism of architects to be made, but actually induce intelligent and sensitive designers to accept it.

In a design process (taking the process to extend from conception to obsolescence) each person concerned has an image of "the problem"; "the task environment" as Newell and Simon (1972) call it. These images are their problem spaces. The problem spaces of individuals may have the usual class relations of inclusion, exclusion and intersection, a point brought out in some detail by Thompson (1977) in discussing lay and professional views of what "architecture" is. One way of describing the consensus which is necessary for design to succeed is to say that there is an adequate overlap of the problem spaces of all concerned. Where this is not the case the problem is "wicked". Where the common problem space is very large, as often happens, the problem is difficult. And where the common problem spaces does not contain a solution, or more accurately a solution space, it is insoluble at least within the current frames of reference of those concerned.

The designer's duty in each of these cases is different. In the case of the wicked problem his task is to achieve a consensus by encouraging rational debate — an issue-based approach to the problem (Heath, 1974b, 1975). In the case of the difficult problem he has to search patiently for a solution. And where it turns out that the problem is not soluble (negative solution space) it is his duty to say so. However, in each case the designer may prefer to invent some scheme without regard to the problem spaces of others, and then to "sell" it, by means for example of massive and apparently highly technical reports, or attractive models or drawings. This is certainly manipulative, whether it is done for the profit and convenience of the designer, or of his employer. If the designer has not been genuinely concerned to find a solution that lies within the user(s) problem space(s) he can reasonably be accused of manipulation, except insofar as he is avowedly acting as an advocate.

There is a qualification that must be made to this. Initially all problems tend to be wicked, in that in their first encounter the individuals concerned do not understand one another's problem spaces sufficiently. This applies not only to design, but to all advice-giving situations. The utility of advice derives from a certain concept of what the situation is on the part of the advice giver; on the other hand, the advice receiver can at least make a judgement as to whether the advice proffered is of use to him (conforms to his problem space). The reasonable man will give advice *along with* some description of the problem as he sees it (his "reasons"). Such reasons will not make the metastructure, the problem space, entirely clear to either party, but by a repeated process of mutual adjustment (admission of the symmetry of ignorance) a common problem space may be achieved.

Advice giving takes place in a person-to-person relationship.

However, as we have already noted, one of the difficulties of architecture is that it may not be possible to establish such a person-to-person relationship with the user. In such cases, to establish a common problem space may require detailed investigations, of the kind generally referred to as environment-behaviour research. Such an *inquiring* process of design, to use Zeisel's term (Zeisel, 1981), may be laborious and expensive, but it must be undertaken if the designer is to avoid the charge of making for others decisions that he has no right to make; and, at a more down-to-earth level, if he is to avoid having his buildings rejected or damaged in use.

Assuming that a common problem space can be achieved, there are two situations that may arise which may be mistaken for manipulation, but which are not manipulative. The first of these is not unique to design, and occurs when the user's problem space can be seen to be a poor representation of the actual situation, and excludes solutions that might be valid. (The same may of course be true of professionals.) Here the professional has a duty to offer his own perspective on matters, which will often be accepted. There is a danger here of "undue influence" being exercised, but it is not fundamental to the relationship.

The second situation is unique to design. It arises because design problems rarely if ever have a unique solution (Heath, 1973; Simon, 1970). Rather, there is a solution space containing a large number of equally valid solutions. Design is concerned with "closure of the terminal state" (Wade, 1977), with deciding to do something specific. To say that a design problem does not have a unique solution is to say that it is not adequately structured. Therefore in order to arrive at a specific conclusion, a "design", the designer must import structure (or "issues"). Newell and Simon (1972) show that this happens even in the well-structured situation of chess playing; actual moves are often arrived at on the basis of "chess values", such as "control of the centre". It is similarly an old maxim in management that "the task of management is to make decisions in the absence of the necessary information"; that is, where the situation is not sufficiently structured for there to be a unique "best" solution. Just as one hears of "styles" of management, so architects and planners make use of styles, modules, proportions, genius loci, or whatever, to structure a solution space sufficiently to reach a unique solution.

This kind of situation has a pathology of its own. Designers habitually and necessarily achieve results by importing values of their own to structure a *solution* space. In the absence of some analysis, such as the present, of what they are doing, they may do the same for the *problem* space, thus disregarding or overriding the user's values. But, precisely because they are aware, at least in a diffuse way, that their conclusions are not reached entirely on rational/empirical grounds they are inclined to reject analysis. They may also suspect themselves of manipulation, even in cases where they have done all that can be done to eliminate it (Weber, 1975). The cure is to recognize, first, that it is normally a part of the professional's duty to import more structure than the task contains, but secondly, that this should not be private or covert but frankly declared and diligently tested against the problem space of the user.

The traditional view of the professional man's duty was that he should act for his client as the client would himself act, had he the necessary knowledge or skill. But this presumes that the professional knows how the client would act. In the practice of design today the ethical problems are compounded by the difficulty of establishing the user's frame of reference, as previously discussed, and by the pressure of time and the need for action. There is a characteristic and widely recognized academic bias towards inaction (Gutman, 1966), which is reflected, and properly, in academic criticisms of practice. The academic is concerned, if not with certainty, then with truthlikeness. But action can seldom wait on such considerations. The field of actions is "where the action is"; and if we cannot achieve a high degree of truthlikeness or a very good description of the user's problem space in the time available, then hypotheses or myths have to be substituted. In some cases, given the limitations of our knowledge and our capacity to handle information, we will be working largely with myth. It follows that action is not risk free. We have to resort to rather primitive and robust bases for action; in particular, perhaps the old English common-law concept of the reasonable man. Faced with the necessity of doing *something*, what would a reasonable man do? He cannot be sure that any proposal in the given field is the best, or even a good idea. But he can test each as severely as the available knowledge, supplemented by debate, allows. And he can make the risks as clear as possible to the decision makers, and perhaps also to the users.

In their paper previously referred to, Rittel and Webber (1974) argue that in the past the problems of the professional were more definable, understandable and consensual than they are today. Historically this seems a doubtful proposition. Social action tends to move from the unknown and unpredictable to the known and predictable. The introduction of public health measures (an example they give) was at the time a much more daring gamble than they suggest; it is only in looking back over a century and a half of success that we are able to perceive it as an ordinary and predictable process. It may be suggested that the high salaries attracted by the learned professions are not solely or even mainly justified by their possession of a unique stock of scientific knowledge, or exceptional empathy for the problems of others. Rather, they do accept, however cautiously and reluctantly, the responsibility for decisions that many other people would not care to make. As Rittel and Webber point out, they do not have the right to be wrong. This applies as much to the doctor or lawyer as to the architect or planner. Therefore, like the sacred king in more primitive times, they are liable to be sacrificed when things go amiss; though the sacrifice is now by way of suits for negligence. In the case of architecture and planning the continued existence of wicked problems means that risk will continue. The argument for making every effort to bring about a match between the designer's and user's problem spaces, for testing as severely as possible, and for avoiding "manipulation", is all the stronger.

4.5   Aesthetic goals

We have seen that empirical study of the professional environment of architecture supports the conventional belief that goals of a kind generally describable as aesthetic rank high with architects. Since clients and users are not definable groups, it is hardly possible to make an equivalent generalization about them. However, both anecdotal and systematic studies of specific groups of users indicate that they too have well-developed aesthetic goals. Reynolds and Nicholson (1969) in a study of a housing estate report that the aesthetic quality of the surroundings in particular was important to the occupants. An investigation of housing choices by office workers moving from one city to another showed that when they were asked to indicate their choice disregarding economic and practical factors, "free" choices were influenced by aesthetic considerations (Bateman, Burtenshaw and Duffet, 1974). But it has also been widely argued that, even though both architects and users may have aesthetic goals, these goals are at present widely different and may perhaps be diverging. Thompson (1977) in a paper which seeks to apply Thom's catastrophe theory to the "crisis in architecture" has suggested that the overlap between "non-architect's architecture" and "architect's architecture", i.e. the aesthetic standards or goals of the two groups, is small or non-existent, and that to avoid a catastrophic collapse the profession "must stop trying to move non-architect's ideas of architecture to theirs and start moving their ideas of architecture towards those of non-architects." Brolin (1976) has presented the aesthetic failures of modern architecture in a way which is the more telling for its naïvete. These criticisms and much other recent criticism of contemporary architecture by architects fail by being too narrow, by assuming that hostility to modern architecture is based solely on formal aesthetic judgements. In this they illustrate that very introversion which is the main weakness of the profession (and perhaps of other professions). In this context Prak (1977) refers to the work of Kaplan, Kaplan and Deardorff (1974), which revealed a tendency in architects to excuse or ignore practical shortcomings in buildings or neighbourhoods that they like for aesthetic reasons; a "halo" effect which was not so significant for non-architects. Heimsath (1977) has treated this whole question in a broader and more satisfactory way than is usual. He draws attention to the gap between current architectural theory and the reality of the user's experience. Architectural theory has either extended Modern Movement ideas, or reacted against them in favour of a narrow view of "popular" aesthetics as the banal or vulgar, or retreated into Utopianism. Theory and method need a view of aesthetic goals that sets them in a social context. An attempt will be made here to outline such a view.

What is an aesthetic goal? As far as the environmental arts are concerned, until recently the established, if seldom expressed, view was that things should be *tidy*; that is, that they should have some simple kind of *order*. As with most established views, there were good reasons for this one: many, even most, environments in the past were so untidy and confused that the appearance of some order here and there must have been very welcome. But in recent years we have taken to reconstructing or constructing substantial areas of our environment simultaneously, and the adoption of such simple goals has produced impoverished environments. Criticisms of these failures have stimulated the design professions into a frenzied pursuit of complexity, novelty, small scale and so on, regardless of context and sometimes even of common sense. It is no doubt possible to see these changes as part of an historical cycle: the neoclassical period at the end of the eighteenth century replaces the rococo and is in turn replaced by the decorative and formal profusion of the picturesque, culminating in the art nouveau; there is then a return to severity, which we call the Modern Movement; after some eighty years this too is exhausted and we stand at the beginning of a new period of enthusiasm for ornament and so on. But such a cyclic account in itself explains nothing: neither why we have aims of the general kind we call aesthetic, such as tidiness, formality, variety, richness, beauty, character and so on, nor how these aims are to be realized in the physical stuff of the built environment. The investigation of these questions is a problem for psychology, and in recent years psychologists have taken up the challenge.

A brief account requires a number of assumptions that would not be by any means universally accepted. First is the assumption that environmental aesthetics is concerned with a class of interactions or relations, between people and things. Further assumptions are that the quality of these interactions is limited but not precisely determined by characteristics of people in general — roughly the perceptual and cognitive abilities of their minds; by physical features of things — shapes, textures, colours, patterns and so on; and by characteristics of the milieu — the previous experience of the people concerned, their roles and expectations, more generally their culture.

It is not necessary to specify that the interactions should be pleasant, or that they should produce aesthetic emotion, or anything of that sort. It has long been recognized that aesthetics should be able to locate the realms of the ugly, the boring and the banal, as well as those of the beautiful, the stimulating and the admirable. And there are good reasons for keeping before our minds many different words of a kind generally associated with aesthetic judgements or situations, rather than sticking to a single word such as "beauty". This is because the science of aesthetics is young and poorly developed, and it has not yet achieved a technical vocabulary that subdivides the physical features "out there" — what the psychologists call the "distal stimulus" — in the same way that people do in experiencing and reacting to it. Our present language is about as well suited to the discussion of aesthetics as that of the early eighteenth century was to the discussion of chemistry.

However, in considering what our aesthetic aims should be in designing or altering the built environment, we will on the whole be looking for environments that are at least comfortable, desirably pleasant, and, in parts at least, rewarding and delightful. Comfort is a very interesting subject in itself, full of technical problems, but it is not really an aesthetic interaction although it may be a precondition of aesthetic interactions. Here it will be more profitable to look first at the question of what makes a stimulus (a building, an environment) rewarding. Some insights have been provided by research on arousal. Behavioural and neurological evidence has accumulated which suggests that the hedonic or rewarding value of a stimulus depends on how arousing or de-arousing it is. There appear to be two distinct mechanisms involved, one of which produces reward when stimulation is decreased after it has risen to the point of being unpleasant or painful, while the other comes into play when arousal is raised to a moderate extent. Berlyne, who took a leading role in this area of research (Berlyne, 1960, 1971), was emphatically of the opinion that it is not the achievement of a constant "optimum state" that is pleasant or rewarding, it is the increments or decrements in arousal. The interaction of the two mechanisms can be represented by a graph, the Wundt curve, which describes the net result of a particular amount of stimulation. The curve shows, first, an area of indifference, when stimulation is below the threshold of response; then a rapid increase to

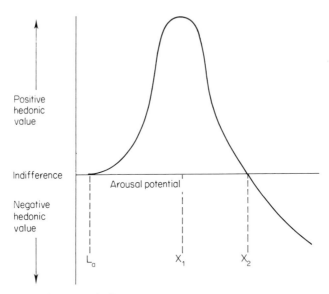

Figure 4.1   The Wundt Curve

a peak; and finally an equally rapid decline ending in negative or aversive responses (Figure 4.1). The part of the curve between the peak and the negative response is of particular interest in that here either increase or decrease in stimulation can be pleasasnt.

Arousal increasing or decreasing characteristics can be divided into the psychophysical, or perceptual, and the cognitive. At the psychophysical level arousal is varied by varying the intensity of stimulation: larger or smaller size, brighter or dimmer lights, strong colours or pastels, and so on. The cognitive variables include the effects of learned associations and of what Berlyne calls the "collative variables": novelty, complexity, surprise, ambiguity. However, the arousal increment or decrement sought will depend on the interests, objects, and generally on the current state of the individual. The environment may be supportive and facilitative or the reverse, but it is not deterministic. This raises issues that go beyond the psychobiological questions to which Berlyne and his colleagues have addressed themselves: issues of behaviour, of interest, of personality.

It is these differences of *interest* and *personality* that have made many people argue that aesthetics is a futile study. But this argument ignores certain feature of the situation. For, first of all, the differences between people are not so gross as all that: there is plenty of evidence that, despite an element of selective attention, by and large people see what there is to be seen. The fact that, in studying aesthetic goals in the built environment, we are mostly concerned with issues and places which are in the broadest sense public, means that there will be some conformity of expectation and attitude, a considerable overlap of schemata. And secondly, and perhaps even more importantly, the effect of human design and control over the environment is to make it act as a sorting device, providing to some extent separately for different interests and personalities, for different environmental objectives. The resulting higher-order relationships between perception, the collative variables and associations can be explored a little further by considering the question of symbolism.

Symbolism, or rather, successful symbolism, may be described as "good fit" between perception and cognition, form and content. What "good fit" means in this context was first suggested by Kant: certain essential relationships are conserved or mapped from one medium to another, in our case from the way an environment is used or understood to its perceived form. An Egyptian temple is not only admirably suited to a religious procession, it is practically impossible to do anything in it but process; the building marches in a straight line and we also march. It is an ideal setting for a certain kind of behaviour. Buildings and urban environments all function as settings or props for behaviour, although not always so obviously. Goffman, in his book *The Presentation of Self in Everyday Life* (Goffman, 1959) and subsequent developments of its themes, has provided a framework for discussing the use of environments as stage sets and props to assist people both in enacting their social roles and in escaping from them. Conversely, Sommer (1974) and Ittelson and his collaborators (1970) have brought out some of the ways in which the administration of public facilities can, by such simple things as the arrangements of furniture, symbolically and practically contradict the official programme of the institution and the intention of its design. There is every reason to suppose that similar kinds of analysis can fruitfully be applied to urban, rural, and even wild environments, though in the wild environment nature provides the framework and meaning is imputed to it by men.

To think in this way about design involves an understanding by the designer of the parts which various environments play for different groups of the population in the enactment of their various life roles. It also involves an understanding both of perception in general, and of the particular perceptual qualities or characters to which such groups are sensitized, which can be effective for them in making the perceived environment a map of the understood role. This connection between role and environment will often be largely a matter of socially established schemata; and it is the mere reproduction of such schemata, regardless of their permanence or their relevance to broader

Court of the Temple at Luxor. An Egyptian temple is not only admirably suited to a religious procession; it is practically impossible to do anything in it but process

aesthetic or ethical goals, that designers have long feared in connection with empirical studies of aesthetic questions. But there is another kind of connection, which is indicated by Berlyne's work. The arousal increment provided by the environment must be appropriate to the role. There are thus two ways in which the environment must relate to the role for it to achieve aesthetic quality at the symbolic level: it must provide overt cues to the appropriate behaviour, or props for roles; and it must provide the right arousal increment for that kind of behaviour. If the two contradict each other, or if one is appropriate and the other inappropriate, the environment will be an aesthetic failure.

Despite the apparent complexity of environmental design, created by the interaction of many different goals and roles, the introduction of a few quite general classifications can greatly simplify the designer's task. First of all, following, and it is to be hoped not too much distorting, ideas suggested by Berlyne, we can distinguish two very broad classes of goal or objective: goals of specific activity and goals of diversive exploration. Goals of specific activity are those places to which we go to *do* something: to work, to eat, to play, to sleep. Evaluation of such places will be in terms of their fitness to the activity: the quality of the sand on the beach, the quality of the turf and the orientation of the cricket oval, the equipment and convenient layout of the operating theatre. Prak (1977) expresses this kind of attitude very well when he says that "users consider the built environment first of all as an instrument or tool." Insofar as such activities are genuinely productive and not ritual or formal, a highly formal or organized setting is not appropriate to them. The activity creates its own order, since human activity is rarely if ever wholly disorderly.

Goals of diversive exploration, on the other hand, are places to which people go to seek an arousal increment (or decrement): to find stimulation and excitement, or calm and peace. Examples are visits to museums and art galleries, window shopping, a stroll in the park or through "picturesque" streets, hiking, a stay in a country cottage. As distinct from the goals of specific activity, a significant element is that of personal choice, of being free to explore new possibilities, or renew acquaintance with old favourites. Variety, to provide both for differences of personality and changes of mood, is essential to diversive exploration.

The physical expression of each of these general kinds of goal or activity is always qualified in some way to indicate its significance in the life of individuals or social groups. There is a ritual element in most activities, but in some the ritual element is dominant. Some places are created as shrines or memorials, and some have this character superimposed on something else: the managing director's office, the board room, the formal sitting room of a private house are often loaded with symbols of importance to the point of collapse, and it is this also that troubles many people about museums, art galleries and opera houses. One universal sign of importance has been described by Pye (1964) as "useless work", and while some useless work goes into everything that human beings make or do, the amount varies quite directly with the mana or social significance of the place. Another such sign is quality of material. Prak (1977) has again drawn attention to the fact that users may be more influenced, at the symbolic level, by quality of material than by the more formal qualities of order and interest. Ritual or symbolic environments also customarily require a special style of behaviour, and this is usually signalled by formality or "good gestalt" in the physical arrangement of the spaces.

These general types of environmental goal, and these qualifications to them, can be found in every culture that has developed artificial

Lincoln Centre, New York. Some places are loaded with symbols of importance to the point of collapse

environments, and they extend into the ways in which different cultures perceive, make use of, and evaluate the natural environment. They make possible, at least as an hypothesis, a framework for environmental design and discussion in terms of four elements or tasks. The importance of the tasks, and the order in which they will have to be undertaken, will vary according to the nature of the design in general, and specifically in relation to the extent to which diversive exploration is an objective. The *first task* is the identification of the specific activities involved and the relations between them — the content of the problem. This is part of method in general, and will not be elaborated further at this point. But it is clear from what has been said so far that form does not "follow" content or "function", it is merely constrained by it. The *second task* is to ensure that the perceptual experience, immediate or sequential, of the finished work can be a map or symbol of the activities and objectives within it for the people who will use it; an aspect of this task is the provision of adequate cues for purposive or goal seeking behaviour, starting with the simplest, such as, where is the entrance? The *third task* is to estimate and provide the amount of stimulation appropriate to the activities, goals and objectives: how formal or informal, quiet or exciting should the place be? This third task amounts to providing

Temple at Somnathpur India. "Useless work" is a universal symbol of importance

appropriate cues for *expressive* behaviour. *Finally*, there has to be an
assessment of the social importance of the place, to be expressed in
terms of "useless work" and quality of materials. If any of these
judgements is mistaken, the design will suffer.

    These four tasks are related in a complex way to two separable
dimensions of behaviour. One of these dimensions is the degree to
which the activities designed for are specified or defined, rather than
free or diverse: "work" rather than "play". The other is the extent to
which the activity is formalized or ritualized, public or "backstage".
The first task, the identification of activities, must include locating
them on each of these two dimensions. The second, the mapping or
symbolic task, also relates both to the provision of cues for practical
behaviour and to the provision of settings and props for ritual. The
fourth task, the determination of the amount of "useless work", again
relates both to the importance given to different ritual activities: not all
rituals are important; private obsessive behaviour, for example, is

ritual but socially deprecated rather than revered. It is the third task, the adjustment of the level of stimulation to the circumstances, which is the most interesting and the most challenging for the designer. In "backstage" places informality is permitted and arousal increment is rarely necessary. As places become more public and what goes on in them becomes more ritualized, there is an increasing demand for formality, that is for an arousal reducing character and "good gestalt". However, the element of diversive exploration, or "play" can vary independently of the demand for formal, ritual, or public behaviour. Thus, some places must provide opportunities for *either* increasing *or* decreasing excitement. It will be recalled that the Wundt curve indicates that this is quite possible.

In the past, architects' aesthetic goals have been restricted to conformity with, or extension of, canons of architectural achievement defined by the profession itself: architects' architecture. But if professional goals are to be made consistent with the goals of users these professional canons must be seen as special cases of a more general activity: the marshalling and mutual adjustment of gradients of stimulation in the service of activities, whether specific or diversive. This mutual adjustment is a matter of order, not in the simple sense with which we began, but in the sense of the formation of supersigns, the notion that is conveyed by "composition" in painting or in traditional architectural writing. Psychology has also cast a great deal of new light on the nature of order. Arnheim in particular has made an invaluable contribution (Arnheim, 1954, 1966, 1977), but this is a matter of aesthetic strategies rather than aesthetic goals, and cannot be pursued further here.

Chapter 5

Problem types and problem spaces

5.1 Introduction

Method in action is the construction and search of specific design problem spaces for specific design tasks. Even if it is conceded that the general goals of design and the general extended problem space of architecture can be described in some such way as has been outlined in the preceding chapters, it need not be admitted that any useful generalizations can be made about the individual case. Method might still be individual and personal, so much confined to the black box of the individual designer's mind that it cannot be explained or clarified. Or it is possible, though on the face of it unlikely, that each new architectural problem requires a new and different method. Or again, method might be specific to building types, so that there would be one method for libraries, another for schools, another for houses and so on, and a separate book, or at least a separate chapter, written by a specialist in that building type, would be required to describe the method for each. This chapter will, first of all, show that it is impossible for method to be wholly or even largely subjective or internal. On the other hand, it will be argued that attempts to construct a single method for all architectural problems have not been wholly successful because there are different types of problems requiring different methods. However, method is not specific to each individual task: there _are_ broad classes of problem, but these classes are not identical with, and are much fewer than, building types. Three classes or types of problem are discussed; and these are shown to be specializations within a general architectural problem space, the structure of which is a homomorph of the roles that various client and user groups may have in society. The nature of a particular problem and the method and programmes appropriate to it can thus be determined at an early stage.

5.2   Critique of "conceptual" architecture

One common and, in a sense, well-developed theory of architecture holds that method is irrelevant if not actually harmful. It is an extreme case of what Christopher Jones has called "black box" theories, theories in which significant, and perhaps all essential, parts of the design process are internal to the problem solver, and unavailable for, or even incapable of, rational or empirical discussion. The inputs and outputs can be discussed, but not the method. This extreme type of black-box theory has here been given the name "conceptual" architecture; for on this kind of view the formation of the "concept" of the building, the governing idea on which all else depends, is hermetic. Robin Boyd has expressed the idea with characteristic precision:

> "... it is the central step of extracting the vision that shapes the building and gives it whatever expression or feeling or poetry it will have. With experience an architect learns to see in the flash when the image forms an entire building complex in principle, including quite intimate details of structure." (Boyd, 1965)

Now this theory is false, and what Boyd describes is impossible. It is important to understand why it is false, and also why it has been widely held. The first of these questions requires a new detour into the psychology of problem solving. Newell and Simon (1972) discuss the abilities and limitations of human minds as problem-solving devices at length. The most important of these abilities and limitations concern memory. Human beings have three kinds of memory: the long-term memory, the short-term memory and the external memory. When we speak of memory in ordinary language, it is the long-term memory that we mean. The external memory consists of any physical or recorded analogue of the problem, attempts at its solution, and so on, such as notes, drawings, models, books, a chess board with chessmen; although Newell and Simon do not say so, in the solution of complex problems it also includes the memories of others. It is, however, the limitations of the short-term memory that are decisive in determining human problem-solving methods.

The short-term memory is the collection of information of which a person is aware at any time: roughly speaking, our "consciousness". It has a very small capacity, of "seven plus or minus two" symbols, characters or elements, in the phrase made famous by Miller's essay (Miller, 1956). In case this limitation should be doubted, a simple experiment will demonstrate it. Have someone read aloud a list of random numbers and attempt to memorize them. Up to six numbers the task is easy; over nine, almost impossible.

Not only is short-term memory small, but it is also virtually incapable of parallel operations; this is what is meant by the "serial character" of the mind. This too is readily demonstrable empirically; for if it were not so, as Newell and Simon (1972) argue, it would take the same time to determine whether the two numbers 69416 and 35642 are divisible by 7, as it would take to make the same calculation for either separately, which is not the case. Thus only *one* "information process" can be executed at a time; an "information process" is any mental operation involving two or more symbols. The rate of processing, however, is very high, of the order of milliseconds where there are two or more symbols.

The capacity and serial character of the short-term memory, which have been very thoroughly investigated empirically, and can be demonstrated even by the simple tests described above, serve together to demolish the conceptual theory of architecture. For, whatever scheme of "representation" we may conceive to be used, it is impossible that the concept of even a very simple building, its plan, sections and elevations, let alone "quite intimate details of structure" should be expressed in less than seven characters, symbols, bits, chunks, or whatever term we care to adopt. Even conceding, what is most unlikely, that the "great" architect might have *double* the normal human information-processing capacity, and further assuming that experience enables him to think in metasigns which compress or summarize much detail effectively into one "character", *still* the thing is impossible. "Conceptual" architecture will not do.

It is not enough, however, simply to dismiss the theory. Boyd was after all an architect of great experience and distinction, and an architectural critic and writer of long standing; and he and a great many other architects whose opinions cannot be lightly set aside have held this theory or something like it. While it is true that many false theories have been held by men of distinction, and that this particular theory is a characteristic member of the group of theories which go to make up the Romantic Movement (specifically theories of "genius"), it can hardly have been totally and apparently inconsistent with experience. It is suggested that the credibility of the conceptual theory of architecture has three main sources. One is the visual character of the thinking of many architects (one would like to be able to say, of *all* architects). Visualization is important in many kinds of problem solving: in chess, according to de Groot (1965); obviously in certain branches of mathematics; and in ordinary life probably much more widely than is commonly admitted. Arnheim, in his pioneering study of visual thinking (Arnheim, 1969), has drawn attention to the weaknesses in both psychological theory and practical education, which arise from the neglect of visual thinking. It is possible that visualization can bring very large bodies of information into a single "character" and make them compresent in the short-term memory. Even so a whole architectural "concept" could not be present simultaneously. Most visualization, Arnheim suggests, takes the form of "flashes" which are to a considerable extent abstracted. No doubt with experience, trained and gifted visualizers can learn to "glance" quickly from one "flash" to another so that an illusion of compresence is created. Introspection confirms that this may be so. But it is to be noted that even the greatest architects have made considerable use of sketches and models — the "external memory" — to aid their powers of visualization.

The second likely source of this particular belief of experienced architects is common to all skilled persons in the exercise of their skills. It consists in the possession of a set of "preprogrammed" (learnt) internalized behaviour or habits, which, when correctly applied, enable them to deal by inspection with many matters which would be a source of difficulty for the tyro. An example may illustrate this point. Hunter (1968) reports a study that he made of Professor A.C. Aitken, a mathematician remarkable for his ability as a lightning calculator. At the time Hunter interviewed him he was 66; amongst other mental calculations, he was able to give on request the fraction 4/47 to 46 decimal places. As an experienced and articulate teacher, Aitken was able to explain to Hunter how he did this; in effect, he broke the problem up into a number of subroutines which he could then solve "by inspection". Hunter gives a number of other similar examples and concludes:

> "The most important general conclusion to be drawn from the study of mental calculation is probably this. Increase in ability concerns the development of techniques which enables the person to make more effective use of his basically limited capacities for handling information."

The experienced architect, though his work is more complicated than mental arithmetic, nevertheless must develop such skills and techniques; he too breaks the problem up and solves it piecemeal, sometimes with surprising rapidity, so that it may well appear, even to him, that a whole "concept" has arrived "simultaneously". But it is the internalized skills and techniques which make such rapid solution, where it occurs, possible; and it is just these skills and techniques with which method is concerned.

A third source of support for the "conceptual" view of design is suggested by a study reported by Darke (1979). Hillier, Musgrave and O'Sullivan (1972) had proposed a version of the Popperian theory of science, outlined previously (section 2.4), in place of the then fashionable analysis–synthesis model of design. Darke's aim was to test this against the practice of designers. She investigated the design processes of the architects of six London housing schemes. In general the results supported the conjecture–analysis model of Hillier and his collaborators. In the course of the study, Darke discovered something that appeared to precede the conjecture, which she calls the "primary generator". This "generator" is a concept or a small group of concepts which serve the architect as a *way in* to the problem. They included such things as expressing the site, maintaining social patterns, and other general values, which were not determined by the investigation or analysis of the design task, but were self-imposed.

Such "generators" provided general guides to action in the initial stages of the design, to enable a start to be made, structuring an as yet unstructured field. Just so, we have observed earlier (section 4.4), the designer may have to import structure or values of his own to *complete* a design that is insufficiently structured. The generators, however, are quite clearly the elements from which an initial *problem space* is constructed; they are the designer's first attempts to answer the question, what *kind* of problem is this? Darke has thus provided empirical support for Newell and Simon's speculation that the initial problem space is either "ready-made" in or is constructed from elements in the long-term memory of the problem solver.

There can be little doubt that a vague and imperfect understanding of the need for the designer to supply something of his own which goes beyond the mere collection and ordering of facts at an early stage in design underlies both the emphasis often placed on the "creativity" of design and also the tenacious defence of the "conceptual" approach to designing. There is nevertheless a very great difference between Boyd's notion, with which we began, of the "concept" as something fairly complete, and the "generator" or "problem space" which exists to be criticized, as a tool of inquiry or heuristic device which will help to reveal facts that may well cause it to be modified or abandoned.

A stock of values or general concepts that can be applied to structuring the initial stages of design, internalized skills and techniques that aid in breaking up design problems into manageable chunks, and considerable powers of visualization are all things that are developed by experience and improved by practice. It is thus not surprising that those who are already expert are often indifferent or hostile to method and prefer the mystique of the "conceptual" theory. The "conceptual" theory is none the less unsound and an impediment to the improvement of architecture in that it obstructs understanding of the interaction between hypothesis and test, conjecture and analysis. In certain cases it is also actively dangerous, since, as we shall see, some of the problems that architects today face are beyond the scope of even the most highly developed internalized skills alone. The business of method is to make external, and thus more readily learned and more testable, what the expert can in many cases do on the basis of internalized experience.

5.3   The recent history of design methods in architecture

Why the *recent* history of design method? The *total* history of design methods, as a recognised subject with an impact on architecture, covers only about fifteen years, starting with the Oxford *Conference on Design Methods* (Jones and Thornley, 1963). Alexander's seminal book *Notes on the Synthesis of Form* appeared in 1964; and the Birmingham Symposium, subsequently published as *The Design Method* (Gregory, 1966), took place in 1965. The first conference to deal specifically with design methods in architecture was held at Portsmouth, England, in 1968 (Broadbent and Ward, 1969), and in that year also the American Design Methods Group held its first international conference at Cambridge, Massachusetts (Moore, 1970). Jones produced a comprehensive and critical review of all this activity in his *Design Methods — Seeds of Human Futures* (Jones, 1970a), and Broadbent did a similar service for the more specifically architectural developments in his *Design in Architecture* (Broadbent, 1973a). So one reason for treating only recent history is that the history of the period 1962–1972 has been very thoroughly and completely written.

The second and more important reason is that the year 1972 marks a decisive change in the direction of thinking on the subject; a point at which certain difficulties that had been experienced in the application of the theories and methods developed in the previous decade were, if not resolved, at least explained, by a new and broader theory. The new theory had been in preparation for some time, but it was brought to general notice by a discussion that appeared in the fifth anniversary report of the Design Methods Group in January 1972 (Rittel, 1972). The participants were Horst Rittel, Jean-Pierre Protzen, and Donald Grant, and what they discussed was a new direction, a "second generation" in design methods. It is the history of the developments of the last decade, and some comparison of the new "second-generation" ideas with those of the first generation which will be undertaken here.

If we follow Wade (1977) in taking design to be describable in the most abstract way as a transformation $A \rightarrow B$, where A is some initial state, B is a terminal state, and the two are linked by a vector represented by the arrow, then first-generation methods had centred on the vector term. That is, they assumed that the present state of affairs and the final goal were known or could readily be discovered and attempted to develop better methods of organizing the transformation of the initial state into the final state. The object of these methods was in fact to find an algorithm, a logically rigorous set of rules for producing a satisfactory, or even optimum, result. This "systems" or "mission-oriented" approach had proved its effectiveness in military and space technology, where the actual goal was extremely simple and precise, though the equipment needed to realize it was extremely complex. The problems, in fact, were very well constrained by the laws of physics on the one hand, and the limits of human psychophysical performance on the other.

In town planning and architecture, on the other hand, the goals are complex and vague, whereas the equipment needed to realize them is extremely simple. The transformation process could certainly be improved, and operations research methods, particularly critical path network analysis and its various refinements, have been successfully applied, first to the construction process and then to the organization of detailed design and documentation. These are not, however, *design* problems. The impact of the new methods on design was limited to the resolution of *puzzles*: such as, given a set of rental returns, a range of cost/unit, and certain regulations as to the minimum number of units of each type, what is the best mix of flats in a new development, in terms of return on investment, where a "best" answer can be obtained by linear programming methods, or the more complex site-feasibility analysis using iterative methods reported by Gero and James (1972); or, given a number of sets of elements for roof constructions, some of which are incompatible, what is the most economic practicable combination? a puzzle that can be solved by the use of the AIDA method (Luckman, 1969). Such methods provide quicker and more reliable solutions to puzzles which would previously have been "solved" by trial and error or guesswork.

In other cases, the new methods did not even reduce design time or cost, and were rather more complicated than those in use. An example is the procedure for the design of a rainwater system for an industrial building developed by the Building Research Station in England (Honey, 1969); though in fairness it must be admitted that this was intended more as an example to illustrate possibilities than for use in practice. It is interesting to note that the whole report, "A study of coding and data co-ordination for the construction industry", of which Honey's paper forms part, does not deal with the "outline and scheme stages of architectural design" but confines itself to the better constrained tasks of detail design. The reason given is that the "sequence of activities was unique to each project and depended very much on the constraint that was the most important, whether stated to be so by the client or selected by the designer." But it is just this question of deciding goals, or "most important constraints", which separates the design problem from the puzzle. In fact, as Rittel remarks (Rittel, 1972): "First generation methods seem to start once all the really difficult questions have been dealt with already."

First-generation methods were suited to the solution of well-constrained or "well-behaved" problems; and as we shall see there are some cases in which the design of a whole building may be a well-behaved problem. But the intention of "second-generation" methods was to extend the scope of method to ill-constrained, ill-behaved or "wicked" problems. In doing so, the aim of logical rigour, which had characterized the first generation methods, had to be given up. Second-generation methods are not algorithmic. The kind of model of the design process exemplified by the RIBA Plan of Work (RIBA, 1967), or in the popular "fact gathering–analysis–synthesis" formulation, is rejected. The overall approach is more in accordance with the current views of scientific method discussed previously; in order to begin, in order to understand the problem, in order to collect facts, we must have a theory of what it is we are trying to do, not a "concept" that is god-given and fixed, but an hypothesis whose purpose it is to be criticized and corrected. That is, second-generation methods are heuristic search processes, which make use of hypotheses and the information that the testing of each successive hypothesis generates to limit the subsequent field of search.

The methods of test explicitly include argument and debate, since second-generation methods admit that part of the problem in design lies in deciding what ought to be done, in what Rittel calls deontics. Each step in the search process is tested instead of reserving the testing to an end-point of "presentation" to a "client", or occupation by a user.

> "The first generation model works like this: you work with your client to understand the problem; then you withdraw and work out the solution; then you come back to the client and offer it to him, and often run into implementation problems because he doesn't believe you. The conclusion of the second generation is that such a sequence is entirely meaningless, and the client is well-advised not to believe you in such circumstances, because at every step in developing such a solution you have made deontic or ought-to-be judgements that he may or may not share, but that he cannot read from the finished product offered in your solution." (Rittel, 1972)

There are six, or perhaps seven, characteristics or principles of second-generation methods which distinguish them from those of the first generation. The first is the assumption of the "symmetry of ignorance". It is not a case of an "expert" confronting a "layman", which implies that the necessary knowledge to achieve a solution is, if not entirely, then very largely in the hands of the expert. But in reality both "sides" have essential knowledge in rather similar amounts; and, correspondingly, both sides are ignorant in some vital areas. This is the logical argument for using participatory and argumentative methods: the knowledge and the ignorance of all parties have to be brought out. And this leads naturally to the second characteristic, the argumentative nature of the planning process, which is represented not as a discovery of facts, but as a process of detecting, defining and deciding issues. The consensual nature of the knowledge used in design has been discussed previously, but this implies that design, as the proponents of second-generation methods contend, is a process of *reaching* consensus, through debate, making use of relatively well-established and tested knowledge and logical methods, including some of those developed in the first generation. The "constraints" on the design problem are *decisions*, and the making of these decisions *is* design.

The third characteristic of second-generation methods is the use of what has been described here as an augmented problem space. The particular issues encountered in an individual design are themselves subsets or consequences of broader issues, and it is always wise, and at times essential, to raise the level of the problem up to the next level of comprehensiveness. This has its dangers; it can become pathological, an excuse for the indefinite deferment of decision and for inaction, as in the typically romantic contention that no limited action can be worthwhile because society is totally corrupt; only revolution can solve any particular problem. But while it is not useful to augment the problem space too far or too often, it should always be possible for the architect to ask himself and others such meta-questions as, "Is it necessary to build a building at all, or would this set of issues be better resolved by some other kind of social action?"

It is also important that the process of decision making, the arguments used, should be as "transparent" as possible. This is equivalent, in terms of Jones' distinction between "black-box" and "glass-box" design methods (Jones, 1970b), to moving the whole process as far as possible into the glass-box realm. There are two interrelated reasons for this. One is that because the process is heuristic each successive step depends on the total of the preceding steps. It is an incremental decision process. If the preceding steps are not clearly understood, the process fails. The second reason is that if the process seems to be leading in the wrong direction, if for example we find that the remaining solution space is negative, that no solution is possible in terms of the decisions or constraints so far established, then we may have to relax some constraints, unmake some decisions, and back-track to a previous "knowledge state". The process of back-tracking can be limited if the argument is transparent, if we can trace it back through the minimum number of steps necessary to relieve the contradictory constraints. But if this is not possible, we may be forced right back to the start; or modifications may be attempted which result in covert contradictions and failure, either at the stage of implementation or in use.

Tied in with the principle of transparency is the principle of objectification. The process of design must not only be transparent, it must be recorded, given propositional form, made part of Popper's "third world". Proper and explicit recording reduces the risk that something critical will be overlooked. It also makes effective criticism and argument much easier. Issues that are vaguely stated may be glossed over, leaving everyone with the assumption that their point of view has prevailed. This is most likely to happen with the most dangerous issues, i.e. those that are both very important for the outcome and subject to a wide range of opinion or outright disagreement between the affected parties. Finally, the process of back-tracking, if it becomes necessary, is much easier if agreement has been in the form of explicit consensus.

The sixth principle is that the delegation of judgement to the professional designer should be minimized. The more clearly any agent in the design process has to spell out his reasons for his decisions, the less opportunity he has to build in ideas about what ought to be the case, what the goals of the design are, which may not be agreed by the other parties. Rittel goes further and argues that the ideal of second-generation designers ought to be self-elimination, that no designing for others should take place. It is doubtful, in a complex and pluralist society, whether such an ideal can be consistently adopted. There is a very great difference between saying that delegated authority should not be presumed upon, or that it should be kept to a feasible minimum, and saying that no-one should ever be prepared to take responsibility for any decision that affects others, which is the force of the wider argument. In practice, what is important is that the scope of delegation should be understood and agreed. This issue has already been argued at some length in section 4.4.

The optional seventh principle can also be seen as a synoptic or overall principle: it is the "conspiracy model of planning". The conspiracy involved is not the "conspiracy against the laity" of the professional, but a conspiracy of designers and users to bring about first agreement and then action. The outcome of such a conspiracy is less likely to fail than the more conventional process in which more decisions are taken by the designer, and the client and users are faced with a proposal that can only be accepted or rejected. It is an interactive rather than a reactive model of the design process.

This, then, is the proposed paradigm change involved in the substitution of second for first generation methods. The new paradigm is based on urban planning rather than on industrial design, which was the practical background from which first-generation methods largely sprang. Rittel's choice of words and of examples makes it clear that he has planning, rather than architecture, in mind. However, both Rittel and what one can fairly call his school of thought have generally held that this is also the right problem space for architecture. But is this the case? Are all architectural problems "wicked" problems?

It is at least possible to argue that they are not. An alternative viewpoint, that there is a range of architectural design problems, only some of which require second generation methods, was advanced in Heath (1972). There it was suggested that architectural problems differ from planning problems on the one hand as they do on the other from industrial design problems. Or, more precisely, that they occupy a middle ground, a range or continuum which extends from tasks that closely resemble product design to tasks that closely resemble planning. There is both a qualitative and a quantitative aspect to these resemblances. The design of building elements such as doors, partitions or fittings may be near to industrial design both in terms of the kind of design approach that is appropriate, the qualitative aspect, and also quantitatively, in that both are concerned with relatively small though perhaps complex units. But the design of certain building types can also be shown to resemble industrial design in the qualitative aspect alone, as will be demonstrated in more detail hereafter. Similarly, some architectural design resembles planning in scale but not in character; small projects, on the other hand, may have more features in common with planning than their size would suggest.

A general description of the characteristics of industrial design that tend to distinguish it from architectural activity may help to bring out some aspects of this design continuum. Industrial design is concerned with objects that are, as has been said, by no means necessarily less complex, as physical systems, than buildings; but the role of these objects in the system of human activities in which they play a part is customarily much more closely and clearly defined in two distinct ways. Firstly, the inputs and outputs required can be stated with some precision, and the boundaries between the physical system and the activity system are clear. In the language of ergonomics, it is possible to specify the feedback loop between user and tool, and their interactions are constrained to ensure that, in general, the only significant interactions are those specified. Of course there will always be people who insist on using chisels to open cans, and children who attempt to use refrigerators as play houses, but these are clearly cases of *abuse*. Further, the industrial design product becomes obsolete in a relatively short time — its response to change is characteristically scrapping — and this is both a consequence of and contributes to the definition of the problem; no-one tries to adapt black and white television to colour reception, but very much of this sort of thing is often attempted with buildings, because of their longer life and looser fit.

Secondly, industrial design works for a market, which by accepting, rejecting, complaining and so on provides feedback and gives further precision to the definition of inputs and outputs required, whereas as we have seen the process of evaluation of buildings is laborious and slow, and even when it is carried out the results sometimes arrive too late. The market for industrial design consists of identifiable groups of people or firms whose opinions can be observed directly by sampling. Market research techniques have been developed and their use is encouraged in many cases by over-supply and competition, which permit the consumer to exercise buying leverage. Because the conditions of use are well defined, it is relatively easy for consumers to envisage them and express criticisms or suggestions for improvement. All this makes possible the existence and success of consumer research organizations, which are able to correlate and codify consumer experience of products in the interests of better buying. Without exaggerating the merits or efficiency of such market mechanisms, it is clear that they contribute much to making the industrial designer's task easier.

The situation of planning and urban design is completely different. From every point of view the problems are ill-defined. We have no general model of society as a system within which to locate the city as a subsystem; it may not even be possible to construct such a model. The boundaries between the physical system and the activity system therefore cannot be clear, and this is illustrated by those models that have been constructed to deal with specific planning problems, such as transportation and shopping behaviour, that include in their inputs both physical and sociological information. The feedback loop between city and inhabitants is not closed, even theoretically, but open: a variety of interactions is not only possible, but certain. Cities, and even parts of cities, last a long time, so that changes in the inputs and outputs cannot in general be accommodated by scrapping. There is a long delay between the completion of even a small-scale planning change and the feedback from its effects. There is no definable client or market; rather, there is a multiplicity of clients and markets, differing in economic status and life style, who can be said without exaggeration to inhabit different cities even though they make use of the same physical facilities. Attempts to test proposed courses of action by public discussion are frustrated by the diffuseness of the "public"; by the remoteness, temporal and conceptual, of the proposals from the consumer; and, as Hoinville and Jowell (1972) among others have pointed out, by the biasing effects of articulate and politically efficient middle-class groups. Nor have attempts to redress the bias by way of "advocacy planning" been especially successful (Blecher, 1971). Thus, instead of consumer organizations, in urban affairs we have pressure groups, more or less overtly political, concerned with arguing their particular point of view or interest. Planning problems are peculiarly ill-defined and wicked problems.

Pursuing this line of argument, it is possible to identify certain cases of building design which approximate to the extremes of industrial design on the one hand and urban planning on the other. Generally, we can distinguish between those building types for which there is a well-defined market, and "one-off" buildings serving complex organizations. Heath (1972) labels the former "commodity" buildings, by analogy with consumers durables, and the latter "systems" buildings because they house and form part of a complex sociotechnic system. Consideration of these types in relation to the range of architectural practice points to the existence of a third extreme type, the "symbolic" building, one of whose prime objectives is to denote or symbolize the social significance of the activities for which it is a focus. The fuller description of these types and the explication of their relationships forms the remainder of this chapter; they represent possible problem spaces for tackling architectural design, and they can be related in a comprehensive problem space which permits a general theory.

The subsequent history of second-generation methods tends to confirm the hypothesis that their application to architecture is in some ways limited. Some distinguished papers on application to architecture have appeared (Weber, 1973, 1975), but is it difficult to detect any significant impact in practice. Both the theory and the techniques of participatory design have developed considerably in the past decade, but this development has not been much influenced by design theory. Rather it is due to the vigorous growth of environment–behaviour research, which has itself suffered an application gap attributable in part to failure to understand the practice of design (Purcell and Heath, 1982).

If, as with first-generation methods, application of second-generation methods to practice has lagged, the most likely reason is that, as with first-generation methods, the benefit to be gained is not clear to practitioners. Stated generally, the theory does not seem to be relevant. However, observations of workshops on policy planning and briefing conducted by the Royal Australian Institue of Architects in 1981 and 1982 suggests that where the application of the theory to particular limited problems is demonstrated, it is perceived as highly relevant. Before attempting to demonstrate just what the range of application of second-generation methods to architecture is, it will be helpful to give special attention to three theories which have undertaken specifically to build bridges between method and architectural practice.

5.4   Three methods: Alexander, Broadbent, Wade

In a sense it is unnecessary to review the contribution of Christopher Alexander to architectural method, because as with first-generation methods generally it has received very thorough treatment in the literature, culminating in an extended criticism and rebuttal by Broadbent (Broadbent, 1973a), and because Alexander himself has explicitly rejected it (Alexander, 1971). But he is a pioneer; his book *Notes on the Synthesis of Form* is still in circulation and rightly so, for it contains many valuable observations on the difference between unselfconscious or traditional design and self-conscious design; and his mistakes are worth learning from. And he contributed not one but two distinct methods, or ideas for methods: that described in the *Notes* and the later design by patterns, which arose from his work with the Offices Development Group of the Ministry of Public Building (as it then was) in England (Alexander and Poyner, 1970). The method proposed in the *Notes* is an almost perfect example of Cartesian rationalism supplemented by modern graph theory and set theory and the use of a computer; that is, it depends on breaking the problem down until single self-evident propositions are reached, and then recombining them systematically. Alexander attempts to meet the objection that the number of possible descriptions or "crude" facts about even a simple object is infinite by his doctrine of "misfits". The designer is to attend only to those features of the existing environment that are evidently failing; these will form a large but finite class of "facts".

The process of breaking the problem down will yield a hierarchy of subproblems, logically connected in the form of a "tree". The process of recombination follows this sequence in reverse. The recombination is done by proposal or intuition: "form diagrams" are invented which summarize the physical implications of the requirements at each stage; each higher stage embodies the form diagrams below it. Many readers took Alexander to be saying that the process of recombination was a mechanical one, a true process of induction. However, there is no warrant for this in the text, although the diagrams are given much less space than other aspects of the process.

Even granting that Alexander did not make the mistake of supposing that design could be an inductive process, there are five criticisms of this theory, which taken together are conclusive. First, it is difficult to be sure we have found all the "misfits". Secondly, information about what "fits" may be just as important; if we ignore what is right about the situation, correcting a misfit may produce another, different misfit. Thirdly, the world is not divided simply into good and bad, fit and misfit. Fourthly, as Alexander himself was to argue in a later paper "A city is not a tree" (Alexander, 1965), real environment–behaviour systems are often too complex to represent in a simple "tree" pattern. Finally, the assumption that it is always possible to find a solution at any level of recombination that does not compromise solutions at lower levels cannot be justified; this is really the converse of the fourth point.

Since the publication of "A city is not a tree", Alexander has been at work on his theory of design by patterns, which seeks to overcome the difficulties that he then recognized. This work culminated in the publication of *A Pattern Language* (Alexander, Ishikawa and Silverstein, 1977) and the associated volumes *The Timeless Way of Building* and *The Oregon Experiment*. In the pattern language, the notion of atoms or ultimates is retained, but the ultimates are no longer "misfits" but systems of interaction between people and environments. Behaviour is seen as forming a field of forces or tendencies-to-action, and the environment may interfere with or facilitate these tendencies. A "good environment" is then taken to be one in which no two tendencies conflict, because they are not "allowed" to by the design. Certain systems of behaviour and certain physical settings are in fact *prescribed* as ideal or ultimate, as "patterns". In *A Pattern Language* the prescriptive intention is quite clear; of some of the patterns at least the authors assert that they are "true invariants", that they are properties common to *"all possible ways"* of solving the stated problem, that they are "archetypal" and that they will be "part of human nature... as much in five hundred years as they are today".

Such claims are very strong. They go far beyond the traditional use of pattern books in architecture, discussed earlier, as exemplars or guides and as devices for saving design time. Inevitably, they have been challenged. The objection that such an approach to design amounts to behaviour control and is therefore deterministic and immoral (Daley, 1969) can be dismissed, firstly on the grounds that, as we have seen, environments do not to any great extent determine behaviour, and secondly, because it is subsumed in more general questions. Of these the most central is the question of conflict.

In real life, the aims and objectives, the desires and interests of different groups, and even the aims, objectives, desires and interests of any one person, conflict. The process of design is largely one of moving sufficiently from conflict towards consensus to permit action; thus it makes sense to treat it as *negotiation* (Cuff, 1982). A deep-rooted distaste for conflict is the other face of Alexander's quest for ultimates. The pattern language simply legislates conflict out of existence. However, it does not answer the criticism already made of the method proposed in the *Notes*; it is simply assumed that there are no possible conflicts *between* "patterns". This difficulty is recognized to the extent that each pattern is supposed to be connected to, or embedded in, other patterns. This does not solve the problem, it simply raises the ante. There *are* no ultimates, no propositions that are simply true and unquestionable, no environments that cannot be the subject of disagreement.

Protzen (1980) has drawn attention to the mandatory and arbitrary nature of the patterns, and has argued that they are not empirically testable and may be obstructive to inquiring design. He has also advanced trenchant criticisms of the use of evidence in *A Pattern Language* and its sister volumes. In replying, Alexander (1980) does not attempt to refute Protzen in detail. He falls back on a form of Platonism, a claim that "...as we become more true to our own selves... we do, without intending to, approach one another... with respect to our essence, ...the extent to which we manage to be united with the Divine void." This is the kind of position to which a doctrine of essences or ultimates naturally leads. However, Alexander also makes it clear that he regards this kind of position as the only alternative to relativistic views of ethics and aesthetics, which he calls "the many-value theory", and which he, rightly, regards as a source of much confusion, and even "nihilism". Why he should object so strongly to relativism in these fields when he himself, as Protzen (1980) shows, takes a relativistic or consensual view of *knowledge* is not clear, but it is certainly important to consider whether this kind of idealism is indeed the only alternative to relativism.

In fact, a qualitative view of all of these matters *is* possible without resorting to idealism. Moore (1903, 1912), for example, developed an empirical and qualitative view of ethics, and Anderson (1962) has shown how such a position can be maintained without Moore's intuitionism. An empirical and qualitative view of environmental aesthetics was sketched in the previous chapter (section 4.5), where it was argued that certain quite specifiable aesthetic properties of situations interact with people's understandings, aims and objectives to produce preferences. These aesthetic qualities or properties are invariant and independent of the observer in the same way as and to the same extent as any other qualities, greenness for example. The understandings, aims and objectives vary with the observer, though in accountable and describable ways, and so do the preferences.

If such qualities exist, they are characteristics of things or situations in general, and our ability to perceive them is not a cultural but an evolutionary phenomenon, and antedates by millenia the kinds of complex cultural constructs that make up Alexander's "patterns". Even if it is argued that the aims, objectives and understandings of individuals are so far determined by evolutionary or cultural factors, that some interactions with aesthetic qualities, some preferences, are inevitable, it seems unlikely that there would be 253 of them, which is the number of "patterns" proposed by Alexander and his colleagues. While it may be that the value that Alexander attributes to the patterns is not aesthetic, the same argument can be applied to any attempt to connect qualities, preferences and artifacts. A far-reaching empirical investigation, on the lines suggested by the Kaplans in their *Humanscape* (Kaplan and Kaplan, 1982), may eventually disclose such "preferred environments"; even then, it is more likely that we shall merely have a more complete knowledge of the aesthetic qualities that can serve commonly occurring interests and desires, rather than a set of "patterns". Lacking such an investigation, we have no reason to believe that any particular set of "patterns" are indeed invariant and not simply a sample of the preferences of a particular group or person, like any traditional pattern book.

In summary, the pattern language does not appear to have any substantial empirical justification, and its author does not attempt to justify it on empirical grounds. His philosophical justification, while it is aimed at countering real evils, does so in an unsound way.

Broadbent's approach (Broadbent, 1973a) can be described as common sense. He does not believe in any one ideal design process; he does believe that we can proceed reasonably, making use of as much well-tested information as we can get, and also of the logical methods of the first generation where these seem to be relevant. He divides goals fairly sharply into "client motivation" and "user requirements". Client motivation is treated with a very broad brush; user needs "will provide a surer guide to how one should design than the client's initial motivation." The process, which Broadbent describes in detail, stems from a consideration of user needs, though he is careful to specify that there are other processes, and he provides a chart of the three essential systems — human, environmental and building — and their elements. Design, he says, can commence at any point in the chart; for example, one may commence "knowing" the system of construction. However, he considers the process that he details the most probable one.

Now what is this "modal" method, if we may call it so? Broadbent suggests that, having established the client's motivation, our early investigations will be guided by precedent — the building type, the client's own building if he already has one. This may lead us to conclude that the needs can be met by an aggregation of Cowan-type 14 square metre rooms, with "average" environmental conditions; or it may indicate the need for more detailed investigation leading to more accurate "fit". In the latter case, a list of activities will be prepared, by consultation with the client and by observation; some evaluation of the importance of activities, perhaps in economic terms, may also be necessary. Then for each activity a planing brief is prepared, setting out the physical space it requires, the environmental conditions, its effect on the structure (or loading) and its relationships with other activities. The relationships have to be considered in further detail. There are physical movement relationships, relationships between environmental conditions, which may be compatible or incompatible as between any two activities, and social relationships. Considered in relation to a given site, this accumulation of data will provide a guide as to where in physical space each activity should be located: in a quiet zone, on the sunny side, towards a view, and so on. It is also possible at this stage to treat the grouping and interconnection of activities systematically, though abstractly, yielding "strings of beads" or flow charts.

A separate line of reasoning, or design development, flows from consideration of the site. The site may be given, or it may have to be selected. In either case, the site being known, its physical characteristics (dimensions, levels, and so on), its "conceptual" characteristics (the legal planning and financial constraints) and its environmental characteristics (prospect, exposure, noise levels and the like) have to be discovered. In the specific case of the design of a small office building, which Broadbent takes as an example, these considerations yield precise constraints. He also discusses briefly the case in which the site is large, open, and generally unconstrained. Here, he suggests, some constraint such as the overall volume obtainable for the envisaged price will operate. Another possibility, which he does not mention, would be some kind of perimeter/area or surface/volume ratio, which is also an economic constraint; and, as he does propose, we may be guided by the aesthetic qualities of the site in establishing a desirable building envelope. All these characteristics of the building envelope or site are then represented in an "environmental matrix" which may be a literal physical model.

These two lines of development are now combined. The "strings of beads" are packed into the environmental matrix, locating the most important beads in the environmentally "best" positions for them. Packing has its problems, because the "beads" may vary widely in their dimensions, including height; because there may be conflict in the environmental conditions — the best view may be towards a noise source, for example; and because there may be strong connections between significant and relatively insignificant activities. Trade-offs and compromises will be necessary. However, it is assumed that these conflicts can be dealt with rationally; some deficiencies will just have to be accepted. At this point the building exists as a sort of diagram in space; now it is necessary to give it physical form.

This process of translation from diagram to physical form must, Broadbent argues, be accomplished by one of four types of design, which he derives from the study of architectural history, or from some combination of those types. The four pure types are pragmatic design, iconic design, analogical design, and canonic design. Pragmatic design is the use of available materials and methods, by trial and error, to establish building form. Iconic design is the literal repetition of a tried and accepted form — the Greek temple, or the public buildings of twelfth century China (Glahn, 1981); some extrapolation in the form of the combination of known elements is possible within this general type. Analogical design is "the central mechanism of creativity"; it is the transfer of ideas from one context to another, or the displacement of concepts as we have discussed previously (section 2.5); architects may draw on the work of other architects, on vernacular building, on natural forms, or on the forms of other artefacts for their analogues. Canonic design involves the use of a geometric grid or proportional system.

Broadbent considers these four types of methods to be of uneven usefulness in present-day design. Pragmatic design will be involved in the selection of the methods of construction. Here we have to consider structural support and space division. Structural support may be mass, planar or frame. Space division may be mass, planar or skin. Some of these methods of construction carry along with them possibilities or difficulties in maintaining the desired environmental conditions. They have to be considered in relation to the anticipated loads, the subsoil conditions, the availability and cost of materials, the availability and cost of labour, the need for environmental control, the expected life of the building, the money available for capital and running costs, statutory controls, and their aesthetic qualities. Here again there may be contradictions, which prevent a clear decision on pragmatic grounds alone; other types of design may also be necessary.

Iconic design he regards as the least useful. Architects today are expected to be "original", so that literal copying is largely taboo. Also it may be difficult to adapt a literal copy to a different site and situation. However, Broadbent here seems to overlook the extent to which iconic design is in fact used; in Australia, both public and "merchant built" production of family houses proceeds almost entirely by iconic design.

Analogic design is Broadbent's favourite. By adapting, rather than copying, some pre-existing form — and built forms will be easiest — to suit the logical structure of the "environmental matrix", an appropriate built form can be produced. To judge by his examples, what Broadbent is really concerned with here is the method of arriving at the external appearance of the building: an aesthetic system to match the functional system, an "architectural vocabulary". But he does not say that.

Finally, Broadbent discusses canonic design. He suggests that, rather than attempt to fit a pre-established mathematically abstract grid to an environmental matrix, a grid may be determined by analysis of the dimensions already fixed in the process of producing the matrix. This approach might lead to the use of a building system. In his "worked example" he develops designs using each of his four methods, and ranks them on a number of criteria: structural practicability; cost; environmental performance; and effectiveness as a symbol. On the basis of this ranking he selects a final design.

Broadbent's approach is obviously much more useful than either of Alexander's methods. It is evolutionary, rather than revolutionary. A problem space is clearly established by the use of precedents. It is progressively constrained by information derived from consideration of the users' activities and of the site; and the final selection of an individual solution within the restricted solution space thus created is made on aesthetic grounds. A wide range of tactics are well and clearly related to the overall strategy; although discussion of this aspect has been omitted here for the sake of brevity. However, despite these considerable merits, the reaction of practitioners has been, as far as one can judge by informal discussion, unfavourable. They feel that there is more to it than that. And, making due allowance for the conservatism of the craft, and for romantic drives for unfettered freedom, it seems that they are right. For Broadbent really considers only the constrained, well-behaved problem; it is significant, as we shall see, that he chooses a small office building as his worked example. He sees very well that lack of constraint is a difficulty, as in his discussion of the site; and he also sees that this kind of sequence is by no means the only possible one. But he does not really provide any alternative. In the "systems" building (it will shortly be demonstrated in more detail) the problem just is to establish the constraints and to rank them. In the symbolic building the problem is so lightly constrained that this kind of approach is not feasible. It is really a method suited only for the "commodity" building, and for that it is, as Broadbent acknowledges in part at the beginning of his discussion, generally over-elaborate. It represents an important step forward in method, in that it summarizes first-generation methods and extends them by relating them to architectural history and the culture or subculture of architecture generally. But it is not complete.

Wade's approach to method is more abstract and comprehensive; academic in the best sense of the word. He constructs a logical framework, carefully developed and drawing on a wide variety of systems theory, psychological and sociological sources. Having identified architecture as a problem-solving process, he takes as his starting point the general problem form A $\rightarrow$ B. Each term of this formulation — initial state, transformation process, and final state — may be in any one of three conditions: known, range, or unknown. These states are numbered for convenience: known = 1, range = 2, unknown = 3. For solution, two terms must be in state 1, known. If two or three terms are in states 2 or 3, the problem is ill-defined, and "closure" is required to bring at least two items into condition 1. Design problems characteristically require closure of the terminal state or goal; that is, they are in states (1, 2, 2), (1, 2, 3), (1, 3, 2) or (1, 3, 3). The terminal state, objective or goal may be strong or weak; the designer may have strong or weak control. Weak control and strong objectives promote a strategic decision or design style, leading to closure of the terminal state; strong control and weak objectives promote an open-ended design style leading to closure of the process term. Final solution is a determinate process with strong control and strong objectives. Closure of the terminal state is the "real" design activity; as the process term grows in importance "information about available processes and capabilities" will exercise a stronger influence on the terminal state, helping to close it.

Goal closure is achieved, then, in part by consideration of what is feasible, both what is feasible to the actor or client and what is feasible to the designer; and also what is feasible given the present state of the world. It will also be guided by typological information, that is, by reference to prior solutions or part solutions. The designer will imagine, and represent in the form of drawings, trial solutions, which are not a priori, but based on these considerations and a multiplicity of others; these drawings or "proposals" make trial solutions objective and permit their critical discussion and the progressively improved formulation of goals. The process may be aided by breaking down the problem into parts: "it is often easier to talk about reasons for parts than about reasons for the whole"; these parts are not, however, in any sense ultimate, but chosen for convenience. The amount of innovation that a particular problem calls for will depend on the aspirations of the client and the designer. Since the process of innovation is itself still a black box, the designer will be wise to concentrate on preparation and testing. Finally, goals may conflict; arguments should be developed for each side so that a better final closure may be achieved. Closure "often occurs only gradually during an extended solution process."

When goal closure has been achieved, the remaining term in the problem, the middle term or transformation process, is derived by abduction. The abduction process involves decomposition or breaking up of the two known terms in such a way that some fit can be discerned between the corresponding parts. This decomposition is in terms of demand statements and supply statments; the fit is established by detailed design. For example, in Honey's (1969) division of design into layout, functional systems design and detail design, layout is a demand statement, identifying the places where functions are required, functional systems design is a supply statement about the physical means of realisation, and detailed designed is the adaptation of one to the other. As it is possible for goals to conflict, so it is possible also for demand and supply statements to be inconsistent; for example, the client may want more than he can afford. Supply systems also may conflict with one another: Wade gives the classic example of the service supply duct running through beams — usually at the point of maximum stress.

The second phase of adduction is means–end analysis. Wade's schema for means–end analysis is the person–behaviour–function–object spectrum. Each succeeding term is a means with respect to the preceding term; an end with respect to the following term. "*Programming* converts *purpose* into *behaviour* information; *planning* converts *behaviour* into *function* information; *design* converts *function* into *object* information." There is a cyclic movement from the general to the specific; purpose is more general than person or institution; behaviour is less general; function more general; and finally the building is specific. Each move from the general to the specific requires *decision*. "Since the demand statements in a means–end analysis are typically at a higher level of abstractness than the proposed element to supply that demand, there is no way to ensure a determinate selection." A choice or decision is required and this should be referred to "the problem authority (usually the client)" at each step. The process is not one of analysis and synthesis; it is analysis–proposal–analysis–fit. Each stage provides a specification for the succeeding one, concluding in the object; each proposed solution can be tested against the preceding specification, though the decision cannot. The final phases of adduction are thus *specification, generation* of proposals, *testing* of proposals against the specification. The testing criteria can be classified under headings summarized in the engaging acronym SOFA: *symbolic, ordering, functional,* and *affective* aspects. Some of these aspects will be factored out in the progress of the design from the general to the specific, because some of the information involved is non-specific; but what has to be omitted should not be forgotten.

The final process in detail design or fitting function to object, specification to proposal, is carried out either by selection or building up, or some combination of the two. The former process, generate-and-test, can proceed step by step to greater and greater levels of detail; at each level the proposal can either be "bought" entire, or broken into its parts, which can in turn be bought or broken. "Buying" implies either that there is some object or system available on the market that meets the specification, or that there is a known fully understood solution. The building-up process proceeds as follows:

"1. Identify the elements of particular systems that are determined by the larger context or have been preselected.
2. Select an element from the most pervasive or most basic system and position tentatively according to known facts and principles.
3. Provide supporting or stabilising elements required by that placement.
4. Check for spatial incompatibilities.
    (a) Is there an easy fit with preselected elements?
    (b) Are auxiliary supporting elements reasonable?
    (c) Is there no interference with paths, continuites of other systems, like plumbing, air ducts, etc?
5. If *yes* proceed to the next most pervasive element.
   If *no* revise placement until *yes* is achieved."

The term "most constrained" may be substituted for "most pervasive" without doing violence to Wade's argument. Either selection or building up permits the assembly of the solution to a complex problem. Alternative possible solution assemblies may be developed and compete. Selection among alternatives will depend on compliance with the specification, on the degree of internal contradiction, and on consideration of elements factored out. Finally, the solution has to be acceptable to the selector (presumably the client) who must be able to identify with it.

It is difficult in a short account to do justice to the careful organization of Wade's argument. He sets out to provide an overview of the architectural design process that is general without being a priori. Something that is not brought out in the summary so far given, although some previous references have been made to it, is his account of the architect's task environment, and specifically the educational and office experience components. In the terms that have been used here, he describes an augmented problem space, and gives an outline of the construction of more specialized problem spaces for particular design tasks; this is the goal closure/means–end analysis/ specification/ proposal/ testing sequence. Finally, he provides a brief but important outline of programmes or search methods: a generate-and-test method, the "buy it or break it" type of design, and an heuristic method, the build-up process.

This logical structure fits both the "symbolic" and the "commodity" building. There are difficulties in applying it to the "systems" building. These difficulties are not inherent in the logic, but arise from the presentation. One group concerns the relations between designer, client and user. Little attention is given to the client/user distinction, or to the possibility of conflicting groups of clients and users, though the existence and inevitability of conflicts at all levels of design is acknowledged. It is not clear how such conflicts are to be resolved; nor is it clear how "identification" of client (and user?) with the final design is to be achieved; that is, the implementation problem is not treated. We may take it that both these obstacles are to be overcome by the process of appealing for a client decision each time generalities are converted to specifics. But cases arise where no "client" in the sense of a person or body able to make and enforce decisions, exists. It is implicit in the argument that this is a "weak control" situation, and that control will have to be improved before design can proceed; but it is important to know how.

A more serious criticism concerns the assumed primacy of the person–behaviour–function–object *sequence* and the corresponding layout–functional system-detailed design and programming–planning–design–object sequences. Wade discusses the mixture of information that may make up the "problem statement"; he makes it clear that such information can range over the person–object spectrum. He also points out as we have seen that goal closure may occur only gradually through the design process. But it follows that what are presented as sequences are not sequences but structures, frameworks which have ultimately to be filled out, and a separate description of process is needed. The final design will be analysable in terms of such sequences, but the actual order of decision, the design *process* will depend on the distribution of well- and ill-constrained elements throughout the structure. It will, therefore, be more like the process that Wade describes for detailed design, or "build-up".

These criticisms will be clarified by the more detailed discussion of the three design types or "problem spaces" and of tactics or programmes which follows. They go to make up an alternative, or rather complementary, model of the design process; a model that is psychological rather than logical, and task-centred rather than designer-centred.

5.5 Commodity building

The idea of commodity building has been briefly introduced. Here its characteristics will be examined in more detail, and the way in which an architectural problem space can be derived from these characteristics will be outlined. It is the simplest of the three types to be discussed, and corresponds to the well-behaved problem. A well-behaved problem, we have seen, is well constrained. Good constraint can arise, as in industrial design, where the boundary between physical and activity systems is clear and interactions can be precisely specified; but such situations are the exception in building, and good constraint is more often a consequence of good consensus: there is a general agreement as to what buildings of that particular kind are "like". Such a consensus is likely to arise in the case of buildings that are being produced in quantity: this gives clients and users the opportunity to make comparisons and to develop standards of their own, either subjectively or in some objective way. However, if there is no feedback loop or the feedback is attenuated, mass production may not lead to consensus, but may rather serve to produce conflict or rejection as in the reaction against much public housing. The existence of a market, whether for rental or purchase, creates a feedback loop, in that there is consumer choice, and this in turn may lead to market research and to the more empirical evaluation of consumer organizations. Quantity production, a market, and feedback systems take time to develop; it is likely that parallel to, but lagging slightly behind, these developments there will be legislative controls on the building type, which become more specific as the communal concern grows stronger and more widespread. The feedback loop is thus positive; the more a building moves towards the commodity type, the more highly it is constrained, and the less it resembles a problem or even a puzzle. If the process continues for long enough, the involvement of professional designers ceases to be necessary, or becomes merely cosmetic.

Such a tight consensus can only be temporary. For reasons that have been discussed in connection with the task environment of architecture, the large-scale production of any particular building type cannot be long continued. The market becomes, relatively quickly, exhausted. Production then drops to replacement level. What was formerly awareness based on choice becomes a conservative acceptance. The period of inactivity may be long, especially if, as is often the case, the collapse of building triggers or follows a general decline in the economy. Meanwhile, social and technical changes continue. Designers and builders cease, through lack of practice, to be skilled in the building type; and by the time a new demand appears their former skills are in any case technically obsolete. Thus when the new demand does appear it is effectively and perhaps actually for a new building type; and a new building type is not a commodity building, since consensus is lacking. We may call this, by analogy with the "building cycle", the "design cycle". The commodity building, while it must always represent most of the design output at any one time (by definition, so to speak), is thus a special or limiting case in the design cycle.

An interesting example of the design cycle is provided in a paper by Ouye (1974). He describes the process of setting up an information system for a firm that had a considerable practice in the design of laboratories. The firm, which had designed some twenty projects of this kind, was feeling the competition of manufacturers of prefabricated systems, who were at least able to represent themselves as able to provide better service in terms of cost and time. Clearly, for one firm to have designed twenty projects of the same kind, there must have been widespread demand; and this is confirmed by the incursion into the field of manufacturers, by-passing the designer of specialist facilities. It is also clear that expectations must have become standardized; otherwise, prefabricated solutions would not be acceptable. The information system devised by Ouye was intended to provide a compromise: more standarization than the traditional system, more flexibility than the prefabricated alternative. Whether or not the solution worked, we see here another feature of the design cycle: as buildings move towards the commodity state designers will be not merely enabled but forced to develop more algorithmic methods in order to meet the increasingly precise demands of the market.

Laboratory buildings are a useful first example because they do not immediately suggest themselves as commodity buildings. In recent years the archetypal commodity building in most major cities has been the rental office building. It may be worth examining the course of a typical "cycle". The following account is based on events in Sydney, but closely parallel sequences of events have occurred elsewhere. The office building boom, from 1960 to 1975 approximately, was initially a product of shortage. The depression, the second world war, and subsequent materials shortages had limited office construction for nearly twenty-five years. Employment in offices was growing in relation to other forms of employment. Existing office space was overcrowded and, for reasons discussed previously, obsolete. Nevertheless, investors were initially cautious, both about constructing new office space of any kind, and more especially about the demand for highly serviced, air-conditioned buildings. Market surveys were commissioned, which reduced the former anxiety, and a government report, which showed improved employee morale and productivity in such air-conditioned buildings as existed, influenced the latter. The first buildings constructed were enormously successful commercially; they revealed the pent-up demand, and served to make the obsolescence of the existing stock more obvious. Standards rose rapidly; air-conditioning, lighting, and finishes, and above all space per person all increased in successive buildings over a short period. Existing regulations limited building heights and did not allow the deep planning which air-conditioning and better artificial lighting made possible. At the same time the professional image of the skyscraper or office tower, standing in urban open space, which was part of current architectural ideology, was popularized; and the regulations were changed to allow both tall and deep buildings. A complex of new problems faced architects: air-conditioned buildings, taller buildings, better finished buildings, buildings that had to be flexibly subdividable to allow for multiple tenancies of various sizes. While many solutions were borrowed from America, equally many were invented. After about eight years the intrinsic problems were largely solved, though not without a number of costly failures; the extrinsic problems, the unintended side-effects, especially the environmental problems of congestion, shading, and wind effects, persisted. Construction continued at a high rate and the absolute size of projects continued to grow, but design processes had become routine: "anyone could do it" and design-and-construct packages became more and more common, except for the largest and most complex buildings. Client and user expectations became more and more exacting and specific: a consumer organization, the Building Owners and Managers Association, was formed and exercised a powerful influence on standards. Finally, it become clear that projects already committed exceeded the demand; at the same time popular pressures generated by the environmental effects already mentioned, not least the nuisance of living in a city constantly under construction, forced increasingly restrictive legislation, first at the city and then at the national level; simultaneously the economy took a decisive turn for the worse. Just as demands for higher standards of quality and space appeared simultaneously with the recognition of shortage, so willingness to accept lower standards for much reduced rentals appeared with over-supply, so that over-supply was exaggerated. Various estimates of doubtful reliability have been made as to how long the slump will last; it may be five years, or ten, or even longer. By that time the realization of energy shortage, expressed in rising costs, will have brought about substantial changes in the nature of the buildings demanded.

Various lessons can be drawn from this experience. For the purposes of method, the interesting point is that the new demand created new problems, for both clients and designers; that at a certain point these problems were "solved", that is techniques and aspirations had been brought more or less into line, leading to a consensus. At this point design no longer required such a high level of skill and was absorbed into the construction process. At the same time theorists began work on algorithms for the design of the building type. The whole cycle is parallelled, again in Sydney, by the booms in "home units" (flats or apartments for sale, not rent) and in "project housing" (off-the-peg individual houses in standardized, but architect-designed models), both of which took place over the same general period. It is not, it must be emphasized, the content of the building, the activities that it houses, which in themselves distinguish the commodity building; it is the existence of a sufficient rate of construction continued over a sufficient period for criteria to be developed and gain some kind of circulation, if only by the migration of designers from one office to another. This is a process quite different from the a priori imposition of minimum criteria which prevails where the user has no economic influence on the outcome; this is to be found either in undersupplied markets, or where supply is in the hands of a bureaucracy (Turner, 1976).

In the well-constrained or commodity building as we have described it, relations between designer, client and user are simplified. Both the entrepreneur-client and the ultimate user or consumer are reasonably well aware of what they can expect to get for their money. They are able to compare and trade off advantages and disadvantages of various designs, and even to evaluate proposed innovations where these are not of too radical a kind. An example is the introduction of "landscaped" office space, which after a relatively short initial period of trial and error became an accepted and at least partially understood possibility in the office space market. Both designer and client are or should be well aware of the ends to be pursued; instead of the symmetry of ignorance, we might speak of the symmetry of knowledge. While there may well be a great deal of work involved in getting from this general initial awareness to a specific design, this work is largely of a routine technical nature, puzzle solving not problem solving, what is sometimes called "grunge". The entrepreneur who employs an experienced architect to design such a building will not expect to engage in a prolonged argumentative process with him. He will want to minimize his holding costs by cutting design time as much as possible; a preliminary design within a month and working drawings within six months is a not uncommon programme. The result of such a process is not necessarily a bad building; neither is it necessarily a good one. It depends on the dedication and aesthetic judgement of the architects concerned and on whether the method used does in fact deal in an effective and orderly way with all the constraints. This is more likely to be the case if the method has been made objective.

When the method has been made objective it will be at least quasi-algorithmic; that is, the bulk of the work will consist of tasks for which algorithms can be written, connected at certain nodes by deontic decisions. As previously remarked, once a problem type has been stated in this form it is possible to write a computer programme for its solution, although the programme may have to be interactive to allow for the necessary deontic decisions; and such programmes have been written for office buildings (Grahame, 1969) and for "home units" or flats (Gero and James, 1972). The cost of preparing such programmes is very great, by comparison with the design cost of an individual building, but where it is justified by a constant through-put of work the rewards are correspondingly great. Even where such a semi-automated system cannot be economically justified, the automation of sections of the design, or simply the use of algorithms to guide the normal process of design in an office, can improve the speed and probability of success of the work. The life of such programmes or algorithms is limited because of technical innovations and changes in the market; this difficulty can be alleviated by making the algorithm and/or programme modular, and thus capable of piecemeal reconstruction. With the knowledge that now exists, it should be possible to automate the design of newly emerging commodity buildings soon after their existence is detected.

While the solution of commodity building problems has been illustrated in general terms in discussing Broadbent's method, a brief description of the main decision sequence in a well-constained problem of a different kind may not be amiss. This is a post-hoc reconstruction of an actual case, but it will serve as an illustration. The building shown in Figure 5.1 is an extension, in the form of an independent block, to a university college for men. Its main purpose was residential; some small teaching rooms were also required, but they were a subordinate element and will not be considered here. The client, the college council, had much experience in administering the existing college; the design architect had also spent a number of years living in a similar college nearby. There was therefore good client–architect communication or consensus on what were the main issues. Funding was provided by a national body, the Australian Universities

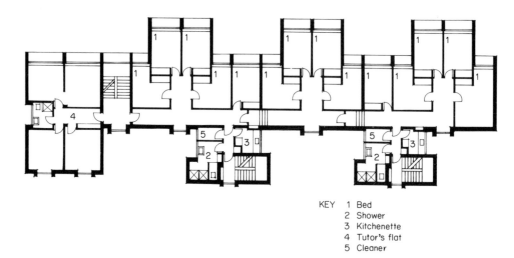

KEY 1 Bed
     2 Shower
     3 Kitchenette
     4 Tutor's flat
     5 Cleaner

Figure 5.1   Plan: college extension

Commission, which laid down somewhat stringent conditions, especially as to room size; but the college was also able to provide funds of
its own, which enabled these constraints to be relaxed in some
instances.

The site selection process was not of much interest and will be
omitted here. The site selected was near the main entrance to the
college, facing a parking area on one side, and on the other a quiet
area of lawn, with some established trees, beyond which was another
earlier residential block. There was a steep fall between the parking
area and the lawn, which then sloped away gently. The lawn face was
north-east, which is the favourable aspect, receiving morning and
early afternoon sun. Immediately to the west of the site was the
original college building, a monumental essay in Scottish Baronial,
constructed of sandstone, now mellowed, with four metre floor-to-
floor heights and steep pitched slate roofs.

The issues that emerged as critical to the design from the client's
point of view (and it must be borne in mind that both client and
designer were well aware of user needs) were: a maximum budget,
consisting of the government subsidy plus the funds that the college
was prepared to invest; room size and suitable environmental conditions for study at all times of the day and night, especially absence of
disturbing noise; arrangement of rooms so that groups of friends could
establish a common territory. The restrictions placed by the funding
body on room size were regarded by both designer and client as too
tight; students differ in sociability and in the amount of equipment they

require for their work, and there is also a student "pecking order" which requires some environmental expression. The college therefore decided to devote some of its funds to paying for some "oversize" rooms to provide a range of choice. Room size, though an important constraint, was therefore not primary.

The primary constraints were environmental, and particularly acoustic. The college had had a great deal of trouble with noise in an earlier extension built in the later 1940s. It was possible to study this building in detail and to identify noise sources and features of the planning and finish which aggravated or failed to reduce the noise. The primary noise sources were footsteps, on stairs and in corridors, conversation and activity in bathrooms and communal kitchenettes, slamming doors, radios and record players in rooms, and impact noises transmitted through the room floors, which were of concrete with a vinyl tile finish. The normal noise generated in these ways was aggravated by the fact that all the rooms, the stairs, the bathrooms and the kitchenettes opened on to a common double-loaded corridor on each level, with hard finished floor, walls and ceiling, so that all noise echoed throughout the floor on which it originated and even, by way of the stairs, on the other levels. In addition, the rooms had light hollow-core doors with glass over the transome, a construction that is for practical purposes acoustically transparent. The conclusions to be drawn were obvious. The new building should be planned so that the common facilities and stairs were acoustically isolated from any common corridors; the corridors and rooms should have a soft floor finish such as carpet to minimize impact noises; and the structure generally and the doors in particular should be sufficiently massive to reduce transmission from room to room and from corridor to room to acceptable levels. Since the over-transome glazing was both a sound transmission problem and almost totally ineffective in lighting the corridors, the corridors must be provided with windows of their own.

The site also contributed to the environmental constraints. As noted, one long side adjoins a car park — a significant noise source. So it was desirable that no students' rooms face in that direction. It was fortunate that the other long side of the site provided the best aspect and the best prospect. The reasonable solution was therefore to locate all noise elements — stairs and common facilities — on the car-park side, and the rooms on the other side. This was not an economical solution in terms of building perimeter, but it was worth exploring, and was in fact adopted. The north-east aspect was good for the winter term, in that the sun would warm the rooms in the mornings, but in the autumn and spring terms the sun would be too hot. With this aspect a simple horizontal projection would shade the windows in the hotter weather while the sun angle was still high.

Exploration of the problem using the constraints of (1) number of rooms required, (2) approximate size of room, (3) decision to locate all rooms on one side, (4) size of site, showed that a three-storey building would be required. Making use of the slope of the site it was possible to have a two storeys up and one down arrangement, and this was tentatively adopted. In order to fit the building between the boundary and the eastern wall of the original college building the rooms had to be overlapped somewhat. Taken together with the demand for social grouping of rooms, this generated the planning unit of four rooms grouped around a short stub corridor off the main corridor; an arrangement that had the added advantage of being less prone to echo than a simple parallel-sided corridor.

Further constraints were suggested by the budget. At best, the building would have to be built cheaply. And it had to be of fireproof construction. The cheapest fireproof construction was load-bearing brickwork with concrete floor slabs. This had the advantage of mass, which again helped with sound transmision problems.

At this point a good deal was "known" or decided about the building. A further constraint was provided by the building regulations: there had to be two fire stairs. After discussion with the client it was agreed that the bathrooms and kitchenettes should also be duplicated, so that there would be two "service blocks" on the south-west side. This was the last of the major constraints which helped to determine the form of the building. It was not, however, enough to "close" the problem, so there was an opportunity to introduce aesthetic considerations. One aesthetic constraint was of considerable importance: since the new block was quite close to the heroically scaled original wing of the college, but was much smaller in its inherent scale — that is, in room size and floor-to-floor heights — it seemed desirable to create larger units in the massing; otherwise the contrast could easily look absurd.

The next stage of design was therefore an investigation of aesthetic possibilities: those inherent in the constraints already discussed, which could be expressed in the form of diagrammatic elevations and block sketches, and others obtained by analogy with admired buildings whose general character was relevant to the problem. Analogies that influenced the final design were Le Corbusier's Pavillion Suisse (the stair and communal facilities grouping); Louis Kahn's laboratory building at Philadelphia (the concept of a group of "towers") and Le Corbusier's Maison Jaoul (the general treatment of the sunshades and wing walls). None of these analogies was used very literally or in any detail. A final decision, suggested by the site and the desire to increase the visual independence of the "towers", thus emphasizing them as

The Thynne Building, St. Andrew's College, University of Sydney, by McConnel, Smith and Johnson

units (the scale problem), was to change the levels between the groups of rooms, following the site contours. There were of course many other detail decisions but at this point the schematic design was complete.

This description of the solution of a very simple well-constrained design problem brings out a number of points. First, the process closely follows Broadbent's method: environmental conditions, site conditions and the budget provide a very large measure of constraint, leaving only a small solution space to be searched or "closed" by postulation and the introduction of aesthetic decisions. Secondly we notice, in accordance with both Broadbent's and Wade's arguments, the importance of an existing model, the earlier extension to the college, even though its lessons were largely negative. Thirdly, conflicts between activities were an important source of constraints, as indicated by Alexander's later theory. Fourthly, several major decisions, those relating to the location of the rooms, their grouping, and the form of construction, were "over-determined" in that more than one line of reasoning lead to that particular solution; this is common in

Pavilion Suisse Paris, by Le Corbusier. The main source for the stair towers and communal facilities grouping in the Thynne Building

well-constrained design problems. Fifthly, the process resembles in a number of points Eastman's (1970) study of architectural design, particularly in the way successive decisions were tested; on the whole, as in that study "the tests applied were overwhelmingly of a binary or threshold nature, corresponding to Simon's notion of 'satisficing'"; there was no attempt to optimize. Finally, it was perhaps worth mentioning that the design process was not only simple but successful in that the rooms were in fact very quiet and proved popular with the students.

5.6 Symbolic building

"Symbolic" building was defined earlier as being required, as one of its prime objectives, to denote or symbolize the social significance of the

Richards Medical Research Laboratories, by Louis Kahn. The source of the "group of towers" concept for the Thynne Building

activities for which it is a focus. Utilitarian constraints, of the kind we have considered in the case of the commodity building, are few or of secondary importance. This does not of itself imply that symbolic buildings are necessarily free from constraint. In traditional societies, where symbolism was, and in some cases still is, a highly developed and systematized way of thinking, the design of symbolic buildings is customarily subject to an extremely rigorous set of social rules or prescriptions. Such buildings are the best examples of Broadbent's "iconic" design: there are three "forms" or "icons" of the Greek temple, or of the classical Hindu temple, and these forms are departed from only under very unusual conditions. The Renaissance, the scientific revolution, and finally the Romantic Movement successively eroded such systems in European and related societies. In modern times, the *invention* of appropriate symbolism is seen as part of the architect's task in designing symbolic buildings. Secondary functional constraints may still apply; in a monument, the extreme form of symbolic building, they may be negligible, but here, significantly, a

Maison Jaoul, Paris, by Le Corbusier. The source of the general treatment of the sunshades and wing walls in the Thynne Building

sculptor is just as likely to be employed as an architect. In the more typical case of religious buildings, there are liturgical and other specifications which must be met. Nevertheless, it is characteristic of symbolic building that it is subject to relatively few constraints: the problem space, the architect's freedom of action, is, comparatively speaking, unbounded.

In the development of the architectural profession, there has been a heavy and continuing emphasis on symbolic building. Until quite recently, few architects would have been able conscientiously to deny that the height of their ambition would be to design a cathedral — and, in England or Australia, be duly knighted on the steps. More seriously, architects were usually employed, if not solely for aesthetic reasons, at least to ensure a quality of execution which would give the building social status or prestige. The legacy of this way of thinking is very much with us. "Architectural design" as it is still taught in many schools, and "high" architectural practice as it remains enshrined in the subculture of professional magazines, are almost entirely concerned with the symbolic/aesthetic aspects of building though they may pay lip service to other matters. This conservatism is understandable and perhaps inevitable. For the schools have not yet found an effective substitute for the Bauhaus methods and the remnants of Beaux-Arts methods to which they are accustomed; and the evaluation of the performance of buildings is a major research task which journals do not on the whole have the resources to undertake.

This established bias has had a significant effect on the development of design method. It would seem that one reason for the widespread acceptance of the fact gathering-analysis-synthesis-evaluation model of design is its fairly good match with the kind of real-life design process which is inevitable in "symbolic" building. For where the architect's main task is conceiving a form that will "carry" the required social meanings, he cannot do this as part of a transparent or "glass-box" process in which the client or users take part dialectically. He must discover the practical limitations on the problem, which may appear to correspond to the information gathering-analysis stages. Then he must go away and doodle or model in plasticine or use whatever other techniques he has acquired to generate "significant form" — techniques which fall into one or other of Broadbent's categories. Thus the Australian architect Roy Grounds is said to have described his "design method" for the National Gallery of Victoria as "a lifetime of experience, two years of discussion, and five minutes drawing with a stick on the beach at Waikiki." Having produced a concept, the architect working in this way has to face the problems of acceptance and implementation: he has to "sell" the design to the client. Thus the analysis–synthesis–evaluation model seems to many architects to be a license to go on doing what they were doing anyway, in space-age fancy dress; hence its popularity.

This kind of "conceptual" designing has been one of the main targets of those who seek new design methods; and insofar as it consistently under-estimates the need for understanding of the systems of which even a symbolic building usually forms a part, and insofar as methods that are appropriate to the category of symbolic buildings have been and are applied to other categories with more or less disastrous results, the methodologists are quite right. But given the premise that symbolic/aesthetic aspects are in a particular case of overwhelming importance, the method is appropriate. Here the designer, supposing him to be in fact a gifted artist, is indeed an expert, and the client may only accept or reject; he modifies at his peril. Exactly the same principle applies, as Townsend (1970) has pointed out, in that home ground of modern symbolism, advertising. So while true "symbolic" building in the sense in which it is being discussed here, forms only a tiny fraction of architectural production, and should certainly not be the model, as it has been in the past, for all architectural activity, an account of design method that does not include this possibility will be incomplete and thus misleading.

The fact that the design of symbolic buildings is in important respects black-box or non-rational does not mean that there is nothing that can usefully be said about method in such cases. There are at least three lines of inquiry, already under way, which, while they cannot be substituted for insight and productivity in the designer, may in due course be useful in bringing about a better match between the designer's skills and the requirements of a given situation. The first of these concerns the psychology of productivity, or creativity. Something has been said about this already, in considering architecture and knowledge. A better understanding of the ways in which ideas are generated may help architects to be more productive of ideas, which increases the chance of finding one that "matches" symbolically the problem in hand; and it may also enable them to choose from among the methods of generation available and ones most likely to result in such a match. Broadbent's pragmatic, iconic, analogic, canonic, classification is useful in this sort of way.

The second line of inquiry has also been briefly discussed in the earlier analysis of aesthetic goals. If we can classify activities and connect this classification with needs for arousal increment or decrement, and this in turn with various physical characteristics of the environment, through perception, then once again we shall be in a better position to match proposals to situations. At present this has not proceeded much beyond speculation, but the means for an empirical investigation exist.

The third line is equally speculative, but again methods now exist by which it could be pursued. It is to investigate and map the relevant "symbolic space" or schemata of the users. This can be done by observation of "popular" or vernacular building (Rapoport, 1969; Venturi, Scott-Brown and Izenour, 1972; Wolfe, 1966) or by experimental presentation (Krampen, 1974; Groat and Canter, 1979). In either case some theory of symbol formation and use is required; Rapoport makes use of anthropological theory, Venturi and Wolfe take an art historical approach, and Krampen draws on semantic theory. Or the question can be attacked at a more fundamental level, seeking to uncover the conceptual system directly, using either Osgood's semantic differential theory (Osgood, Suci and Tannenbaum, 1957) or Kelly's personal construct theory and the repertory grid method (Kelly, 1955). Since these methods are verbal, there is a difficulty in applying the results to the physical world; this has been overcome heuristically by Wools (1970) using successive drawn presentations or proposals guided by the verbal data. The point of such studies, whatever the theory and range of evidence used, is not to reproduce the schemata of potential users, whose symbolic space is likely, on the one hand, to be narrower than that of the professional designer, and on the other, to be too imprecise to yield any kind of definite proposal, but to ensure the final proposal contains the user's symbolic spaces as a specialization; in fact this is a special case of the more general problem of designing for others.

A short case study of a conventional process of design for a symbolic building may, once again, be helpful. Again, this is an historical reconstruction. The building concerned was a very small Presbyterian church in an outer suburb of Sydney; a new church for a new suburb and a newly formed congregation. The congregation was small and relatively poor, which is the usual case. The Presbyterian rite imposes few restrictions on the plan, and these are mainly concerned with the relations between holy table, pulpit, lectern and elders' chairs. Apart from that, the congregation must be able to see and hear, and there must be two vestries, for the minister and the choir. There is an emphasis on simplicity, both in the form of service and its setting. The architect's approach is simulated in the page of sketches (Figure 5.2). It is a conscious, if not especially self-conscious, application of Bauhaus "fundamental design" principles to the problem of finding a suitable form for the building. It might be said to be a sort of hybrid of Broadbent's analogic and canonic procedures, since what is being sought is a geometric form that will have some kind of analogy with the physical and symbolic requirements. There is also an analogy with Wright's Unitarian church at Madison but this did not really influence

Unitarian Church, Madison, by Frank Lloyd Wright. Despite certain similarities this well-known church did not significantly influence the design of the Presbyterian church illustrated below. Analogy is the most important, but not the only, source of form.

the solution; the method was essentially search among geometric forms. The designer here largely disregards pragmatic issues, assuming, correctly as it turned out, that the technical problems of constructing such a small and simple building would not be overwhelming. The design proved a popular success, and become the iconic model for a series of similar churches with a slight variation in plan and detail.

   We may contrast this case, in which the scale and complexity of the problem were such that this abstract and purely aesthetic design method was successful, with the history of the Sydney Opera House. Joern Utzon's approach to his original competition design seems to

Presbyterian church, Sydney, by McConnel, Smith and Johnson. The method of design for this church and its sister churches was essentially search among geometric forms

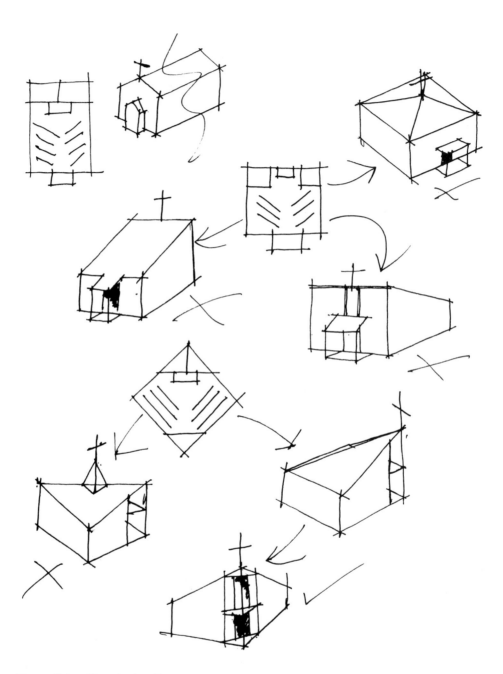

Figure 5.2 Church doodles

have been for all practical purposes identical to that just described. That is, he sought a series of striking forms which would contain and symbolize the complex uses that were intended. This is of course what the whole notion of a competition for such a building implies. But the difference between the Opera House and the little church lies in the validity of the assumption that the detailed adaptation of the activities and techniques of construction to the form proposed would prove feasible. It turned out to be impossible to build the forms that Utzon at first envisaged; drastic changes to the design were required, and there also proved to be serious conflicts between the demands of the users and the restrictions imposed by the form (Baume, 1967). These difficulties were at length overcome, but only after a long delay and at great additional expense; the issue became a political one, Utzon resigned, and the building was completed by other architects. It is possible that a different method would not have produced such a fine work of art. Yet the executed building does in many important respects represent an adaptation of the original proposal to constraints which

Sydney Opera House, by Joern Utzon. Utzon's design approach seems also to have been one of search amongst a range of geometric forms

the designer subsequently discovered; so that it is legitimate to wonder whether, had the constraints been known first, an equally successful work might not have resulted, without quite so much difficulty and disturbance. In other words, the Opera House was not really in the terms used here, a symbolic building, and the method appropriate to symbolic building was bound to encounter great difficulties or fail when applied to it.

5.7 Systems building

The term "systems building", as it will be used here, does not refer to industrialized or prefabricated systems, but to a particular kind of relationship between the building fabric and the activity system that it exists to serve; that is, it is being used in the sense that we find in "systems theory". This class of building is not so readily defined as those previously discussed; the earlier statement that the systems building is "one-off" and serves a complex organization is inadequate. Using Wade's (1977) logical classification of problems we may say that the systems building is a problem which suffers from lack of closure in all its terms: the initial state, the final state or objective, and the transformation term. Another way to express this is to say that consensus is lacking; and there will be a corresponding lack of relevant models. Thus, it is important to note, whatever their other characteristics, buildings that are of a type new to designer, client and user must be treated as systems buildings. But in order to appreciate the nature of the systems building problem we need a more detailed and explicit account, dealing with the relation of the systems building and the organization it serves to the social environment, the characteristic structure of the organization that requires a systems building, and the role of change in the design of systems buildings.

To being with the relation between the organization and its environment, the first danger signal is the involvement of the organization with other organizations in a complex ramified network. Of course *all* organizations are involved with other organizations; but the kind of organization we are considering is richly interconnected with a large number of other organizations which are themselves large. By contrast with the "placid clustered environment" in which the commodity building exists, the systems building is part of a "turbulent field" (Emery and Trist, 1965). As an illustration of this concept, consider a teaching hospital. It is a node in the health care system of a city and perhaps a region, since teaching hospitals commonly provide specialized medical services to an area much wider than their basic catchment. It is thus subject to more or less unpredictable variations in the pattern of health service demand, for example a rapid decline in the occupancy of maternity beds due to population shifts and or changes in contraceptive practices; to changes in official attitudes to health care delivery, which may suddenly lop or enlarge certain of its activities; and to fluctuation in the available resources due to quite extraneous factors such as the relative political power or sensitivity of different electorates. And as an industrial organization it is likely to be plagued by labour shortages and recurrent unrest, breaking out occasionally in strike action. These sources of uncertainty which exist for all hospitals are compounded by the teaching function, which may involve a strong connection with another large and complex organization, a university, and also connections with government agencies concerned with education; so that the teaching hospital may be simultaneously under pressure to limit or reduce the number of beds, in the interest of maintaining a pattern of expenditure laid down on demographic grounds by one government department, and to increase or maintain them, in the interests of increasing the number of trained doctors and nurses, to meet the objectives of another.

This complex and turbulent external social environment is paralleled by an equally complex and sometimes equally turbulent inner life. Because the organization is large, and has many purposes, it will have many subsystems, richly interconnected with each other. The number of subsystems and the complexity of their connections make the overall structure, as distinct from the structure and operation of the parts, difficult to understand, and it may not in fact be understood by anyone, since such understanding is not essential for effective operation and requires an additional level of theory over and above the knowledge necessary for operating the parts. (We may compare this with the earlier discussion of craft knowledge in the individual.) This lack of understanding is illustrated, as Beer (1966) argues, by the formal organization charts common in large organizations, which disregard the redundance of communication and the multiple interconnections of the informal network of personal contacts which alone permit such institutions to function. Further, it is likely that the organization will not be fully integrated, so that there will be cross-purposes and oppositions between its subsystems: what we may call "internal politicization". Differences of opinion will arise from real conflicts of aims between the different subsystems, and there will also be merely factious differences, and it will often be hard to tell which are which. The formal structure of such an organization is rarely suited to the task of self-analysis. Resounding titles of authority often and quite reasonably accompany an extensive ignorance of the detailed machinery and workings of the institution, or, perhaps worse, knowledge some years out of date; moreover, it is one of the objects of formal management to smooth over and conceal just those disagreements and issues which must be located and resolved if a design is ultimately to gain acceptance. Taking again the example of a teaching hospital, at the very least we can identify half a dozen main systems or classes of activity: being treated for and recovering from illness; nursing; medicine; teaching; administration; maintenance. Each of these has in turn many subdivisions each in itself a complex activity. In this rich and diverse society heads of departments exercise the uneasy authority of a paramount chief over feuding clans, and the administration treads the devious course of a mediaeval bishop trying to maintain religious power in a violent and secular world. The larger and more important the hospital, the worse the internal divisions are likely to be.

The third set of characteristics of the organization requiring the systems building concerns its exposure to change. Its turbulent environment implies, as we have seen, a good deal of external change: changes that arise because of the high social importance attached to the activities that the organization pursues. These external changes may produce correspondingly radical internal changes. In addition, however, the organization itself is likely to be future-oriented; its subsystems and the organization as a whole may be actively pursuing institutional and social changes of one kind or another, so that change will also be generated from within the organization. And this is likely to go along with the use of advanced technology and a concern for *technical* innovation; a further source of rapid change which inevitably has many effects on the operation of the organization. Once more we may take the teaching hospital as an illustration. All major hospitals depend heavily on advanced technology and seek to adopt the latest and most efficient methods. The ingrained disposition of almost everyone in the organization is to use the best methods available. In the teaching hospital there are additional pressures; they are heavily involved in research, in the attempt to advance medicine; and they also have the function of training the doctors and nurses of the future, and seek to expose them, not to the standard practice of today, but to the likely standard practice of some years hence. The teaching hospital is thus future-oriented; there is a crystal ball in every briefcase, and what is happening now is only rarely acceptable as an indication of what ought to happen in some proposed new facility; all planning is planning for change.

The methods appropriate to the systems building would appear to be those of the second generation. Let us review the features of these methods and see how they correspond to the organizational characteristics just described. First of all there is the assumption of the symmetry of ignorance. In the kind of situation we have been considering, *no-one* knows "all about" the organization: not the architect, not the administration, not even the cleaners. Knowledge and ignorance are both distributed over a large number of individuals; and so a success-ful design process will require the co-operation and participation of a large number of individuals. Secondly, there is the argumentative structure of the process; if the organization's external environment is turbulent, if it is future-oriented, if there are internal political divisions, then there are not so much "facts" about its operation which are "known", as key issues, over which there will be dispute, and which have to be decided. Thirdly, there is the possibility of regarding any issue as a symptom of another one; often the only way of resolving a disputed issue will be to look up to the next level of organization, to see if there is some fact or decision there which will enable a consensus to be reached. Fourthly, there is the ideal of the transpar-ence of arguments; in the process of heuristic search we have to be able to go back and reconsider previous decisions if a given line is blocked, and since we will be dealing largely with decisions and not with well-tested facts or matters of social consensus we cannot simply refer back to sources external to the design process; we must be able to retrace the decision process and the reasons and arguments advanced for each decision. Fifthly, there is the principle of objectification, the explicit and blunt statement of objectives or issues, so that they can be as thoroughly debated and well tested as possible. Sixthly, there is the control of delegated judgement; since the designer is not in this case an expert, he has no right to assume or build in judgements about what ought to be the case; all such judgements have to be stated as issues and properly debated. And finally and perhaps most importantly, there is the conspiracy model of planning; the implementation problem, the problem of securing agreement to a final design, which is obviously a very real one where there is internal politicization and external uncertainty, is overcome by securing the commitment of the con-cerned parties to the decisions taken during the design itself; final acceptance then becomes a "rubber stamp" matter.

Whilst the examples so far given, and the more extended example that follows, are taken from the design of hospitals, hospitals are not the only building type that may have the systems character. Indeed in our age we may regard the systems building as being the general type of the design problem, with the commodity building and the symbolic building as special cases, even though by definition commodity buildings will be produced in greater quantity. Thus Weber (1973) has criticized the implication in Heath (1972) that it is proper for designers and producers to have "confronted habitation as a 'commodity'". While the intention of the original paper was to argue that such an attitude was only proper where there was in fact competition, as in middle-class market housing, the further argument of Weber's paper, that there may be cases in which housing would not be a commodity type of building at all, but would require to be dealt with by second generation methods, is clearly correct. Some buildings almost inevitably have the systems character besides hospitals: theatres and concert halls, airport terminals, some industrial buildings such as pharmaceutical factories, some educational buildings, and no doubt others. That we can name building types within the class may suggest that the problems are being exaggerated, that models exist; but while such complex systems may resemble one another in many respects, the fact that the overall structure of the organization is on a different level from that of the parts means that such resemblances are likely to be superficial and misleading; systems buildings tend to be unique. "Generations" of hospitals or airports, for instance, succeed one another with bewildering rapidity, so that only a national or even an international design organization could have sufficient through-put to produce more than a very few examples according to any one model. Each building is in fact a "one-off" design, which brings us back to the original, simplified description of the systems building.

It is difficult to give an example of systems building design processes because of their extreme complexity. However, a case study by Heath (1973) of the design of a small hospital operating theatre suite can be used to illustrate some of the features we have been considering. The example is simplified in three ways: the institution concerned was small, and relatively unpoliticized, though its external environment was extremely turbulent; some substantial constraints existed; and only the main decision sequence is considered. Finally, this is again an analysis after the fact. The new operating theatre suite was required to replace previously existing theatres which had been destroyed by fire. The architects, while not unacquainted with technically complex buildings, were inexperienced in this field and the clients had no recent experience of building. Figure 5.3 represents the essential decisions taken in planning the main floor of the new unit, in the form of a precedence diagram. Elements of Figure 5.3 will hereafter be referred to by number, F/1, F/2 and so on. Elements F/1 to F/7 can be passed over briefly; they culminate in the establishment of site constraints (F/6). The effect of these decisions was that the area available for building was strictly limited on all sides by existing buildings and roads, and that the main floor had to be located 4.5 metres above actual ground level. These site constraints lead to the rejection of a prefabricated system which at first (F/4) appeared to offer speedy relief for the hospital's emergency, and a convenient evasion of the architect's design problem. This brings us to the search for models on which to base the new design (F/8).

For reasons too involved to be worth setting out here, but connected with the convoluted finances of Australia's federal system of govern-

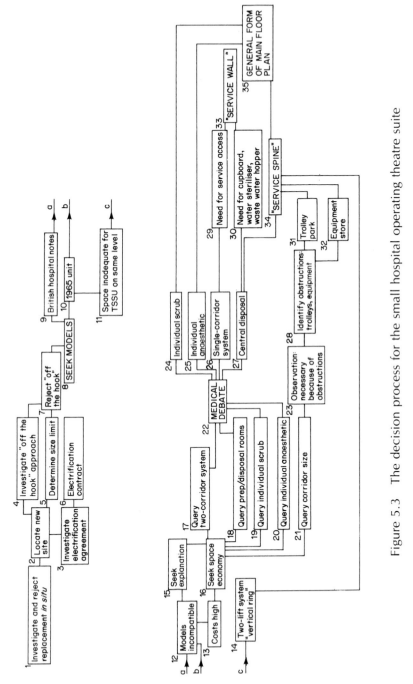

Figure 5.3   The decision process for the small hospital operating theatre suite

ment, few hospitals had been built in the state for a considerable number of years and the supply of local models was not large. Of the local and overseas models investigated, only two had any considerable influence on the final design: the Hospital Building Notes prepared by the British Department of Health and Social Security (F/9) and a professorial surgical unit at a large Sydney teaching hospital, designed by the Government Architect of New South Wales and completed in 1965 (F/10). With the study of these models, attention, which had initially focussed on the theatre itself (the Dr. Kildare syndrome), gradually expanded to include the complex back-up services. As a result, the investigation split into parallel streams. Reasonable brevity and simplicity forbid our following all these streams through, but it is important to record that, while they were parallel, there was also some hierarchy among them; thus some streams dealt with overall layout, others with the features of particular departments or spaces; generally the latter were in this case less significant and completed later in the design process. Figure 5.3 in general represents the "highest level" stream for the main floor only; the exception is the theatre sterile supply department, the significance of which will emerge shortly.

At this point it may be helpful to say a brief something about the activities of a modern operating theatre suite, as a preliminary to further description of the main models and their differences. First, the patients: they arrive, usually under sedation; they are "held" within the theatre suite until the theatre is ready for them; they are anaesthetized; they are operated on; they are "held" again, this time in a special recovery ward under watchful attention; if they recover satisfactorily they are removed, either to an intensive care ward or to the ward from which they came. Second, the staff: they arrive, change out of their ordinary clothes into clean protective clothing, enter the theatre suite, and in the case of the surgeons wash and don sterile clothing within the suite; at intervals during the day's work they leave the suite to eat, rest, or answer the calls of nature and at these times they wholly or partially repeat the re-clothing and washing processes. Finally, goods: a quite surprising quantity of sterile instruments and linen is used during the day's work, something in the order of a couple of cubic metres per theatre. This has to be supplied, removed when used, and washed and sterilized for re-use. The washing and sterilization of instruments and linen is the work of the theatre sterile supply department. There are many subtleties, complications and variations to this general scheme, but as an introduction for those not acquainted with the problem, and a background to the further discussion, it may serve.

Returning now to the two main models which influenced the design: at the broad level with which we are concerned, study revealed both conflicts between the models and a common use of space which could not be contemplated within the restrictions of the site and the budget. Of the conflicts between the models, the most important concerned the concept of sterility. The Hospital Building Notes envisaged a system under which the three flows, of patients, staff and goods, were clearly separated; each passed through successive processes of purification up to the "sterile" zone of the theatre itself, and then left again by a separate disposal exit or corridor. The flow of each stream was clearly one way, up the "hill" of sterility and then down again on the other side. The whole thing appeared highly *rational*, with the clarity that Descartes held to be an index of truth.

The local professorial unit, hereafter referred to as the 1965 unit, was quite different. Everything except the used goods simply went back the way it had come; wastes that could not be disposed of in the utility rooms, which each pair of theatres shared, went out with the goods. This might of course have been due to the cultural backwardness and geographic inversion of Australia, but it deserved investigation. Settling the question was obviously beyond the competence of the architects, who then encouraged and became the interested audience of a medical debate (F/22). The outcome of the debate, in which the leading voices were naturally those of authorities on pathology and post-operative infection, was the revelation that many, though not of course all, of the devices used to separate operating theatres from the everyday environment were in the nature of taboos, ritual or magical rather than practical in character. There were, so the consensus held (but clearly a different group might have decided differently), good reasons for reducing air turbulence in the theatre and therefore for air conditioning and pressurizing the space and reducing the number of doors; and also for the changes of clothes, washing, capping and, possibly, masking. But there was not held to be any real reason why people, and wastes in suitably covered receptacles, should not return "upstream", and there was a considerable potential saving in space in eliminating the additional corridors. The "single corridor" system was therefore adopted in place of the "two corridor" system (F/26).

The "success" of this investigation initiated a similar process of critical appraisal for all the ancillary spaces. The very considerable debate engendered within the hospital needed organizing, formalizing and recording, and the client, with some prompting from the architects, decided to appoint an officer at a senior executive level, with the title project manager, to focus and control this activity. The architects were thus not called upon to moderate the debate, though they did contribute to it, mainly by proposing economies of various kinds.

Besides the two-corridor system, four common features of theatre layouts, which were to be found in various forms in the models, were radically examined. These were: the provision of a separate anaesthetic room, used as the name implies for the induction of anaesthesia, next to each theatre; the provision of a scrub room, for final hand washing before the operation, next to each theatre; the provision of a work room for minor storage, minor sterilization, the preliminary post-operative cleaning of instruments, next to each theatre; and the provision of very wide corridors (F/18/19/20/21).

The last of these questions was answered fairly simply by observation (F/23). The need for very wide corridors, wider, that is, than the reasonable minimum required for two trolleys to pass, arose because the corridors were used as trolley parks and equipment stores, and even patient-holding areas (F/28). By designing a proper flow system for trolleys, with a parking area at the point of origin, and providing a bulk equipment store not too far from the theatres this constraint was removed (F/31/32). The scrub and anaesthetic rooms presented more complex problems. A little work study showed that the induction of anaesthesia was much quicker than most operations, so that two anaesthetic rooms would be sufficient for three or more theatres. The same was true of the "scrubbing" process. Further, it emerged that both scrubbing and the induction of anaesthesia are sometimes done in the theatre itself. Thus there was a matrix of nine possibilities: each of the two activities could take place in the theatre, attached to the theatre, or remote from the theatre. Medical debate rapidly reduced this number to three by linking the two functions; a consensus of surgeons preferred to be able to watch the patient while anaesthesia was induced and they scrubbed up, though no very clear medical reason for this emerged. Further, while scrubbing, the surgeons splashed vigorously and waved their arms about, which was undesirable in the theatre, because of the scattering of water and the air turbulence involved, and even more undesirable close to the patient, so that anaesthetic room and scrub room could not be combined in one; their connection had to be by a suitably placed window. This left two possibilities: anaesthetic and scrub room en suite but remote from the theatre, or en suite but associated with it. Remote location was subject to two criticisms: surgeons disliked travelling more than a few steps after their final "purification", and anaesthetists wished to minimize the time between disconnecting the patient from the equipment in the anaesthetic room and re-connecting in the theatre — not unreasonably, since with some procedures the patient is for all practical purposes dead and entirely dependent on these life-support systems. There were ways round these problems, but the balance of the discussion led to the retention of individual anaesthetic and scrub rooms next to each theatre (F/24/25).

The work room, or disposal room (F/18), also generated lengthy debate. Here, however, it was concluded that staff, equipment, and space could be saved by centralizing most of the functions that these rooms normally performed, particularly the setting up of instruments for subsequent operations, preliminary washing of instruments after operations, and emergency sterilization of dropped instruments. The saving in space meant that these functions were effectively little further from the theatre than before. There was still need for some minor storage, for a supply of sterile water, and for waste-water disposal in the theatre itself; these matters could be provided for by cabinets recessed in one wall of each theatre.

One logical element of importance has so far been passed over. It was realized quite early, from the study of the models, that the site area was insufficient to allow the sterile supply department to be on the main floor next to the theatres (F/11). However, the 1965 unit demonstrated that this department could satisfactorily be located on another floor connected to the main floor by "clean" and "dirty" lifts; that is, supply and return lifts. This solution was adopted; and it followed that, in order to keep the production line in the sterile supply department as straight as possible, and thus reduce the risk of goods skipping one or more stages in the cleaning and sterilization process, the lifts should be a certain minimum distance apart. Further, the fact that the sterile supplies and the main sterilizing facilities were on a different floor created the need for a store at the head of the supply lift, in case of system failure. The whole goods supply system thus became a "vertical ring" (F/14). The central disposal room, of course, formed part of this ring, at the head of the return lift.

This lengthy, but still abbreviated, account, outlines the main decisions that established the general form of the plan (Figure 5.4). This consists of a sandwich; in the middle are the theatres, with the single corridor connecting them; on the other side of the corridor is the "service spine" containing the bulk equipment store, the "clean" store with its supply lift, the disposal room with washing and emergency sterilizing facilities and return lift, and one or two other ancillary spaces (F/34). At the back of the theatre is the "service wall" containing the main air-conditioning ducts and supply pipes to the theatre; into this wall, which is a large duct or narrow passage, are built the storage cupboard, waste-water hopper and ultraviolet water sterilizer required in each theatre. All of these services are accessible from the corridor serving the staff lounges and change rooms, without entering the

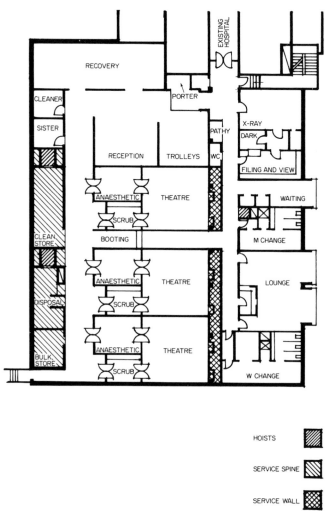

Figure 5.4   Plan of the operating theatre suite

theatres. The staff areas, the reception and recovery areas for patients and a small X-ray suite are "tacked on" to the main sandwich as site conditions and connections to the existing building permitted. Thus we come to the "as built" plan, which was indeed built and functioned satisfactorily as intended.

In this example we must note the political or consensual character of many of the constraints, even those that might at first appear deterministic; the hospital board might have made other decisions than to demolish the coal-fired boiler house, electrify the services, and build on the land thus made available (F/3), to take only the most fundamental. The significance of debate is still more obvious in the series of vital decisions at F/17/18/19/20/21. The final plan could clearly have come out in totally different ways depending on which of a number of different medical opinions carried the day. The symmetry of ignorance is also manifest; the architects could propose models, point to savings that might be made, and encourage and record debate, but they could not lay down the law. The doctors, on the other hand, had to rely on the architects for information about certain limitations imposed by building regulations, plumbing requirements and so on, though they could and did question and ask for further information on these points. All this means that the very form of the problem is non-algorithmic; the decisions involved are not reducible to either simple yes/no alternatives or arbitrary choices; even a formalized description of how the problem was in fact solved, such as Figure 5.3, does not guarantee that the same path could or would be followed on any other occasion. While it is still the case, in accordance with the previous general argument, that design must proceed by progressive limitation of the problem space, the limitations are political or consensual decisions, not "facts" or states of nature. The design procedure is clearly heuristic; successive decisions close the objectives and limit the problem space, and each decision creates the conditions for further decisions; but the course of the process cannot be predicted in advance.

Another way of looking at this, which gives further clarity to the distinction between systems and commodity building, is to say that the models available are visibly defective. As we have seen in connection with the Hospital Building Notes, this is not a consequence of any lack of care or intelligence in the development of the models themselves, but of the inherent complexity of the system served, which defies a priori description. Models can here only be guides, in the sense that one can have a guide to dangerous and hostile territory, which neverthelesss remains hostile and dangerous; whereas the commodity building can be compared to the local bus route, without even so excluding the possibility of an accident, or, more prosaically, of catching the wrong bus. Further, models are not only inherently unreliable, they are impermanent, and as previously pointed out, in the case of any attempt at large-scale systematic building of generalized models, it requires a very considerable through-put to get an economic return on the effort and expense involved. This does not mean that attempts at model building are completely useless, but it does suggest the use of rather rough and broad strategic models.

5.8   The general architectural problem space

So far the three "classes" of symbolic, commodity and systems building have been treated as wholly distinct. This is an oversimplification, intended to ease the task of explanation. In fact at the general level of problem classification, or problem space formation, they represent the boundaries of a continuum; and at the level of development of programmes or tactics for an individual design task the various subsystems may have characteristics different from those of the system as a whole. Any particular problem is likely to be impure or mixed, and different approaches may be required at different stages and for different parts. The interrelation between the three classes at the problem space construction level can be brought out by considering the architectural design space as an information space, or as a knowledge space. We have already discussed the variable quality of the knowledge available to architects; these variations however are not random, but systematic; they can be described and modelled. Figure 5.5 is such a model. Architectural design space is represented as having three dimensions: knowledge about the significance, value or symbolism of the work to be undertaken; knowledge about the mode of operation of the system designed for and the resources available; and estimates of the uncertainty or unreliability of this knowledge, the amount of "noise" that it contains, to make metaphorical use of a term from communication theory. Or, putting it another way, information may be taken to refer to the amount of data available that might be relevant to the problem, noise to the degree of subjective or objective

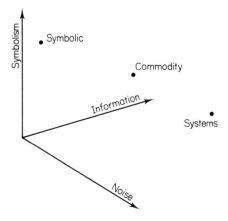

Figure 5.5   The general architectural problem space

uncertainty as to the relevance or reliability of the data, and the dimension of symbolism as the extent to which imageability is important in the solution. Clearly in such a space, problem difficulty increases with the increase in each dimension: the more symbolic significance, the more information, and the more uncertainty the problem involves, the more severe it is, and the less the likelihood of reaching a successful solution.

If we now map our three former "classes" on to this space, what has been said about symbolic buildings corresponds to a case in which symbolism is high, but information and noise are low; the commodity building will be moderate to low in symbolism, moderate to high in information, and low in noise; and the systems building will be moderate to low in symbolism, high in information, and high in noise. The novel building that turns out to be well constrained might be moderate in information and symbolism, but high in noise. The Sydney Opera House, to which we have previously referred, was probably a case of a building high in all three dimensions. This generalized problem space thus provides another way of looking at problems, supplementary to the lists of characteristics previously given for the three classes or boundary conditions, and explanatory of the way in which those characteristics help to determine the proper approach to a given design. With this picture in mind, we can examine a task and form estimates of its difficulty, of the kind of model that may be useful, and of the relative importance of proposal, algorithmic methods, or heuristic search in its solution.

Turning to the detailed structure of individual problems, it has been suggested that the parts of a problem may have a different character from the problem as a whole. What, in this context, is meant by the parts of a problem? We have seen that problems have to be broken up in order to reach a solution, but how is this to be done? It may well be the most important task facing the designer. The detailed tactics will be considered in the next chapter, but we need an image of problem structure to focus the discussion. A suitable image is the stochastic network (Figure 5.6). Any organized activity can be represented in terms of such a network, and if we know enough about the organization it can be developed into a predictive model (Beer, 1966). Architects rarely have the time or opportunity to develop a detailed model of the organizations they serve, in the way that operations researchers can do. Still, the picture is useful. We can, first of all, imagine that the network is a picture of society at large. The nodes are organizations of various kinds, using organization in its most general sense to include any co-operative grouping of people. The lines indicate two-way interchanges of some kind: information or goods or travel. Then we can enlarge the scale. Now some of the internal

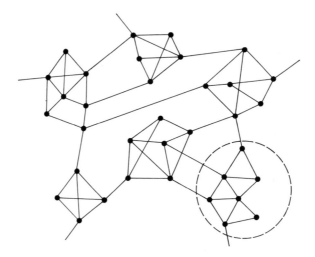

Figure 5.6   The stochastic network as a model of a system

structure of a particular organization appears: within the dotted circle in Figure 5.6. And at this scale we can see, in system terms, why we refer to "an organization", how we distinguish it from the larger society of which it forms a part: it has more numerous and stronger "internal" links than it has "external" links. If this were not the case we should not regard it as a separate organization. Now let us enlarge the scale once more. The whole of Figure 5.6 is now just one organization, and it is clear what is meant by a part of the problem: subsystems within the organization that have more and stronger internal than external links — links, that is, with the organization as a whole.

Now we can look again at the methodologically mixed or impure character of design problems. Almost every building, certainly every building that is likely to require the attention of an architect, has its symbolic aspects. Every building serves some kind of dynamic system which will produce some uncertainty, though in some cases this is small enough to be disregarded. And even the most technically complex building for the most politicized and unstable organization will have parts or subsystems that are conventional and well-defined and can be handled quasi-algorithmically. Thus we have referred, in considering aesthetic goals, to the work of Goffman (1959), and it is clear from his study of the use of building as stage sets on which people enact their social roles that this aspect will be significant in, for example, factories, as well as in buildings where role playing and symbolism are more conspicuous, such as churches or banks. Again, a church, which has been treated here as typical of symbolic building, may form part of a quite complex system of activities which is the life of the congregation, and have to act, not only as a backdrop for a variety of different highly formal rituals, but also as a place for formal and informal teaching, for quiet meditation, and for more secular social activity. Failure to understand this system on the part of the designer can produce an operationally unsatisfactory building, even though the symbolic needs of the congregation have been met. And the systems building will contain elements, such as cafeterias, toilet blocks and vertical circulation systems, not to mention many technical elements, whose design is quite routine; indeed if this were not so the design of such buildings would be hopelessly uneconomic. We recall Wade's observation that it may often be easier to agree on the purposes of parts than on the purposes of the whole (Wade, 1977); most of the parts of most design problems are likely to have the commodity character, to be well-constrained, well-behaved problems.

This can be brought out in more detail by a further consideration of the small operating theatre block used as an example of the system building. Within this design there were elements of symbolism, and also elements that could be solved algorithmically. The taboo or magical character of some of the barriers between the "sterile" or "clean" theatre and the outer world was mentioned. This was not something that could be simply disregarded in the design. The social reason for such barriers is a sound one: a more careful and ritualized style of behaviour really is required of the staff in their working environment, and reminders of the need to abandon ordinary behaviour and adopt this special style are needed. Such reminders can be symbolic, however: in the building we are considering they take the form of literal physical barriers or stiles which must be climbed; they are painted bright red, and the colour of the flooring changes at that point, which is also the point for donning caps, masks, and overshoes. This device has proved an effective substitute at the social level for the two-corridor system. Many other symbolic features, some of them therapeutically counter-productive, can be identified in the tradition of hospital design. This systems building also has many commodity aspects or subsystems. As an example, we may take the design of the several toilet blocks. Expectations of toilet blocks and change rooms are highly standardized, and are in fact the subject of numerous regulations and recommendations by public agencies. Debate is unnecessary, though careful and systematic attention in following a model is required. The problem is well defined: the number of WCs, showers and basins, the size and shape of compartments, the number of lockers and their size and shape, the area of the rest room are all laid down; add in the clearances between the fittings indicated by anthropometric data, the plumbing requirements, and the requirement that area be kept to a minimum, and there is a fully constrained, perhaps over-constrained problem, for which an algorithm could be constructed, though since it is a simple problem it is usually solved by trial and error, aided by model layouts. We should bear in mind that all this depends on the assumption that regulations are accepted as constraints. Such an assumption in turn depends for its validity on the truth of the assertion that expectations of this kind of room are in fact standardized. If this ceased to be the case, for example as a result of a confrontation between unions and employers, or because of a change in hygiene standards in the community, or some technical change in plumbing practice, the character of the subproblem would change. Conversely, of course, should the general layout of operating theatre suites become constrained by tradition or regulation, it might cease to be a wicked problem and become a well-behaved one, though any attempt to impose such regulative constraints is likely to enjoy only short-lived success so long as hospitals continue to exist in a turbulent field.

It follows from what has been said about the continuum or generalized problem space for architectural design, and from the impure or mixed character of the detailed structure of individual problems, that the typology of buildings cannot be mapped with com-plete congruence on to the typology of methods. By the typology of buildings is meant the collection of names we ordinarily give to buildings, which identify them by "function". Any architectural library will contain many volumes dealing with the design of specific building types: theatres, offices, old peoples housing and so on. These may be mere pattern books or they may attempt to provide the designer with a set of procedures for generating new designs. Nevertheless a brief examination of most of these works will reveal that within the given building type there are examples that would be widely spaced on the continuum of methods. In other words, naming a building does not automatically tell us how to design it, even though it is a necessary preliminary in the process of achieving adequate definition or closure of the terminal state for design.

In summary, then, how can we classify a particular problem in advance, so to speak, and what are the predictions that will result from such a classification? It would seem that classification will be made by considering the relationships between the organization the proposed building will serve (using organization in a very broad sense) and its social environment, the activities themselves as systems, and the relationship between the activities of the organization and the fabric of the building. Where the organization and its activities have high symbolic importance for the community, where the activities themselves are ritualized, and where the relations between activity and building are loosely determined and generally governed by symbolism, we will expect to approach the problem by postulation, as discussed for the symbolic building. Where the organization–society relationship is relatively stable and placid, where the activities concerned are of a routine or predictable kind, and where the activity–fabric relationship is insensitive or loose fit, there will, almost inevitably, be a considerable volume of production and a large number of such buildings in use, and probably a small number of standard types, so that design can proceed by the adaptation of known models and procedures, and potentially algorithmically. Where the organization–environment relationship is richly interconnected and turbulent, and the activities concerned are complex and form a politicized system with many subsystems, so that there is noise, unpredictability and uncertainty, and where the activity–fabric relationship is sensitive, we shall have to proceed heuristically, by debate and decision. Our logic will not be the "hard" logic and quasi-algorithms suited to yes/no choices between specifiable characteristics, but the "soft" logic of system theory, the logic of relations, which specifies inputs and outputs, but not form. At the tactical level we will seek for elements or subsystems that are relatively insensitive and weakly connected to the whole, and which may thus be well-behaved problems; definition of these subproblems will help to constrain the whole solution.

There is an obvious need for further research, closely linked with practice, into the kinds and mixes of strategies and tactics in architectural design method, in relation to the problems presented by different building types. This must be carried out by practitioners who are experienced and successful in particular fields and who can contribute to the more detailed methodological mapping of those fields, either by themselves becoming more familiar with theoretical levels of discourse, or by collaborating with specialists. The next chapter, on programmes and tactics, will indicate some directions for such further investigations, and attempt to remove some obstacles created by traditional attitudes and beliefs.

Chapter 6

From method to design

6.1 Introduction

Between the level of strategy, the level of the generalized problem space, and the construction or selection of a problem space for a particular task, and the level of tactics, of detailed application of specific techniques such as network analysis, the use of dual graphs in planning, and the many other tools that have been developed to aid in the solution of aspects of detailed design, there is a level of operations or programmes: overall algorithms or heuristics. Since heuristics are the most general and most interesting case, this chapter will largely be concerned with them. It will not of course be possible to describe every heuristic that might be of use in the solution of architectural problems, but certain main areas and approaches can be identified and outlined. Something will be said about decision structures, from the social as well as the logical point of view; about the general question of briefing or programming as it is called in America; about the forms that information may take in the design process and the interaction of different forms of information; and about detail design. And finally an attempt will be made to bring all of these aspects together, to give an overall picture of architectural design method at the operational level.

6.2 Decision structures: the brief

It is often helpful to start with a conventional view. The conventional view of the design process in architecture is that it starts with the client giving his architect a brief or programme. Sometimes the client is not able to give attention to this task, and then the architect, or some other architect or specialist, is employed and paid an additional fee. At its simplest the brief may specify only the type of building and its size; a more elaborate version lists rooms and their area; and for complicated buildings an indication of operational policies, or how the building is to be used, may also be provided. Like motherhood, democracy and the mixed economy, the preparation of briefs is often taken to be good in itself. As with many other aspects of architectural practice it has evolved without ever being given much intellectual precision. Yet it has implications for the whole process of design, some of which are quite misleading. It is worth looking, first, at the origins of the idea, in order to understand what these implications are. In fact, the two words, brief and programme, have different origins and implications, which have been conflated to some extent.

The idea of the brief originates in British legal practice. A solicitor receives instructions from his client. He learns what matter is in dispute, and what, at least in his client's view, are the facts of the case. He writes all this out in a suitable form for study by a barrister, who uses this "brief" as the basis for his pleading in court, together of course with his knowledge of legal precedent. The implications in the use of this word are, first, that "the facts of the case" are known in advance: they have happened, they are a matter of history or evidence; and secondly, that suitable precedents exist, which combined with these facts will give a desired or at any rate a conclusive result. It is doubtful how clearly these implications are understood by most of those who use the term; law is an older profession than architecture, and it is probable that architects simply borrowed the rough general idea of taking some notes of what the client said he wanted, and calling it a brief.

The origins and implications of the "programme" are more straightforward and more specifically architectural. It goes back to the Ecole des Beaux-Arts and the training it gave, which was aimed first and foremost at the winning of architectural competitions. Such competitions were a test of the competitor's ability to combine essentially conventional material, the "elements of architecture", in a striking and appropriate way. That is, they were concerned entirely with symbolism, and symbolism within a quite definite and limited aesthetic vocabulary. It was not necessary for the competitors to be informed in detail about the activities that would take place in a Palace of the Arts or a National Bank. A list of names of rooms and some indication of their areas was sufficient since competitors and judges shared a set of assumptions as to what was essential and what was non-essential; assumptions clearly revealed by the study of the prize-winning entries for the Prix de Rome (van Zanten, 1976). This curious and unworldly system ultimately became enshrined in various codes of professional practice, for the same reason that, as we have seen, it was so influential in education, namely that it was the only system available; and so we find fee scales which set a price on an activity called "taking client's instructions" and forms of contract between architect and principal which lay down that the principal shall provide the architect with an adequate brief, or words to that effect.

Animal species do not survive the disappearance of their ecological niche. The same, alas, is not true of ideas, which can long survive any vestige of the situation in which they were generated, and continue to obstruct the efforts of subsequent generations. Nevertheless, if there were no correspondence at all between the idea of the brief or programme and anything that ever happened in practice, it would no doubt have fallen into desuetude, if not become extinct. And in fact there are situations which this traditional picture fits more conveniently than more sophisticated accounts, just as Ptolemaic astronomy is still used in navigation. In the symbolic building, as we have defined it, aesthetic considerations are dominant, and the designer's task thus resembles that of the Beaux-Arts student in significant ways. Similarly in the commodity building, while it may be fruitful to examine and test the bases of the consensus that exists it is usually unnecessary to do so, and a very simple description may serve to communicate to all parties what is desired or intended. The persistence of the conventional notion of the programme as a mere schedule of rooms and areas is, it may be suggested, justified insofar as it really is applicable to what is, economically speaking, the most significant segment of building construction.

Nevertheless, the commonsense traditional view of the brief is in some respects seriously misleading. It helps to support and confirm a mistaken view of what "design" is. It would appear that underlying this kind of view is the belief that designing is what designers do, and that architects are designers, while other people, if they are allowed to do anything at all, prepare briefs. Yet on reflection designing appears just to be the making of decisions that determine the physical form of the building. In some cases, it has been argued, the decisions are largely made in advance, by some form of consensus. In others, the symbolic buildings, some of the key decisions have to be made by the architect and presented as proposals. But in every piece of architectural design there are decisions that are not made, and cannot be made by the architect; indeed we often hear the complaint that the architect is powerless and that the really important decisions are made by others. So it would seem that all decisions about a proposed building, at whatever point in time they are made and whoever makes them, may be considered to be design, and that there is no point at which we can drive a wedge between the brief and the design. The notion that some things about the design process are "facts" or "given" and that other things are design and therefore under the control of the designer glosses over the difficulties about the quality of knowledge available to the designer which have been brought out earlier. In the case of the systems building, this is positively dangerous.

It is interesting to see what happens when a practising architect with a thoroughly sophisticated view of his task sets out to defend the brief as a separable stage of design. Heimsath (1977) describes the "programming phase" as consisting of four elements:

"1. A clarification of goals for the project and the background of the organisation and the participants.
 2. A definition of the area requirements in terms of physical space, tools, participants, and activities, including anticipated flexibility.
 3. Development of adjacency matrices based on the adjacency of social activities, environmental criteria, and servicing proximities.
 4. Establishing alternatives in terms of activities, personnel, size of units, and relationship to site and community."

Here items 2 and 4, particularly, take us well into what would be conventionally regarded as design, though they are certainly preliminary to the generation of plan proposals or schematic design. However, Heimsath is thinking in terms of these activities being carried out by the design team, which would include behavioural scientists; he argues explicitly against the preparation of programmes by clients. His real objective in retaining the notion of a briefing or programming phase is to use it as a lever to induce clients for complex buildings to pay for the services they need, particularly those of behavioural scientists; and this is indeed the way it is often used in practice, and the argument most often advanced for its retention. But we should not rely on bad arguments for good objectives; and the arguments against retaining this distinction, especially just in those cases in which an extended design team of the kind Heimsath wants is most necessary, are strong.

It is easy to show that the more conventional kind of brief is not an appropriate device for attacking wicked problems, by reference to the characteristics of second-generation design methods, which we have seen to be appropriate to their solution. For, first of all, a brief, in the form of a schedule of rooms and areas, is not transparent; it does not in itself make clear how the decisions were made, or by whom, or what arguments were advanced to support them. The programme is objective, but to test or reconsider any part of it will involve retracing step by step the process by which it was generated; insofar as it acts to stimulate doubt or criticism it undermines itself. And it certainly provides no indication as to which are the controversial issues; in fact it is not issue-based at all. Thus if any difficulty whatsoever arises the programme does not allow the propositions it contains to be considered at any higher level of comprehensiveness, because it represents itself as conveying "facts" which are not hierarchical and mutually dependent outputs of nested decisions, but atomic and ideal.

It an architect accepts such a brief for a building of this kind, his work is bound to be frustrated and ultimately to fail. For at some point he will have to present a "design", that is a proposal embodying the directions contained in the programme, and at that point all the issues the programme presents as resolved will be raised as criticisms; but instead of being recognized for what they are, unresolved differences within the organization, or between the organization and major forces in its environment, they will be regarded in a much more comfortable way, as evidence of the architect's incompetence. This will be so even if the design follows the brief with impeccable care; but since the rationale of the decisions will not have been clear to the designers, it is quite likely that technical and economic factors will have encouraged departures from the brief, so that it will not even be necessary for the brief itself to come under fire. The brief or programme, to summarize, is a collection of "facts" of the kind that may be assumed to underlie first-generation design methods, and it leaves the designer with the nightmare of implementing a design to which no-one concerned need admit that they have consented. In attempting to overcome the resulting storm of criticism the designer will at best be forced back over every step of the ground the brief is supposed to have covered, re-negotiating every issue. At worst, he will simply be told to try again, with the *same* programme, and neither encouragement nor facilities offered for testing or re-negotiating its provisions, so that the same pattern will, in all probability, repeat itself. Anyone who doubts that such things really happen should consult O'Reilly (1973), where such a sequence of events is described in depressing detail. There is no essential difference between this and design by postulation.

These difficulties will not automatically be overcome by using second-generation methods in preparing the brief, which would require that it be prepared by argumentative methods, acknowledging the distribution of knowledge and ignorance between the programmer and the various individuals and groups involved, and recording the arguments presented and the decisions reached in a transparent and objective format. For in practice these conditions are unlikely to be met. They require confrontation between the various factions within the organization, and in the interest of day-to-day convenience these factions will inevitably have developed techniques of a more or less subtle kind for avoiding confrontation. The formal organizational structure is similarly more likely to have developed methods for deferring and defusing than for promoting confrontation. Thus, whether the brief is prepared "in-house" or by an outside agent, there is likely to be considerable resistance to be overcome. Sheer lack of time, in the case of in-house preparation, and cost in the case of an outside agency, will discourage the adoption of argumentative methods and encourage those charged with preparing the brief to fall back on precedent and their own powers of invention. Delegation of judgement will take place inexplicitly, and by default.

Even supposing that these temptations are sternly resisted, and that briefing or programming is carried out strictly by second-generation methods, the concept of a brief is, in this kind of case, inherently self-destructive. For it is, as we have seen, often in the interest of those concerned to defer confrontation and decision to the last possible moment, both to avoid the essential but distasteful process of reaching a consensus, and to gain or attempt to gain political advantage for their own party or point of view. This is in fact sound management: in a ramified system which is directed towards some terminal node or event, which is a reasonable representation of the process of design, the situation becomes clearer as the goal is neared (Beer, 1966), and decisions made nearer the terminal point are more likely to be correct. But since a brief is, rightly, seen as not being conclusive, as not being a design, the argumentative process, however carefully initiated and monitored, will be falsified, either by compromises that are not sincere, or by the giving or withholding of information for political reasons, or by some combination of these strategies on the part of subsystems of the organization. Thus, while it may appear that argument is taking place, that the distribution of knowledge and ignorance is being respected, that decisions are being reached and recorded by transparent and objective processes and so on, all this is really being done tongue in cheek, without any real commitment to the resulting decisions, because of a conscious or intuitive recognition that the whole process is not final, that there will be an opportunity to re-open issues, perhaps on more favourable terms, when the time comes to receive a final "design".

One solution to the objections so far raised might appear to be the description of operational policies as part of the brief; that is, giving "reasons" as well as, or in support of, "facts". But this does not overcome either the objections to the "commonsense" "factual" brief, or to the more complex argumentative process. For, in the first case, it does not overcome the objection that the brief is not transparent or issue-based. Why was one operational policy chosen rather than another? In a complex organization there will certainly be legitimate, as well as merely factious, disagreement over which of a number of possible policies or methods is the best to pursue now, let alone some years hence. As with programmes of the simpler sort, the programme with operational policies at once poses for the architect the question of the method by which the programme was produced. Indeed, the inclusion of operational policies may be regarded as a special danger signal, a sign that the compilers of the brief were themselves in doubt about its reliability, and wished to justify or defend it in some way. But for the reasons already given, these policies, just as much as the room and area provisions, are likely to be disowned at a later stage. The same applies to the more complex argumentative process; the development and agreement of operational policies will certainly be part of the decision process, but once again because the brief is not final, part or all of these policies will be agreed to with the fingers firmly crossed behind the back.

Thus it is not only that one or another form of brief or programme is unsuitable as a device or tool for attacking the design of the systems building; it is the very notion of the programme as a stage in the work which is somehow complete in itself and yet not a final design, which is inimical to the proper resolution of the difficulties the systems building presents. This applies just as much to the sophisticated procedure carried out by the design team that Heimsath describes as it does to the preparation of briefs by agencies other than the designer. The distinction leads, not perhaps inevitably, but with a high probability, to wasted work and time, the time and cost involved in the preparation of the brief being largely wasted, since eventually all the issues will be fought through again, and the time and cost involved in any design based on the brief completely wasted. It is for this reason that most descriptions of architectural work that include a briefing phase also describe the next phase with the euphemism "Respond to the brief", which in fact means "Invent a courteous formula by which the brief can be scrapped and a new start made."

Nevertheless buildings, even systems buildings, do get designed and built and are even sometimes successful, as we have noticed before. This must mean that there are ways round these difficulties — methods — and that it should be possible to describe those methods. This the next section will seek to do.

6.3   Decision processes: inventing the client

If, for the various reasons that have been advanced in the preceding section, the traditional procedures for starting the building design process are inappropriate to the systems building, it is desirable to find alternative procedures. We have seen that in such cases deontics, questions of what ought to be the case, are the essence of the problem, and that therefore what is being sought is not a set of "facts" but a series of decisions as to what the limits of the problem are to be. All such decisions in reality rest on consensus; the distinction between the commodity building which can be treated quasi-algorithmically and the systems building which cannot, lies in the degree of consensus, the extent to which essential decisions are pre-empted or predetermined by the existence of general agreement or established expectations, or "ideas in good currency" to use Schon's term (Schon, 1971). In the case of the systems building, consensus does not exist or is inadequate to define the design, and we are faced with the task of *establishing* a consensus, a task to which facts in the scientific sense of well-tested empirical propositions are relevant only insofar as they may serve to test some of the positions taken in the argumentative process.

The process of establishing a consensus is neither easy nor straight-forward. The natural resistance of the formal hierarchy of an organiza-tion and its subsystems to the process of locating and defining issues will not lightly be overcome. The dynamic conservatism of the organization will at first be directed towards maintaining the illusion that no issues exist, since the smooth running and even the continued existence of large organizations depends on the collective social control of areas of disagreement. They are encapsulated in a polite system of evasions, and formal discussion of them is effectively taboo, though they will quickly appear in informal "off the record" ex-changes. The strategy for overcoming this resistance is here called "inventing the client". This phrase gives forcible expression to the fact that, in the circumstances we are considering, no person able to make the necessary decisions, or to ensure that they are made, is likely to exist. The symmetry of ignorance applies not only to outsiders involved in the design process, but also within the organization. It applies also to the relations between the formal hierarchy of the orga-nization and its subsystems. Knowledge and ignorance are distributed throughout the organizational network. Thus the formal hierarchy of an organization is a very bad source of design information. For, firstly, its members or representatives inevitably lack much essential informa-tion, but are likely to be unwilling to admit this, and may not even realize it themselves; and secondly, as already argued, they are actively dedicated to suppressing and minimizing just those conten-tious issues that are likely to have the most critical influence on design. A new client structure, independent of the formal hierarchy, and capable of reaching out widely into the organization and tapping its resources of knowledge, or, rather, exchanging its knowledge for that of the professionals in order to reach informed collective decisions, is required, and this has to be invented for each situation.

Since the point is essential, it is worth making it again in a slightly different way. The design process can be seen as an analogue of the control or management process of the organization. The formal control process of the organization will be expressed in terms of a management chart of the traditional bureaucratic kind, with clear vertical and horizontal divisions; a "tree" diagram, in fact. Between the various levels in such an organization an enormous amount of information is lost. Thus Beer (1966) gives figures which show that, for example, 88% of foremen believe they understand the problems of the workers while only 28% of workers believe that the foremen understand their problems; for general managers and works managers the figures are 100% and 59%. Besides indicating that self-confidence is one of the attributes required for a general manager, this illustrates the distribution of knowledge and ignorance. It also shows that while the distribution of knowledge and ignorance is in fact probably symmetrical, it is not *perceived* symmetrically; the reliability of information falls with social distance.

Fortunately, the real pattern of communication, and therefore the real control system, within an organization seldom resembles the management chart. An enormous number of unofficial communication channels exists, which enables much of the control and decision to take place "on the spot", by-passing official channels and disregarding the rule book where its requirements are impractical. The real organization is not a neat tree but a complex net. The importance of these informal information and control networks is one of the best established outcomes of management research; the effectiveness of "work-to-rule" strikes regularly reveals the extent to which the success of institutions depends on management decisions taken informally at the workface. All this can be summarized or stated formally in the form of Ashby's Law of Requisite Variety: the complexity of the controlling agency must equal the complexity of the thing controlled.

Now, as has been said, the design of a new building for a complex organization is an analogue of this control or management process. There is no one person or group who knows the detailed workings and needs of every section of the organization. Indeed the subsections of the organization may not know them themselves; they may be operating on craft knowledge. For the right decisions or, what is rather different, adequate decisions to be made about each aspect of the design, each segment or subsystem of the organization must both receive information, about the limitations imposed on its decisions by external constraints and by the needs and decisions of other subsystems, and also give information about its current work methods, likely changes, aspirations, and so on. For this to take place, the design organization, like the management organization, must be at least as complex as the organization designed for. Since design must be carried out at a reasonable cost, this means that the design process must consist in tapping the informal management network of the organization.

Even to tap in to the informal management organization in this way will be beyond the capacities of an individual or a small group. The working group or design team will have to be quite large, since the task of its members will be to pry and gossip, to act as *agents provocateurs* by providing papers for circulation and discussion, to arrange and record innumerable meetings and to nag people at all levels into either accepting minutes and papers as their own decisions or participating in renewed debate. In order to communicate success-fully with the many different skills and interests within the organiza-tion, the design team will need to have a range of expertise: returning to the example of a teaching hospital, medical, nursing, management, engineering and architectural skills will be required as a minimum. The advantage in having engineering and architectural skills involved from the start lies, first in the ability to consider the physical, technical and economic consequences of decisions, and secondly in the ability to distinguish those issues that actually affect the design of the fabric from other equally hotly contested issues which do not. For fortunately the design task, while analogous with the management task, is not quite so complicated. As we have noted earlier, even in the systems building the fit between activity and fabric seldom or never has to be everywhere exact; it is often possible to provide for quite different and even opposed operational policies within the same built envelope. A further advantage in having engineers and architects involved from the start lies in increasing understanding, forgetting less, and error reduc-tion generally, which result when those who are to be concerned with the physical execution of the decisions made in the early stages have some idea of the way in which the decisions were made.

All the necessary skills for a design working group may be available within the organization, but this is unlikely unless the staffing is highly redundant. Membership of such a group is, at least for the majority, a full-time job. Not only is establishing the necessary contacts through-out the organization a major task; reports and working documents have to be prepared and distributed so that the design process advances; and some at least of the team members must always be available to receive comments, afterthoughts, complaints, off-the-record dissenting opinions and other vital information which contri-butes to the argumentative process. For the process is not, as must be clear from what has gone before, simply one of gathering information that is available, waiting to be collected; much of the wisdom of the organization is unconscious craft knowledge, which has to be brought into consciousness by proposal and discussion. Even good consensus, where it exists, needs to be probed and tested, since it may conceal, unconsciously, quite different functions and procedures. Persuading busy people to give attention to this kind of investigation, in addition to carrying out their day-to-day tasks, is difficult; if the designers are on hand only part of the time the system is likely to fail. So part-time staffing from within the organization is not sufficient. And there are advantages in introducing at least a leavening of cynical outsiders who see the organization, if no more correctly than, at least differently from, those immersed in it. To provide the necessary productive capacity and balance of viewpoints, a team might contain a mixture of seconded permanent staff, to provide the initial internal contacts, contract staff and outside consultants, including, desirably, behavioural scientists. The many cogent arguments for the inclusion of behavioural scientists in the team have been reviewed by Zeisel (1981).

It follows from the argument thus far that if the titular authorities of the organization prepare a brief or engage in design through the formal structure available to them, the outcome is likely to bear little relation to the reasonable needs and wishes of many of the users. The formal structure of the client organization has a vital role to play in the design of the systems building, but that role is not design; it is, rather, to authorize the setting up of a largely separate, design-oriented structure, in the form of an information and decision network of the kind described, which is diffused down into the organization so that every decision can be taken as far as possible by the people most affected by that decision; and subsequently to exercise its formal powers to legitimate the decisions that emerge from the network and see that they are carried out. This exercise of power, however, should not be in the nature of a "gate" which the design must pass. Difficult as it may be, the formal hierarchy must be persuaded to recognize its own incompetence to test in any detail the quality of the decisions the network produces; though they may and indeed must make spot checks and comment on their own areas of expertise, particularly those relating to the external constraints on design and to the constraints of cost and time. In general, however, legitimation should be made an automatic consequence of the operation of the network.

If the output of the network is not to be tested in detail by the formal hierarchy of the organization, the network must incorporate its own testing system, of sufficient stringency to ensure that the resulting design for each subsystem and for the system as a whole lies within the appropriate problem space. That is, the network must include "filters" to eliminate the "noise" in the system. The output of the system cannot be made completely reliable; but errors must be held within limits which will either prove to be acceptable or be subject to easy correction. One kind of noise in the system consists of markedly eccentric or personal opinions, perhaps those of an individual who is able to sway others by reason of his position or personality or both. This kind of noise must be filtered out by some kind of technical review. To an extent this will be provided by the design team themselves; but in the process of establishing the design network, the members of the design team will themselves become involved in alliances and oppositions, so that they too require checks and supports to keep them from making partisan or arbitrary decisions. Often technical review is provided by government agencies concerned with standardization or normalization; but where this is not the case, separate provisions for technical review may have to be made; whether by individuals or committees will depend on circumstances. Another kind of noise arises where the objectives or aspirations of some subgroup or subsystem of the organization differ from those of the administration or of the organization as a whole, even though the objectives themselves may be technically impeccable. A policy review body or filter is therefore required as well as a technical filter.

Further, not all decisions that the network must reach will be able to be reached by consensus. Some disagreements will be irreconcilable; as has already been argued in connection with design objectives in general win–win strategies are simply not feasible in all cases. To take a simple example, it may not be possible to build both a new operating department and a new radiology department for a hospital within the available funds; and the compromise solution of building parts of either or both may lead to an unworkable system. Thus for its successful operation an argumentative information and decision network must include a judicial function; and this judicial function may also include the function of policy filter. Like all judicial bodies this group must be as far as possible impartial and protected from political tampering with its deliberations and decisions; it should also desirably be small enough to reach decisions quickly. The requirement of small size will prevent the judicial group acting as a technical review body, since to provide adequate technical representation of a variety of disciplines will in most cases require the involvement of a considerable number of different experts. While it may appear that the introduction of such a judicial function creates a situation not very different from design by administrative fiat, this is a mistake. There is a fundamental difference in the quality of decisions as between those reached by administrative methods making use of the inadequate formal channels of information, and remote from the detailed problems, and those based on the detailed knowledge and considered arguments of those operating the system; the difference between tyranny and justice.

The process of inventing the client thus consists in establishing an information and decision network by grafting on to the existing informal network of the organization a design team; and of establishing technical review and policy review/arbitrating bodies to monitor, filter and legitimate the output of the network. The establishment of this network and the search for issues will lead directly to many of the decisions necessary for design to progress. In identifying the main forces in the external environment of the organization and in its internal structure and securing their representation on the judicial/ legitimating body, principal constraints such as budget, siting and broad objectives of the design will emerge either as the subject of consensus or as issues, and if they are issues the procedures and the groups and personalities who must be involved in the process of debate and resolution will also emerge. It is fortunate that, as has previously been pointed out, not every subsystem of the complex organization will itself be turbulent or unpredictable; in some at least there will be good agreement as to what ought to be done and these sections of the problem will be able to be solved with comparatively little fuss. While such areas of consensus should not be altogether immune from probing and testing, they should in general be viewed with gratitude rather than undue suspicion. When, on the other hand, there is disagreement, revealed by the existence of factions, the attempt to define the issues will also reveal the areas of consensus, since the definition of issues just consists in the drawing of distinctions between contentious and non-contentious methods and procedures.

So far we have considered and described in outline the process of inventing the client in the case where an organization already exists. But what of the case in which the organization does not yet exist? New hospitals, new universities, and new institutions of even less well-understood kinds are from time to time established, and very often the construction of buildings is necessary before the organization can, properly speaking, come into being. And there are other cases, such as public housing, in which almost by definition no social organization can exist until after the design event. The simplistic view is that in such cases building should simply not take place: the establishment of the organization, even in temporary or unsuitable premises, should always precede new construction. In the case of housing the corresponding argument is for gradual replacement of existing housing areas with maximum consultation with the residents. Authors with otherwise widely diverging viewpoints, such as Turner (1976) and Jameson (1976), have argued strongly against large-scale public housing on the essentially similar ground that no design process mediated by a bureaucratic hierarchy can ever be successful in designing for the real needs of the user population. We have seen that there are excellent reasons in pure management theory for supposing this to be true. Nevertheless the tendency to bureaucracy, which is so strong a force in modern society and its architecture, will not lightly be set aside; and from time to time essentially bureaucratic organizations, of the kind we have been discussing, will have to be set up and housed as a more or less simultaneous operation. Can anything be done to improve the outcome in such situations?

We have seen that there are two essentials for a successful design process: a design organization which equals the complexity of the organization designed for, and commitment to the design on the part of the users. In the case of the *de novo* or "green fields" design these two problems are distinct. With an existing organization, it has been suggested, the subsystems of the organization itself should be involved in the design so that the design network reaches the necessary level of complexity. If the actual organization and the actual users are not available, the only alternative is to model them. That is, existing organizations, or parts of organizations, and existing populations of users of similar facilities must be used to represent the organization that does not yet exist and the users who have not yet been identified. The risks of such a procedure are obvious. It adds to the error inherent in the design process the danger that the wrong model will be selected, or that the information gained from it will be wrongly interpreted. As a secondary strategy, one of the various methods of designing for change may be adopted; but this depends on at least identifying the kinds of change that may be expected, and this in turn will depend on the model chosen for study.

In modelling, there is a distinction to be drawn between those cases in which the organization consists wholly of informal groups of users, as in housing, and those in which the organization to be modelled is more or less formal or bureaucratized. In the former case a population as like as possible to the prospective users can be sought out; in the latter like organizations or parts of organizations can be used as models. Environment–behaviour research has developed an extensive battery of techniques for the selection and investigation of appropriate models, which have been admirably reviewed by Zeisel (1981).

In making use of an existing organization as a model, the lack of realism and commitment is to some extent compensated by the more objective viewpoints which become possible when the specific internal political tensions of the organization are not seen as being involved. If key figures of the proposed new organization have been appointed and can also be involved in the design, so much the better, but we must recall once more the distribution of knowledge and ignorance; these people, however knowledgeable and experienced, will not possess enough information to act, by themselves, as an effective client.

Where a like population, rather than a like organization, is the model, the designer may find special problems in communicating with the users' representatives. Their values, preferences and trade-offs can be investigated interactively, by gaming or even physical simulation

(Brealey, 1972; Lawrence, 1982). The point of such simulation is, again, that it permits exchange of information; it provides the "users" with information about such things as cost and physical practicability which enables them to make their own judgements and engage in their own design process. More sophisticated tools, offering a still broader and richer problem space, could undoubtedly be devised.

Securing a reasonable simulation of the complexity of use in the design process does not, however, secure commitment of the users to the building. The problem of user involvement is transferred from design to management. The completed building must be "sold" to the users. This at once raises questions of morality; how far are we justified in persuading people to "like what they are given"? Immoral persuasion, by the techniques of the estate agent, is certainly possible and may be effective up to a point. The mere effort to persuade and the display of concern which it requires will have a certain influence, a "Hawthorne effect". But there is such a thing as legitimate, moral persuasion: persuasion by telling the truth. The methods of design or modelling used, and the resulting assumptions and decisions can be explained to users, provided of course that they have been properly carried out by second-generation methods and are therefore known. The possibilities for flexibility, change, and personal initiative which may have been incorporated into the design can also be explained. From published accounts, these methods seem to have been used with some success in, for example, Ralph Erskine's design for the Bygger development in Glasgow, and the Centraal Beheer office building by Hertzberger in Apeldoorn.

Nevertheless, indirect design, if carried out on these lines, is likely to be considerably more expensive and less reliable than direct design. It is therefore even more likely to meet with resistance than the method of working directly with existing organizations and social structures. In particular, the nature of the models required is often misunderstood, both by client and designer. The role of built models in the design of commodity buildings is often confused with the quite different role of models in the systems building; in the latter case it is the organization or the social structure, not the building it occupies, that is important. Often long and costly journeys to like or hypothetically like buildings are undertaken, but the building is visited far too briefly for any understanding of the organizational problems, let alone for any involvement of the parallel organization in the design process to take place; little of value is learnt about physical detail, and nothing about the fundamentals of the design.

In conclusion, then: in the case of the systems building it is necessary to invent the client; that is, to construct a design network of complexity equal to that of the social structure which will inhabit the

Bygger housing, Glasgow, by Ralph Erskine. User involvement can be secured by telling the truth; the methods of design used, and the resulting assumptions and decisions can be explained to the users

building in use, either directly or by modelling; and to devise methods of ensuring understanding of and commitment to the methods by which the design decisions were reached and their outcome.

6.4 Form information and system information: the content of design

So far we have been investigating the form of the design process: both its logical form and its social form. But the purpose of these networks is to process information and to arrive at decisions. While all the many kinds of information necessary cannot in practice or even in principle be considered here, it is possible to describe two broad kinds or classes of information which will always be required to complete a design: form information and system information.

Form information, as the name implies, consists of physical descriptions of objects; every kind of object, from a coat-hook to a room to a complete building. For example, "The minimum clear dimensions for an operating room are 6 m × 6 m × 3 m high." Form information, however, is not necessarily confined to the quality of extension. Information about the desired ambient temperature, lighting levels, the colour and imperviousness or absorbency of surfaces, and acoustic qualities is also form information. It is the kind of information that makes up the greater part of the content of the drawings and specifications from which buildings are built. Such information may be qualified, by giving tolerances for example, or expressed in a variety of different ways, by written descriptions, models, drawings and so on, but this does not change the principle. We are told something which purports to be definite about the quantity and quality of the finished building.

Ignoring for the moment the sense in which such propositions may be true or false, they are clearly distinct from another kind of proposition, which deals with relations and connections, inputs and outputs: "Direct access is required between the area in which anaesthesia is induced and the operating room ; "Provision must be made for maintenance of all services to the operating room without entering the operating suite"; "Flows of sterile goods and wastes must not intersect." Information about flows tells us nothing about shape or even direction; it is topological rather than metric, though energy losses, friction, waiting time, voltage drop and so on, may impose limiting lengths of flow. Other propositions about inputs and outputs, such as the supply of fluids, gases and power, the removal of wastes and heat, the arrangement of means of escape, and the containment of nuisances or dangers such as noise, fire and poisons, are also part of the system information. And since they involve inputs and outputs, so is information about prospect, aspect, ambient noise levels, and some other features of the site. Neither of these two kinds of information is complete in itself: both are required.

In a systems building such as a teaching hospital, many, though not all, subsystems are complex networks of activities with highly specific relationships between people and between people and physical objects, such as room enclosures and pieces of equipment. In an operating room with lateral laminar flow air-conditioning, for example, the distribution of the air current around patient and medical staff is critical; the orientation and placing of the operating table with respect to the air inlet is therefore fixed. This in turn constrains the position of the surgical team for various operations and hence the location of exits and other services. Not only the spatial pattern of activities, but also their timing, may literally be vital; as in the case of the time taken to bring a resuscitation trolley to a patient suffering cardiac arrest, which constrains the distance from patient to trolley storage bay. Form information at any level cannot be understood without system information.

It is also the case that form information at a given level depends on both system information and form information at the next level of detail; in a hospital ward size and shape depends on the number and size of beds, and on the nursing and teaching activities performed and the spaces and clearances allowed for them. It is thus impossible to treat any form information as an issue without introducing system information. In the case of ward size, debate might focus on nursing procedures, teaching procedures, bed size, or all three; but if there is debate on bed size, which is form information, this in turn can only be resolved by reference to more detailed nursing and medical proce-dures, to patient behaviour, and to the anthropometrics of the patient population.

The distinction between form information and system information is similar to that drawn by Pye (1964) between the principle of operation of a device and its various physical expressions. The principle of operation is dynamic, topological and non-metric; it can exist in numerous superficially distinct forms. Information about the principle of operation is system information. Similarly the dual graph of a plan is system information. March and Steadman (1971) have shown that a number of apparently different house plans by Frank Lloyd Wright have the same dual graph; the dual graph represents the connections or flows which underlie or form the "deep structure" of the plan.

How is this distinction useful in design? What does it tell us about method? Simplifying somewhat, we may say that the better the consensus the more completely the constraints on the problem can be expressed as form information. Conversely, as argued above, debate will lead to a demand for both form and system information. But if there is little or no doubt about the working of, let us say, a nursing station, then it will be possible to describe it simply as a physical object, in terms of dimensions, clearances, service points and so on, with tolerances if any to permit it to be adjusted in its relationships with other elements. It is also likely, if there is such good agreement, that there is somewhere available a working example, which has established itself by its performance as a standard. It will be highly desirable for those working on the design to understand how the nursing station is used, but this requirement does not differ from the understanding that they should have of, say, a water chiller or any other piece of equipment which is not in itself specially designed but simply incorporated in the building. Such understanding is necessary to avoid contingent errors such as neglecting maintenance clearances or failing to provide a drainage outlet. That is, it is essential to know how the unit fits into the system. The method appropriate where form information is sufficient will be the very simplest: either selection or quasi-algorithmic commodity design. This is conveniently summarized in Wade's aphorism "Buy it or break it" (Wade, 1977). If it is not posible, at least in principle, to buy what is wanted as a unit or going concern, it is necessary to break it down to the next level of detailed form and system information.

A special case of system information, the system character of which may not at first be apparent, is the structural system. The fact that it is customary to speak of a structural *system* should perhaps be a sufficient indication of its nature, but it may still not be clear how this is related to other kinds of system information which, as we have seen, are networks or flow diagrams representing various inputs and outputs to the building system. However, further reflection will disclose that the structural system is exactly like this. The "real" structural system is in fact a network of inputs, in the form of loads, dead and live, and of outputs in terms of the resistances or stress generated in the members. This network can be made apparent by, for example, photoelastic analysis, a beautiful laboratory technique in which a transparent material of appropriate characteristics is placed between two polarizing filters and stressed; light transmitted through the system then forms moire fringes connecting points of equal difference between the principal stresses. This pattern itself is scale free, so that it meets the other condition for system information, that it is primarily topological rather than metric.

One of the difficulties of design is that the various systems described by the system information have to be co-ordinated and may conflict. Le Corbusier is reported to have observed "Pour Ledoux c'était simple; pas de tubes." The increase in the number of service systems which must be incorporated in a building, and the "tubes" which are their physical form, increases the probability of conflict at the technical level, just as the increase in the number of organizational and social systems served by a building does at the level of layout. In theory, these systems, not having fixed form but only fixed relations, have a high degree of adaptability. However, the realization of the systems in practice depends on the available technology, on the adjunct system of the building industry and its capabilities. It is also governed, as previously noted, by the need to avoid excessive losses in the system.

Thus the adaptability of an air-conditioning layout to the activity systems that it serves is restricted both by the kinds of ductwork available and by the need to reduce turbulence and friction in the movement of the air through the ducts; these factors restrict the number and shape of the bends in the ductwork. Similarly, conventional drainage and sewerage systems, which operate by gravity, are extremely inflexible and limited in their capacity to adapt to the needs of other systems.

This brings out the point that *the process of converting system information into form information just is the process of design*, or, more exactly, the end towards which design aims. Thus the purpose of the design process and the design organization which we have been discussing is firstly the collection of system information, and secondly and emerging from that its conversion into form information. This process is camouflaged by the tendency of design professionals to think of form and system together; an aspect of their craft ways of thinking. The architects tend to think of plans as arrangements of rooms, structural engineers of the structure as a steel or concrete frame, mechanical engineers of ducts, pipes and wires. These concrete ways of thinking are not necessarily contrary to the interests of good design; but for method to progress we must learn to separate the abstract and the concrete elements, the system and the form it ultimately takes. It may be useful here to return to the earlier criticism of the brief or programme. Briefs, it was suggested, tend to be in the form of a list of rooms — so many, of such a size, with names indicative of their purpose; and it was argued that this kind of information is misleading and dangerous, and that it is not improved by the inclusion of operational policies. From the point of view of form information and system information, this can be understood in somewhat more depth. A list of rooms and areas is form information; any system information is implicit. But unless the form information has been tested against the system information, that is, unless the practicability of carrying out the proposed activities in the proposed rooms has been thoroughly investigated, contradictions are likely. If this testing has not been done during the preparation of the brief, the attempt to reconcile the form information and system information during design will reveal the contradictions, which will in turn require that the issues be re-opened, with the results that we have seen. The inclusion of system information or operational policies does not improve matters because the implicit system information in the form information contained in the brief may contradict the express system information in the operational policies; further, the operational policies may well contradict each other.

If, on the other hand, the form information and system information are reconciled during the programming, which is what the argument so far would seem to suggest, then what has been done is to produce a design. A correct and non-contradictory combination of system information expressed as form information is already a plan, or what the conventions of architectural discourse would name a schematic design. A plan *is* a model of a set of elements and their relations. This is not a merely theoretical or semantic point. It is a matter of observation, at least anecdotally, that when a briefing team attempt to carry out their work thoroughly, they end up producing plans, usually to the considerable irritation of the architects who have to work from the resulting brief, and who feel, not unreasonably, that they are merely being employed as draughtsmen, or as exterior decorators in the Victorian manner. Here again there is waste of resources, though of a slightly more subtle kind, in that two sets of people are being employed to do one job. It is obviously no better if the briefing team attempt to convert their conclusions back into words and figures; even more effort is wasted, and while it is quite likely that another group of designers receiving such a brief will generate a *different* plan, it will not be a *better* one, since by definition each plan meets the criteria established for the brief, and there can be no other criteria (other perhaps than aesthetic ones) for saying that one such plan is better than another; once such a plan exists, it should be adopted without more ado.

This last point is of considerable practical importance. Because unique solutions to design problems, that is, solutions which are fully determined by well-agreed constraints, are the exception rather than the rule, it commonly happens, especially at the level of detail design, that competing solutions will be developed which do not differ as to merit, though they may have considerably different emotional importance to individuals; the designer grows to love his design. Where design *is* pursued with love, and not as a mere means to an income, such disputes arise constantly and waste a great deal of time. It is desirable for design management, and in practice this means for all designers, to understand this, and to be able to recognize when it is happening, so that their efforts can be directed to the resolution of genuine difficulties.

With the distinction of form information and system information at least partly explained, and the significance of system information and, particularly, the combination of system information, in the design process established, it is possible to look again at the detail of the design process, already illustrated in the discussion of examples in the previous chapter.

6.5   Design: eliminating the impossible

"Eliminate the impossible, and what remains, however improbable, must be the solution." In those words, or something like them, the Great Detective described the essence of his method; and it is a very good general description of the method of establishing a problem space. Design begins with the construction of the problem space, and proceeds initially by the reduction of the boundaries of that space to the narrowest limits possible, without the space becoming negative. Earlier the process was described as one of definition, which is usually represented by the intersection of a series of closed curves; but we may equally imagine the space to be an area defined by a series of boundary lines, as in the graphic method for the solution of linear programming problems or, more accurately, as a "volume" in space defined by the intersection of planes of various shapes. Even more correctly, we might take the defining elements to be "fuzzy sets" in which case the solution space would not have precise boundaries but be determined by something like a density gradient, a gradient of "truthlikeness". For the purpose of this discussion, any mental map can be used that enables us to imagine the constraints on the design as a system progressively defining or enclosing a solution. (More precise models will of course be required if a mathematical solution of a problem is to be attempted.)

If we use the simplest model, an area bounded by straight lines, it can be seen that there are three possible conditions: a solution space of positive area, in which there must theoretically be an infinite number of point solutions; a solution space of zero area, that is, a single or point solution; and a solution space of negative area, where there is no solution (Figure 6.1). The first type is under-constrained, the second fully constrained, and the third over-constrained; a constraint is the dividing line drawn between the possible and the impossible. These distinctions yield another view of the difference between commodity buildings and buildings of other kinds: the commodity building is more fully constrained, and the constraints are themselves better identified, and it is this that allows the quasi-algorithmic solution of such problems. An information network such as has been discussed in the preceding sections is a device for discovering constraints that are not well identified. The process of ensuring a proper overlap between the problem space of the user and the problem space of the designer is thus a process of agreeing on constraints and testing them through debate. The constraints themselves will, as we have seen, consist of form information and system information, and in general the system information will be dominant.

We can divide the constraints on the system designed for into external and internal constraints; roughly these correspond to the task

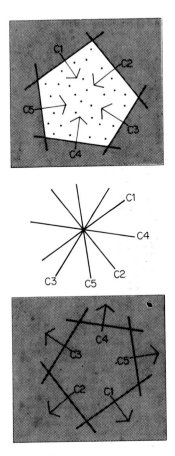

Figure 6.1   Constraints and solutions

environment and the task itself. The system designed for is part of a wider social system and it will exchange inputs and outputs with that system. The wider system cannot be known or understood in its entirety, or even to any large extent, but only through its interaction with the system designed for. It will impose both system constraints and form constraints on the design. The system constraints are the purposes or goals of the organization: what it exists to do. As discussed previously, overall goals may not themselves be clear; but they will be clearer in the case of formal users, such as hospitals, factories and offices, and less clear in the case of amorphous users, such as the inhabitants of housing estates. And since the goals of the user system help to locate and explain the necessary physical inputs and outputs of the system — goods, utilities, people, wastes, vehicles, services and so on — it is more difficult to determine these also in the case of the amorphous user. It may be that many of the failures of housing design spring from this difficulty; at any rate it is common to find in the literature reports of housing that has failed at least in part through neglect of exchanges with the external social system, such as transport linkages and the availability of schools shops and entertainment.

In the case of the structured user organization, the process of setting up the information network will itself reveal many of the external constraints, since the information network is a model of the system with equivalent variety. In the case of the amorphous user, the external system constraints will have to be investigated by simulation, as with the internal constraints: an "estate planning game" perhaps, to supplement the "home improvement game" (Brealey, 1972). One of the most important, if not the most important, of the external constraints is usually the amount of the resources available for construction. While there are cases where resources are, at any rate in relation to the scope of the problem, unlimited, these are very rare, and will mostly be symbolic buildings; even in such cases there is usually an unexpressed order of magnitude of resources to be expended which underlies the decision to proceed, and where, as with the Sydney Opera House, this is exceeded, trouble results. More commonly, if the resources available cannot be determined, at least in their general order, design cannot progress. Knowledge of the available resources, taken in conjunction with information about the current state of the industry, in the form of cost data (another external constraint), effectively limits the range of possible forms of the proposed building. That is, it permits selection, amongst the variety of structural systems, amount and quality of servicing, qualities of finish, and so on, of certain ranges of possibilities, which in turn serve to constrain form. We have seen this process at work in the case studies in Chapter 5. There is some danger that too much will be inferred, that too many constraints will be deduced too quickly from this, and indeed from other constraints as they emerge, to the exclusion of possible solutions; it is for this reason that at the preliminary stages of design it is important to bear in mind that the process is one of exclusion, of eliminating the impossible.

The external constraints will also include form information. If the site is known, the physical extent and characteristics of the site will be one such constraint; though like most other constraints these will interact with the resource constraints; if sufficient resources are available, it may be possible to buy additional land, excavate, build high, remodel land forms, or otherwise avoid site restrictions. If the site is not known, it is the external system requirements of the organization served, primarily accessibility, and the resources that will influence its selection. A less flexible set of external form constraints are the planning laws which may limit in more or less explicit ways the size and shape of the building that may be erected on the site selected. There may also be external constraints, in the form of laws or regulations, on the kind of accommodation to be provided, for example the Parker Morris housing standards in England, or the requirements of the Australian Universities Commission for student housing discussed in section 5 of Chapter 5. Somewhat bizarre external form constraints may be created by the intrusion into a site of elements of the service network of the external social system: rights of way, main sewers, railway tunnels and even microwave relays. The point, however, is not to list every kind of external form constraint that may be encountered, but to recognize their existence as a category. Unlike the external system constraints, they are not necessarily located by the process of setting up an information network; they will have to be found by a separate search process, a process which relies for its effectiveness on the experience and skill of the designer, that is, on his professional extended problem space.

In setting up the information network, the main subsystems of the organization will be identified. Its *first task* is then to identify the most constrained subsystems, since these subsystems will be less capable of adaptation and adjustment; by definition, as it were, their needs must be met first. Because they are relatively well constrained, they will yield a relatively high proportion of form information; they become building blocks which help to describe the total system. To take simple examples, the students room in the college complex, or the basic ward types in a hospital become, as we saw in the last chapter, such blocks; they have a certain limited flexibility, but nevertheless these units and their combinations tell us much about what the final form of the building must be. Not only their form, but their location may be determined, as Broadbent argues in his account of method, by their inputs and outputs: avoidance of noise, requirements for sun penetration, outlook and the like, as well as their connection to the communication system. These inputs and outputs provide their external system constraints; and they will also of course have internal constraints, arising from the nature of the activity in the subsystem — internal system information. Throughout the preliminary design it is the activity system information, information about what the users do or plan to do, which is most important, since as we have seen the other systems that make up the building are relatively able to be subordinated and adapted to these systems.

Each subsystem has to be examined in the light of the distinction previously made between the different kinds of design. A whole complex may have the symbolic, commodity or system character, but this does not mean that every one of it subsystems has the same character. Indeed we have seen that this is not so: a systems building may have parts which have the commodity character. Similarly it may have subsystems of a symbolic character: the chapel of a hospital, for example, or its main entrance hall. It follows from the arguments advanced so far that the most constrained subsystems, those which most nearly approximate complete form information, will have the commodity character; though there may also be less well-constrained subsystems which can still be treated as having this character: a toilet block, for example, is usually a commodity design problem, but less constrained than, say, an operating theatre. However, both subsystems that have the systems character and those that have the symbolic character have special problems which cannot be simply dismissed to a later stage of the design. In the case of those having the systems character, the degree of constraint will not disclose itself to inspection; there will have to be detailed investigation. This means that each such subsystem, when identified, has to be treated as a design problem in itself, and the kind of analysis described up to this point must be repeated for each, so that their degree of constraint with respect to the overall problem can be determined. Similarly, ideas and proposals will have to be generated for subsystems that have the symbolic character, for if these subsystems are simply allowed to be constrained in their form, location and so on by the other, more rational subsystems, which can all too easily happen, then the development of an appropriate expressive form, in the terms discussed in section 5 of Chapter 4, may well prove to be impossible.

The *second task* of design is, then, to identify the subsystems of the total system, to classify them according to their general type, and to rank them approximately with respect to their degree of constraint, or, if one prefers to look at it in that way, in order of their adaptability; this last operation may require the detailed investigation of some subsystems. By this time they will be taking on some physical form, as rooms, departments, wings or "blocks". The requirements of the most constrained, and therefore most constraining, subsystems, the resource constraints, and the other external constraints in conjunction will usually restrict the problem space sufficiently for the development of building shape options: notional or diagrammatic buildings which carry with them some preliminary idea of the hardware involved in their realization — structure, communication and service systems. They are preliminary models which can be tested — hypotheses. The *third stage* of design then consists of generating hypotheses. This is, if not in the terms in which the word has been discussed in Chapter 2, a *creative* process, at least a *productive* process. The number and variety of the hypotheses generated will depend on the designer's ability to move freely between his stock of models, the extended problem space which is his knowledge of the universe of architecture, and free and playful experiment with the combination and recombination of the building blocks derived from the various subsystems.

When a hypothesis, or a stock of hypotheses, has been generated, it has to be tested. Testing consists of the search for system conflict. Even though direct conflicts between chains of decisions coming from different parts of the organization may have been filtered out or adjudicated by the operation of the decision network, conflicts are still inevitable. This follows from the non-algorithmic form of the solution for the systems building, which can be expressed in a different way by saying that it is not fully susceptible to "tree" analysis, that chains of decisions cannot be kept mutually independent; each overlap is a likely point of conflict. It is, indeed, this very feature of the problem which makes the generation of hypotheses necessary. The effect of each overlap between chains of decisions is to produce local over-constraint, that is, subproblems with negative solution spaces, or system conflict. To revert to the example discussed in section 5.7: a sterile supply hoist, located in what appears to be a thoroughly satisfactory position in the operating department, may prove to force a totally unsatisfactory flow pattern on the sterile supply department below, which in turn is closely constrained by the requirements of other, even more highly constrained departments surrounding it. Hypotheses that involve numerous conflicts of this kind will be rejected.

However it is extremely unlikely that any hypothesis can be generated which is totally free from conflict. The progressive process of generating and testing will eventually reduce the supply of hypotheses to one, and conflicts within that hypothetical system will have to be resolved by the relaxation of one or more constraints. In the example given, we might ask: Is a hoist essential? Can it be relocated? How inflexible are the shape and size constraints of the other departments? If the argumentative process of the decision network has been properly recorded, the record will suggest directions which can be explored by reference back through the network and a further process of debate. If the hierarchy of more and less constrained decisions has been correctly established and followed, such contradictions will rarely lead to more than local revision of previous decision processes; the unravelling will speedily run into higher-level decisions which no-one is prepared to revise. The situation in which something has got to give, that is, a decision has to be made between lines of decision both of which are supported by consensus after careful retesting, has to be dealt with by the arbitrating function of the network. Such situations present a special difficulty in the case of the amorphous user, where the decision network is merely simulated and there is no arbitrating function; to avoid settlement by administrative fiat, arbitration too can be simulated by a jury of user-surrogates.

It should be emphasized here that the loops or regressions in the design process which such conflicts engender are not something to be cheerfully accepted. On the contrary, they are pathological, the kind of thing which design method should be seeking to eliminate, not encourage. It is for this reason that the heuristic proposed here, which actively seeks to defuse such conflicts before too much work has been done, is to be preferred to any programming or briefing process, or any process of conceptual design, in which such conflicts may remain concealed like unexploded bombs, threatening the whole design built upon them. No method can eliminate them completely; but a method that recognizes and indeed centres on conflict is better than one that ignores or attempts to conceal it (Heath, 1982).

The systems building suffers from over-constraint; paradoxically, it is also likely to suffer from under-constraint. This also follows from the non-algorithmic pattern of problem solution. An algorithm yields a unique solution; and conversely, problems that have unique solutions can be reduced to algorithms. In the case of the systems building there will be subproblems that are over-constrained, leading to negative solution spaces; but the remainder of the problem will be under-constrained. The distribution of over- and under-constraint may be such that it is not even possible to reduce the number of hypothetical overall solutions to one; or alternatively one surviving overall hypothesis may admit of a considerable number of variants. However, a unique solution has to be reached. How then is the problem to be closed? The supply of problem structure in the task environment, which has been represented in the problem space, through the operation of the information network and its decisions, is exhausted. Of course it is possible that this is not really the case, that some structure has been overlooked. But if diligent search does not reveal any further clues or cues, we are left with a problem which is partly amorphous, a system which has not been fully converted into form.

The only way in which this difficulty can be overcome is by importing additional structure. In fact this has already happened once, at the stage of hypothesis generation; as we saw, the hypothesis is not a necessary induction from the problem structure, but is constructed or invented by a combination of trial and error, or playful recombination, and the use of models from the designer's extended problem space which are, quite clearly, imported structure. The additional structure now required will take the form of rules or decisions which in relation to the problem are arbitrary. They may in fact *be* arbitrary. The introduction of a module, where it is not strictly demanded by the technical requirements of production, is an example of such an arbitrary rule; and it is a solution which will, one fears, continue to appeal to designers with limited resources on which to call. In principle, it would also be possible to make decisions completely arbitrarily and this is sometimes done too; an example, not strictly in the field of architecture, but not totally irrelevant, was the choice of a site for Canberra (Johnson, 1974). However, consciously making an arbitrary decision is difficult, so that it is not done very often. In fact, the usual solution is to introduce aesthetic criteria. Architects prefer not to think or speak of such criteria as rules, but from the point of view of method, that is what they are. They may be in the form of proportional systems or rules — Broadbent's canonic design (Broadbent, 1973a); or analogies from other forms, built or not — his analogic design; or a personal style, more or less adapted to the work in hand, which is something between the two. Ideally, the choice of aesthetic structure should be guided by the considerations outlined in Chapter 4; that is, it should be directed by some sense of the relationship between activity and perceived form.

The heuristic method described here, of establishing constraints, generating hypotheses *within* those constraints, and closing the problem by the introduction of aesthetic criteria, has analogies with the analysis-synthesis model of design. That is, the setting up of the information network and the establishment of constraints might be taken to be analysis, and the remainder synthesis. This analogy is not surprising: analysis-synthesis is a widely popular model, and would not have achieved such popularity if it did not seem to fit in with observation. Nevertheless, there is an important difference: the process we have been considering is guided throughout by models, by a problem space, at first vague and general, but becoming increasingly specific as the work progresses. The information network itself is a model of the organization, and the design is progressively matched to it. And further, the "synthetic" process is not one of induction, but of importing structure, specifically aesthetic structure, so that a clear and essential place is made within method for aspects of design well known to exist, but whose role in the analytic-synthetic view is mysterious.

On the other hand, the use of models conceived of in this account is also quite different from "conceptual" design. In conceptual design the importation of structure takes place once and for all at the beginning, and constrains the other parts of the design process, which must adapt to it. It is obvious that in the systems building which is liberally provided with internal constraints, this must lead to an excess of over-constraint and to numerous conflicts, in which both the user system and the intended aesthetic effect are likely to suffer more or less acutely. To reiterate, the models used in this heuristic are initially very vague, inexact, and plastic, and attempts to give them too much precision too soon must be strenuously resisted; it is worth noting that such attempts may come from the client as much as or even more than the designers, since tolerance of vagueness and ambiguity is not an outstanding characteristic of the bureaucratic mind.

A concluding word on the art of architecture may be appropriate. It will be deduced, by those who follow the argument closely, that buildings designed according to this method are not likely to be great works of art. Great works of art demand a far more rigorous and exclusive dedication to aesthetic ends than this heuristic allows. But it must be borne in mind that this discussion has concentrated on the systems building, and has set itself to answer the question of how the complex practical problems which such buildings pose can be methodically and effectively resolved. The limitation on the role of aesthetics is built into the problem posed. Nevertheless, aesthetics have been given an important role; it has been shown that they cannot in fact be excluded from the solution of such problems. But the greatest achievements of the art of architecture belong to another type of problem, the symbolic building, in which aesthetic considerations are properly dominant. Architecture has a range of problems, and we must understand the range in order to solve them all as well as possible.

6.6   Detail design

The heuristic for design described in the last section is a model of the preliminary design process, what is usually called schematic design. Just how far this process extends is difficult to specify in general; it depends on the nature of the activities designed for and the constraints they generate. In some cases the size and position of, let us say, a window or a door may be critical; even smaller elements may have to be exactly located and their detailed form decided in preliminary design. In other cases it may be sufficient to know that an element can be provided, but its detailed location and mode of operation may not be critical; in this case it is of course under-constrained. We have seen, too, that the distribution of constraint is likely to be uneven. A rough distinction can be made, however, between overall or schematic design, which is concerned with the definition and arrangement of major elements, and detail design, which is concerned with such things as the exact shapes, profiles and methods of assembly of the various building materials, components and subassemblies from which the major elements are constructed.

As with the overall design, some general model of these aspects, varying in its degree of definition, but still incomplete, will exist in the designer's mind before detail design commences. He will be aware of general classes of solution to these problems, as part of his professional extended problem space, and will also perhaps have some more definite idea as to the specific class of solution; for example, he may be thinking of metal-framed windows, out of the general class of windows which include frameless, timber frame, and so on; and within metal-framed windows he may even more specifically have in mind aluminium-framed windows, as distinct from steel or bronze; and still further he may be thinking in terms of reversible windows, rather than casements or double-hung windows or other possible modes of action. As with overall design, a process of successive definition is involved. And in principle, the general heuristic here described, of locating constraints, generating hypotheses within them, searching for system conflicts, eliminating hypotheses, relaxing constraints where conflicts cannot otherwise be resolved, and closing the problem by the introduction of aesthetic criteria, applies also to detail design. Since the constraints on detail design are in general more technical, the balance of decision will shift towards the professional designer and away from the information network; but this is a shift in balance only; there is no design decision which is without consequences for the user, and some quite detailed matters, although they do not constrain the overall design, may be of the first importance for the effective operation of the finished building. In fact, user complaints are much more often concerned with matters of detail than with overall design; it is leaks, cracks, doors that rattle or will not close, mechanical failures, deteriorating finishes, and other "minor" ills of building which cause the greatest unhappiness and resentment.

Failures arising from faulty materials or execution can never be wholly eliminated. Again, Ashby's Law of Requisite Variety warns us that supervision or control of execution can never be sufficient to ensure perfection; and in other industries the statistical nature of quality control is well established (Heath, 1974a). Nevertheless, many detail failures arise from ill-considered design, and method should have something to say about this, and be able to suggest ways in which it can be reduced, if not completely avoided; human error on the part of the designers is also inevitable. It might appear that no general statement, other perhaps than that architects should be well informed in their subject and guided by caution and common sense, could be of much use or application, when the instances are so heterogeneous. But it can be argued, on the contrary, that failures in detail design invariably arise in the same way, regardless of the particulars of each case: they are all failures to conceive of the building and its parts as a dynamic system, constantly interacting with each other and with their environment, which include both the physical environment and the activities of those who produce, use and maintain the building. It is not ignorance alone which causes failure, but inappropriate method; for no designer can know everything that might at some time be useful for him to know; a proper method reveals and overcomes ignorance, by leading us to ask the right questions. An architect may be abundantly supplied with knowledge, he may be familiar with every type of construction used since time immemorial, and yet his designs will fail if he does not understand these techniques as attempts, more or less successful, to cope with dynamic situations.

To illustrate this point, let us consider a few examples of actual failures. These examples are all taken from a single study of public housing in Melbourne (Stevenson, Martin and O'Neill, 1967). They are not spectacular failures, but small nagging deficiencies which served to make people's daily lives less pleasant.

- Bathrooms in the high-rise flats were unpleasantly draughty. No doubt for reasons of economy, toilets had been included in the bathroom and gas hot-water heaters were used. The building regulations required a certain amount of fixed ventilation in such circumstances, and fixed lourvres were accordingly provided, which admitted draughts. The technical problem was "solved" but the bathroom as a system-in-use failed.
- The walk-up flats, which were intended for and occupied by, families with children had laundries on the roof. No lifts were provided. To reach the laundry, to shop or take out the garbage four flights or up to seventy-seven stairs in some cases had to be negotiated by women, some of them pregnant, carrying heavy loads, and often with small children. The designer of such a system had clearly never pictured it in operation.
- Again in the walk-up flats, noise was a serious problem. What was said in the flats could be heard on the landings, and noise from the landings seemed to be in the flats themselves, to the extent that it often disturbed sleeping children. To add to the problem, the metal stair balustrade and the letter boxes resonated when knocked accidentally. Again the interaction of the physical system and the activity system has not been properly considered.

These examples of failures have been chosen from a larger number reported by Stevenson, Martin and O'Neill, not because they are unusual, but because they are the kind of things that occur again and again in the literature of building evaluation, and in the records of disputes between clients and architects. Whether it is correct to call such mistakes "negligence" is open to question. It is likely that great care and consideration were given to the designs. Neither are they strictly due to ignorance; most of the architects concerned would "know" of these possibilities item by item as it were; but they have somehow failed to acquire the habit of thinking of them as unified systems. Their problem space is wrongly constructed. They do not identify the systems at work and test their interactions.

It may be of some interest to compare the view of the problems of detailed design given here with another account of essentially the same problem, by Hillier and Jones (1977). They argue that many of the current difficulties of architecture arise from concurrent changes in both the vocabulary and the main building forms, and that this has stirred up "a hornet's nest of technical problems which had been forgotten because their solution had become a matter of habit." Information about these problems is available, but not sufficient guidance as to when a particular piece of this information will be needed. They distinguish information from knowledge. "Information is what we look up; knowledge is what we learn." They suggest "a direct correlation between the degree to which the design process depends on looking up rather than learning and the probability of failure." And they propose that what is needed is "knowledge of good ways of achieving objectives by combinations of materials and details that can be confidently handled by the constructional skills available, and easily maintained...", for which they borrow the anthropological use of the term "technique". It is an area of knowledge not well covered by either building science, or manufacturers' literature, or reference information; something "between scientific or technological knowledge and the simple repetition of standard solutions".

The problem they identify is much the same as what has here been called detail design. Their solution, however, corresponds to an increase in what has been discussed previously as craft knowledge, though perhaps at a higher level of technical sophistication. And this does not seem to be adequate to avoid the kinds of failures described. The "alphabet" of materials and details is extended to a "vocabulary" but the sentences and paragraphs need to be included. A different level of thought and discourse is needed: an overview of the building-in-use as a dynamic system, and a meta-language for talking about it. It is in fact a problem not of knowledge but of method. And method consists in modelling, in the process of design, the situation being designed.

6.7 Method summarized

Rather than repeating the story so far, in briefer and perhaps no more intelligible terms, this concluding section consists mainly of three

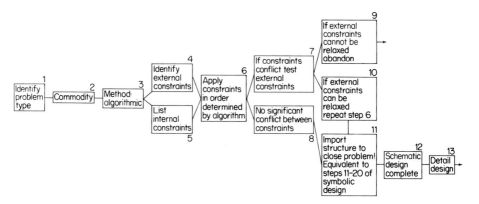

Figure 6.2   Structure of the design process for the commodity building

charts or precedence diagrams, which summarize the processes that
have been described and justified in the preceding sections and
chapters. Each diagram describes the overall method for one of the
three main problem types previously described: commodity buildings
(Figure 6.2), symbolic buildings (Figure 6.3) and systems buildings
(Figure 6.4). Though much simplified these are not ideal or a priori
schemes; they represent, in accordance with the previous arguments,
the logical forms of actual design processes, made transparent and
explicit instead of as usual, operative and inexplicit. The business of
method in architecture is not to invent in the abstract, but to hold up a
mirror to reality, a mirror whose only magic is to eliminate the
contingent and the inessential. It is for this reason that each of these

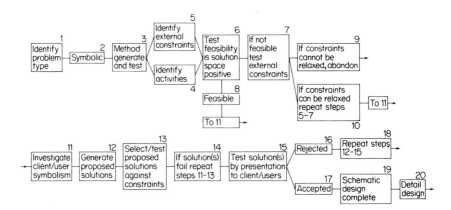

Figure 6.3   Structure of the design process for the symbolic building

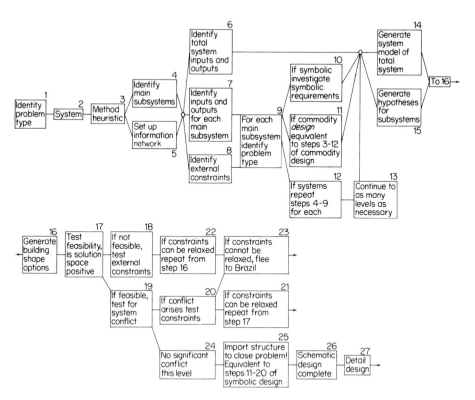

Figure 6.4 Structure of the design process for the systems building

processes includes explicitly the possibility of failure. In real life one cannot "win them all"; a successful design can only be produced if the task environment, the world of people and events which surrounds and intermeshes with the process of design, will permit it.

The task environment is represented only as the set of external constraints. This disregards the role of the professional and office environment in the generation of models. To show this properly, there should perhaps be an overlay on each diagram indicating the existence and progressive modification of models at each successive step. Similarly, the incidence of change and tests for sensitivity to change have been omitted; and this too would require an overlay, since such considerations interact with the process at many points.

The simplification within the diagrams, already mentioned, consists not only in the omission of specific detail of the kind that would be necessary in describing the progress of an actual individual design, but also in the suppression of some logical possibilities, or cases which might, exceptionally, arise, and even of some that occur regularly.

Thus the symbolic and commodity diagrams do not show the possibility that the system may include subsystems which are problems of one of the other types; although this is shown in the systems diagram because here such "maverick" subsystems are extremely likely. And in the systems diagram only the activity system stream of design is shown; whereas a more correct representation would include parallel schemes for service and structural systems branching from step 7 and interacting with the others up to step 15. Further, some steps of the commodity and the systems diagrams compress a whole series of steps which are represented in more detail on the other diagrams into a unit.

Detail design is also represented as a single step in each case; whereas it is a multistage process applied to many different elements and groups of elements. However, the design of each detail element as a dynamic system is generally a problem of the commodity type; the external constraints of each element being the actions of the activity system, the physical environment and the neighbouring elements, and the internal constraints the behaviour of the element in itself. The detail design of each element also extends into the design of subelements and subsubelements, down to whatever level is necessary for design by selection to become possible. As with commodity design generally, final closure may require the importation of structure. To represent all this even in outline would greatly complicate the diagrams without adding much to understanding.

Finally, every step of a complete representation would show an armoury of specific tools or tactics appropriate to that particular task. The classification and description of such tools or tactics is certainly part of method, but an ephemeral part as new and sometimes better techniques are developed quite frequently. Like all the other omissions, this one is made with a clear conscience. A summary such as this need not (and indeed cannot) show the variety of the real world; it should show only what is requisite for control.

At this point we may return, for the last time, to the fact gathering-analysis-synthesis-evaluation model of design. It will be seen that many of the step descriptions begin "IDENTIFY"; these steps are analogous to fact gathering-analysis. Generally following these are steps beginning "GENERATE" which might be seen as synthetic. And towards the end of each sequence are steps beginning "TEST": perhaps evaluations. This does not mean that analysis-synthesis-evaluation is right after all. We have seen that analysis is not possible without models; that generation of proposals is not synthetic; and even evaluation is by no means the same thing as testing, since the scope of testing is limited by the previous process, while evaluation may well imply an impossibly laborious process of matching an endless list of criteria to an equally substantial list of proposals and elements. Nor, to conclude, is analysis-synthesis-evaluation a model of the design process in the sense that these diagrams are models; at best it is a list of names or operations and a crude indication of their sequence, and this is its main failing.

Another more general query may occur to the discerning reader. The three diagrams represent the three classes of problem which, it was argued in section 5.8, are only zones or tendencies within a general problem space of three dimensions, each class representing emphasis on one of the dimensions. This implies that there must be intermediate cases, cases whose location in the general problem space is on or near the diagonals. The question then arises, What method is appropriate to such cases?

Four situations have to be considered: a relatively close balance between commodity characteristics and symbolism; a similar balance between systems characteristics and symbolism; a balance between commodity and systems characteristics; and finally the case in which all three elements are present to almost equal extent. The case in which there is both good constraint or consensus and an important element of symbolism, the commodity-symbolic mix, is in practice unlikely to arise, unless the symbolism is also largely conventional, that is, in the case of iconic design. Clearly if the constraint on other aspects of the problem is good the scope for the symbolic use of form will be limited; symbolism will probably be confined to "useless work": high-quality materials, high finish, high definition of detail.

The other three cases all imply a significant amount of "noise"; that is, lack of certainty about the relevance of the information available. The relevance or otherwise of the information can only be tested by obtaining a deeper understanding of the social system designed for. Thus, without any detailed discussion of the probability or possibility of any of these states occurring in practice, it can be concluded at once that the appropriate method is that outlined for the "systems" case; that is, heuristic search, though it may turn out to be considerably abbreviated. It is in fact the general case, the other methods having applicability limited to those zones of the general problem space in which their particular features are clearly dominant. From the point of view of method, in practice the general problem space is anisotropic; the utility of the various methods is not of equal probability. A representation of the space in terms of the proportion of individual problems requiring each kind of method, that is in terms of probability, would show the volume of commodity or quasi-algorithmic cases as by far the largest, systems or heuristic approaches next, and symbolic or generate-and-test methods occupying the least volume. Drawing such a representation would be an interesting exercise in geometry, but of no great use. We conclude that, in cases of difficulty, the "systems approach" is the correct one.

6.8   Conclusion

The appropriate method for any given architectural task is defined by the social nature of that task. There is no *one* method that can be used on all occasions. However, this does not imply that there are as many methods as there are tasks. Design processes fall into one of three general families or classes, each of which can be formally described. Within these families there are many variants, but these variants are, again, not random but predictable. It is thus possible to plan strategy and select tactics in advance for any design. Such planning can shorten design time and reduce the risk of error.

A theory which claims to be scientific cannot also claim to be final. Theories exist to be tested, and refuted, modified or elaborated. For reasons given previously, it is unlikely that practitioners will of their own initiative undertake the testing of any theory. There are, however, signs that a new field of practice research is emerging. The further development of method requires increased collaboration between practitioners and researchers on case studies of actual design processes, a collaboration for which this work may provide a basis.

Bibliography

Alexander, C. (1964, 1971) *Notes on the Synthesis of Form*, Harvard University Press, Cambridge, MA.
  (1965) 'A city is not a tree,' *Architectural Forum*, **122**, April 58–62, May 58–61.
  (1980) 'Value', *Design Studies*, **1** (5), 295–298.
Alexander, C., and Poyner, B. (1970) 'Atoms of environmental structure,' in *Emerging Methods in Environmental Design and Planning* (Ed. G. Moore), MIT Press, Cambridge, MA, pp. 308–321
Alexander, C., Ishikawa, I., and Silverstein, M. (1977) *A Pattern Language: Towns, Buildings, Construction*, Oxford University Press, New York.
Anderson, J. (1962) *Studies in Empirical Philosophy*, Angus and Robertson, Sydney.
Appleyard, D., and Lintell, M. (1972) 'The environmental quality of city streets: The residents' viewpoint,' *Journal of the American Institute of Planners*, **38** (2) 84–101.
Arnheim, R. (1954) *Art and Visual Perception*, University of California Press, Berkeley.
  (1966) *Towards a Psychology of Art*, Faber and Faber, London.
  (1969) *Visual Thinking*, University of California Press, Berkeley.
  (1977) *The Dynamics of Architectural Form*, University of California Press, Berkeley.
Aron, R. (1967) *Main Currents in Sociological Thought*, Vol. 2, Penguin Books Ltd., Edn. 1970, Harmondsworth, Middlesex.
Australian Bureau of Statistics (1975) *Official Year Book of Australia*, No. 60.
Banham, R. (1960) *Theory and Design in the First Machine Age*, Architectural Press, London.
Banham, P.R. (1965) 'Where are you Universal Man now that we need you...?' *RIBA Journal*, No. 7, 295.
Bateman, M. Burtenshaw, D., and Duffet, A. (1974) 'Environmental perception and migration: a study of perception of residential areas in South Hampshire,' in *Psychology and the Built Environment* (Eds. D. Canter and T. Lee), Architectural Press, London, pp. 148–155.
Baume, M. (1967) *The Sydney Opera House Affair*, Thomas Nelson Ltd., Sydney.
Beer, S. (1966) *Decision and Control*, John Wiley and Sons, London.
Bell, D. (1973) *The Coming of Post-Industrial Society*, Penguin Books, Edn. 1976, Harmondsworth, Middlesex.

221

Berelson, B., and Steiner, G. (1964) *Human Behaviour: An Inventory of Scientific Findings*, Harcourt Brace and World, New York.

Berger, P., and Berger, B. (1972) *Sociology: A Biographical Approach*, Basic Books, New York.

Berlyne D. (1960) *Conflict, Arousal and Curiosity*, McGraw-Hill, New York.
(1971) *Aesthetics and Psychobiology* Appleton Century Crofts, New York.

Blake, P. (1977) *Form Follows Fiasco*, Atlantic-Little, Brown, Boston.

Blecher, E. (1971) *Advocacy Planning for Urban Development with Analysis of Six Demonstration Programs*, Irvington Pubs., New York.

Boyd, R. (1952) *Australia's Home*, Melbourne University Press, Melbourne.
(1965) *The Puzzle of Architecture*, Melbourne University Press, Melbourne.

Brealey, T.B. (1972) *Living in Remote Communities in Tropical Australia: 1. Exploratory Study*, Division of Building Research, C.S.I.R.O. Report TB27–1.

Broadbent, G. (1966) 'Creativity', in *The Design Method* (Ed. S.A. Gregory), Butterworth, London, pp. 111–119.
(1973a) *Design in Architecture*, John Wiley and Sons, Chichester.
(1973b) 'Learning from new research', *RIBA Journal*, May, 228–230.
(1975) 'Its time to stop bashing the schools of architecture', *RIBA Journal*, December, 14–18.

Broadbent, G., and Ward, A. (1969) *Design Methods in Architecture*, Architectural Association Paper No. 4, Lund Humphries, London.

Brolin, B. (1976) *The Failure of Modern Architecture*, Studio Vista, London.

Bromilow, F. (1969) 'Contract time performance: Expectations and the reality,' *Building Forum*, **1** (3), 70–80.

Brown, J.A.C. (1954) *The Social Psychology of Industry*, Penguin Books Ltd., Harmondsworth, Middlesex.

Campbell, Colen (1717) *Vitruvius Britannicus*, or The British Architect.

Canter, D. (1970) 'Need for a theory of function in architecture,' *Architects Journal*, **4**, 299–302.

Chomsky, N. (1965) *Aspects of the Theory of Syntax*, MIT Press, Cambridge, MA.

Churchman, C.W. (1976) 'Morality and planning,' *Design Methods and Theories*, **10** (3), 165–181.

Clarke, J.H. (1969) 'The effect of certain background sounds on the efficiencies of groups of university students engaged in intellectual tasks,' unpublished PhD Thesis, University of Sydney.

Coleridge, S.T. (1817) *Biographia Literaria*, 2 vols., 2nd edn., 1847, London.

Cowan, P. (1964) 'Studies in the growth change and ageing of buildings,' *Transactions of the Bartlett Society*, **1.**

Cowan, P., and Nicholson, J. (1964/5) 'Growth and change in hospitals,' *Transactions of the Bartlett Society*, **3**, 63–68.

Crichton, C. (1966) *Interdependence and Uncertainty — A Study of the Building Industry*, Tavistock, London.

Crowther-Hunt, Lord (1976) 'Whitehall: Just passing through,' *The Listener*, 16 December, 772–774.

Cuff, D. (1982) 'The context for design: six characteristics,' in *Knowledge for Design*, Proceedings of the Thirteenth International Conference of the Environmental Design Research Association (Eds. P. Bart, A. Chen and G. Francescato), EDRA Inc., pp. 38–47.

Daley, J. (1969) 'A philosophical critique of behaviourism in architectural design,' in *Design Methods in Architecture* (Eds. G. Broadbent and A.

Ward), Architectural Association Paper No. 4, Lund Humphries, London, pp. 71–75.

Darke, J. (1979) 'The primary generator and the design process,' *Design Studies*, **1**, 36–44.

De Groot, A.D. (1965) *Thought and Choice in Chess*, Mouton, The Hague.

De Zurko, E. (1957) *Origins of Functionalist Theory*, Columbia University Press, New York.

Descartes, R. (1637) *Discourse on Method.*

Durand, J.N. (1809) *Précis des Lecons d'Architecture, Données a l'Ecòle Polytechnique.*

Eastman, C. (1970) 'On the analysis of intuitive design processes,' in *Emerging Methods in Environmental Design and Planning* (Ed. G. Moore), MIT Press, Cambridge, MA, pp. 21–37.

Eberhard, J.P. (1970) 'We ought to know the difference,' in *Emerging Methods in Environmental Design and Planning* (Ed. G.T. Moore), MIT Press, Cambridge, MA, pp. 363–367.

Edwards, M. (1974) 'Comparison of some expectations of a sample of housing architects with known data,' in *Psychology and the Built Environment* (Eds. D. Canter and T. Lee), The Architectural Press, London, pp. 38–47.

Ehrenzweig, A. (1967) *The Hidden Order of Art*, Weidenfeld and Nicolson, London.

Eisemon, T. (1975) 'Simulations and requirements for citizen participation in public housing — the Truax technique', *Environment and Behaviour 7*, (1), 99–123.

Emery, F., and Trist, E. (1960) 'Socio-technical systems,' in *Systems Thinking* (Ed. F. Emery), Penguin Books, Harmondsworth, Middlesex, 1969, pp. 281–296.
(1965) 'The causal texture of organisational environments,' *Human Relations*, **18**, 21–32.

Emery, F., and others (1974) *Futures We're In*, Centre for Continuing Education, Australian National University, Canberra.

Francis, M. (1975) 'Urban impact assessment and community involvement,' *Environment and Behaviour*, **7** (3), 373–404.

Galbraith, J.K. (1967) *The New Industrial State*, Hamish Hamilton Ltd., London.
(1977) *The Age of Uncertainty*, British Broadcasting Corporation and Andre Deutsch, London.

Gardner, H. (1973) *The Arts and Human Development*, John Wiley and Sons, New York.

Gero, J., and James, I. (1972) 'An experiment in computer-aided constraint oriented approach to the design of home units,' in *Environmental Design Research and Practice*, a joint programme of the third annual Environmental Design Research Association Conference (EDRA 3) and the eighth annual AIA Architecture Researchers Conference (AR–8) (Ed. W.J. Mitchell), University of California, Los Angeles, pp. 20–1–1 to 20–1–9.

Getzels, J., and Jackson, P. (1962) *Creativity and Intelligence*, John Wiley and Sons, New York.

Giedion, S. (1941) *Space, Time and Architecture*, Harvard University Press, Cambridge, MA.

Ginzberg, E. (1976) 'The pluralistic economy of the US,' *Scientific American*, **235** (6), 25–29.

Glahn, E. (1981) 'Chinese building standards in the twelfth century,' *Scientific American*, **244** (5) 162–173.

Glass, D.C., and Singer, J.E. (1973) 'Experimental studies of uncontrollable and unpredictable noise,' *Representative Research in Social Psychology,* **4**, 165–180.

Goffman, E. (1959) *The Presentation of Self in Everyday Life,* Pelican Books, Harmondsworth, Middlesex, 1971.

Golembiewski, R.T. (1962) *The Small Group,* University of Chicago Press, Chicago.

Gordon, W.J. (1961) *Synectics,* Collier-Macmillan, London, 1969.

Grahame, B. (1969) 'Computer graphics in architectural practice,' in *Computer Graphics in Architecture and Design* (Proceedings, Yale Conference on Computer Graphics in Architecture, New Haven, 1968) (Ed. M. Milne), Yale School of Art and Architecture, New Haven, pp. 23–30.

Grant, D. (1974) 'The problem of weighting,' *DMG-DRS Journal,* **8** (3), 136–141.

    (1977a) 'How to contruct a morphological box,' *Design Methods and Theories,* **11** (3), 129–158.

    (1977b) 'How to construct to a morphological tree,' *Design Methods and Theories,* **11** (3), 159–184.

Gregory, O. (Ed.) (1966) *The Design Method,* Butterworth, London.

    (1969) 'Morphological analysis, some simple explorations,' in *Design Methods in Architecture* (Eds. G. Broadbent and A. Ward), Lund Humphries, London, pp. 103–108.

Groat, L., and Canter, D. (1979) 'Does post-modernism communicate?' *Progressive Architecture,* **12**, 84–87.

Gropius, W. (1935) *The New Architecture and the Bauhaus* (trans. P.M. Shand), Faber and Faber, London.

    (1956) *Scope of Total Architecture,* George Allen and Unwin, London.

Guilford, J.P. (1957) *The Relations of Creative Thinking Aptitudes to Non-Aptitude Personality Traits,* Report of The Psychological Laboratory, No. 20, University of Southern California.

Gutman, R. (1966) 'The questions architects ask,' *Transactions of the Bartlett Society,* **4**, 47–82.

    (1981) 'Architecture as a service industry,' *Casabella,* No. 475, November, 28–32; No. 476, December, 108–109.

Handler, B. (1970) *Systems Approach to Architecture,* American Elsevier Publishing Co., New York.

Harvey, J. (1950) *The Gothic World,* Batsford Ltd., London.

Hassid, D. (1964) *Development and application of a System of Recording Critical Evaluations of Architectural Works,* College of Environmental Design, Berkeley, CA.

Heath, T. (1967) 'The storage requirements of old people,' *Architectural Science Review,* **10** (2), 39–43.

    (1970) 'The algorithmic nature of the architectural design process,' in *Emerging Methods in Environmental Design and Planning* (Ed. G. Moore), MIT Press, Cambridge, MA, pp. 57–68.

    (1972) 'Second generation design methods and architectural practice,' *DMG-DRS journal,* **6** (3), 91–98.

    (1973) 'Case study: The design of a small hospital operating suite as an illustration of the range and power of two methodological concepts,' *DMG-DRS Journal,* **7** (3), 201–206.

    (1974a) 'Supervision inspection and quality control,' *Architectural Science Review,* **17** (3), 60–62.

(1974b) 'Programming and user involvement: An issue based approach, *Industrialisation Forum*, **5** (6), 3–8.

(1974c) 'Should we tell the children about aesthetics, or should we let them find out in the street?' in *Psychology and the Built Environment* (Eds. D. Canter and T. Lee), Architectural Press, London, pp. 179–183.

(1975) 'Getting started: "Is your programme really necessary"?' *DMG-DRS Journal*, **9** (2), 196–199.

(1982) 'Design in the organisational setting: Managing communication and conflict,' in *Knowledge for Design*, Proceedings of the Thirteenth International Conference of the Environmental Design Research Association (Eds. P. Bart, A. Chen and G. Francescato), EDRA Inc., pp. 26–34.

Heimsath, C. (1977) *Behavioural Architecture*, McGraw-Hill, New York.

Herrmann, W. (1962) *Laugier and Eighteenth Century French Theory*, Zwemmer, London.

(1973) *The Theory of Claude Perrault*, Zwemmer, London.

Hillier, B., and Jones, L. (1977) 'Architecture at the crossroads,' *New Scientist*, **74** (1052), 390–392.

Hillier, B., and Leaman, A. (1973) 'The man-environment paradigm and its paradoxes,' *Architectural Design*, No. 8, 507–511.

Hillier, W., Musgrave, J., and O'Sullivan, P. (1972) 'Knowledge and design,' in *Environmental Design: Research and Practice*, a joint programme of the third annual Environmental Design Research Association Conference (EDRA 3) and the eighth annual AIA Architecture Researchers Conference (AR–8) (Ed. W.J. Mitchell), University of California, Los Angeles, pp. 29–3–1 to 29–3–4.

Hoinville, G., and Jowell, R. (1972) 'Will the real public please stand UP?' *Official Architecture and Planning*, **35** (3), 159–161.

Holt, E. (Ed.) (1947) *A Documentary History of Art*, Vol. 1, Princeton University Press.

Honey, C.F. (1969) *Architectural Design: A Study of Coding and Data Co-ordination for the Construction Industry*, BRS Current Paper 4/69.

Hopkinson, R.G. (1963) *Architectural Physics: Lighting*, HMSO, London.

Hovey, H.B. (1928) 'Effects of general distraction on the higher thought processes,' *American Journal of Psychology*, **40**, 585–591.

Hudson, L. (1962) 'Intelligence, divergence and potential originality, *Nature*, **196**, 601.

Hume, D. (1739–40) *Treatise on Human Nature*.

Hunter, I.M.L. (1968) 'Mental calculation,' in *Thinking and Reasoning* (Eds. P.C. Wason and P.N. Johnson-Laird), Penguin Books, Harmondsworth, Middlesex, pp. 341–351.

Hutton, J. (Ed.) (1970) *Building and Construction in Australia*, W.F. Cheshire, Melbourne.

Illich, I. (1971) *De-Schooling Society*, Harper and Row, New York.

Ittelson, W., Proshansky, H., and Rivlin, L. (1970) 'The environmental psychology of the psychiatry ward,' in *Environmental Psychology* (eds. H. Proshansky, W. Ittelson and L. Rivlin), Holt Reinhart Winston, New York, pp. 419–439.

Jackson, A. (1970) *The Politics of Architecture*, Architectural Press, London.

James, J. (1972) 'The contractors of Chartres', *Architectural Association Quarterly*, **4** (2) 42–53.

Jameson, C. (1976) 'Enter pattern books, exit public housing architects: a friendly sermon,' *The Architects Journal*, 11 February, 268–269.

Johnson, R. (1974) *Design in Balance*, University of Queensland Press, St. Lucia.

Jones, J.C. (1970a) *Design Methods — Seeds of Human Futures*, John Wiley and Sons, New York.

    (1970b) 'The state of the art in design methods' in *Emerging Methods in Environmental Design and Planning* (Ed. G. Moore), MIT Press, Cambridge, MA, pp. 3–8.

Jones, J.C. and Thornley, D.G. (Eds.) (1963) *Conference on Design Methods*, Pergamon Press, London.

Jonson, Ben (1633) *Tale of a Tub*.

Kahn, H., and Wiener, A. (1967) *The Year 2000*, Macmillan, New York.

Kaplan, R., Kaplan, S., and Deardorff, H.L. (1974) 'The perception and evaluation of a simulated environment,' *Man–Environment Systems*, **4**, 191–192.

Kaplan, S., and Kaplan, R. (Eds.) (1982) *Humanscape: Environments for People*, Ulrich's Books Inc., Ann Arbor, Michigan.

Kelly, G. (1955) *The Psychology of Personal Constructs*, Vols. 1 and 2, Norton, New York.

Kennedy, W.B. (1970) 'Productivity research and innovation,' in *Building and Construction in Australia* (Ed. J. Hutton), F.W. Cheshire, pp. 228–253.

Koestler, A. (1964) *The Act of Creation*, Hutchinson, London.

Koffka, K. (1935) *Principles of Gestalt Psychology*, Routledge and Kegan Paul, London.

Kohler, W. (1925) *The Mentality of Apes*, (trans. Winter), Penguin Edn. 1957, Harmondsworth, Middlesex.

Krampen, M. (1974) 'A possible analogy between (psycho-) linguistic and architectural measurement — the type-token ratio (TTR), in *Psychology and the Built Environment* (Eds. D. Canter and T. Lee), Architectural Press, London, pp. 87–95.

Kuhn, T. (1962) *The Structure of Scientific Revolutions*, The University of Chicago Press, Chicago.

    (1964) 'The essential tension,' in *Scientific Creativity: its Recognition and Development* (Eds. C. Taylor and F. Barron), Wiley New York, pp. 341–54.

Lakatos, I. (1970) 'Methodology of scientific research programmes,' in *Criticism and the Growth of Knowledge* (Eds. I. Lakatos and A. Musgrave), Cambridge University Press, Cambridge, pp. 91–196.

Laratos, I., and Musgrave, A. (Eds.) (1970) *Criticism and the Growth of Knowledge*, Cambridge University Press, Cambridge.

Laugier, M.A. (1753) *Essai sur l'Architecture*.

Lawrence, R. (1982) 'Designer's dilemma: Participatory design methods', in *Knowledge for Design*, Proceedings of the Thirteenth International Conference of the Environmental Design Research Association (Eds. P. Bart, A. Chen and G. Francescato), EDRA Inc., pp. 261–271.

Le Corbusier (1923) *Vers un Architecture*, Editions Crés, Paris.

Lee, T. (1971) 'Psychology and architectural determinism,' *Architects Journal*, August 4, 253–262.

Likert, R. (1961) *New Patterns of Management*, McGraw-Hill, New York.

Lipman, A. (1970) 'Professional ideology "community" and "total" architecture,' *Journal of Architectural Research and Teaching*, **1**, 39–49.

    (1976) 'Professional ideology: The architectural notion of "User requirements,"' *Journal of Architectural Research* **3** (2), 12–27.

Locke, J. (1690) *Essay Concerning Human Understanding*.

Lovejoy, A.O. (1948) *Essays in the History of Ideas*, John Hopkins Press, Capricorn Books Edn., 1960.

Luckman, J. (1969) 'An approach to the management of design,' in *Design Methods in Architecture* (Eds. G. Broadbent and A. Ward), Lund Humphries, London, pp. 128–135.

MacEwen, M. (1974) *Crisis in Architecture*, RIBA Publications Ltd., London.

Mackinnon, D.W. (1962) 'The personality correlates of creativity: a study of American architects' in Proceedings of the Fourteenth Congress on Applied Psychology, Vol. 2. Munksgaard, pp. 11–39.

MacLeod, R. (1971) *Style and Society*, RIBA Publications, London.

Mainstone, R. (1977) 'Brunelleschi's dome,' *Architectural Review*, No. 967, September, 157–166.

Mann, T., and Bender, R. (1972) 'The role of research in the development of performance standards,' in *Environmental Design Research and Practice*, a joint programme of the third annual Environmental Design Research Association Conference (EDRA 3) and the eighth annual AIA Architecture Researchers Conference (AR–8) (Ed. W.J. Mitchell), University of California, Los Angeles, pp. 9–1–1 to 9–1–7.

Mant, A. (1975) 'The manager as professional,' *Management Today*, September, 58–61.

March, L., and Steadman, P. (1971) *The Geometry of Environment*, RIBA Publications, London.

Markus, T. (1970) 'Building appraisal: St. Michael's Academy Kilwinning,' *Architects Journal*, 7 January, 9–50.

(1975) 'Education and training: Long live the difference,' *RIBA Journal*, December, 18–21.

Miller, G.A. (1956) 'The magical number seven, plus or minus two,' *Psychological Review*, **63**, 81–97.

Ministry for Housing and Local Government (UK) (1961) *Houses for Today and Tomorrow* (The Parker-Morris Report), HMSO, London.

Moholy-Nagy, L. (1928) *The New Vision*, Revised edn., Wittenborn and Co., New York, 1946.

Moore, G. (Ed.) (1970) *Emerging Methods in Environmental Design and Planning*, MIT Press, Cambridge, MA.

Moore, G.E. (1903) *Principia Ethica*, Cambridge University Press, Cambridge. (1912) *Ethics*, Oxford University Press, Oxford.

Moore, O.K., and Anderson, A.R. (1969) 'Some principles for the design of clarifying educational environments,' in *Handbook of Socialisation Theory and Research* (Ed. D. Goslin), Rand McNally, New York.

Murdock, G.P. (1956) 'How culture changes' in *Man, Culture and Society* (Ed. H.L. Shapiro), Oxford University Press, New York, pp. 247–260.

Newell, A., and Simon, H. (1972) *Human Problem Solving*, Prentice-Hall, Englewood Cliffs, NJ.

O'Reilly, J.J.N. (1973) *A Case Study of a Design Commission: Problems Highlighted; Initiatives Proposed*, Building Research Establishment Current Paper CP23/73, Department of the Environment, Watford.

Osborn, A.F. (1963) *Applied Imagination*, Scribner, New York.

Osgood, C., Suci, G., and Tannenbaum, P. (1957) *The Measurement of Meaning*, University of Illinois Press, Urbana, Chicago and London.

Ouye, J. (1974) 'A building planning information system,' *DMG-DRS Journal*, **8** (2), 90–98.

Panofsky, E. (1955) *Meaning in the Visual Arts*, Doubleday Anchor Books, New York,

Parkinson, C.N. (1957) *Parkinson's Law*, Penguin Books, edn. 1965, Harmondsworth, Middlesex.

Perin, C. (1970) *With Man in Mind*, MIT Press, Cambridge, MA.

Perrault, C. (1683) *Ordonnance des Cinq Espèces des Colonnes selon la*

Méthode des Anciens.

Pevsner, N. (1949) *Pioneers of Modern Design from Willian Morris to Walter Gropius*, The Museum of Modern Art, New York.

Poincaré, H. (undated) *Science and Method* (trans. F. Maitland), Dover Publications, New York.

Polya, G. (1945) *How to Solve It*, Princeton University Press, Princeton, NJ.

Popper, K. (1963) *Conjectures and Refutations*, Routledge and Kegan Paul, London.

(1972) *Objective Knowledge*, Clarendon Press, Oxford.

Prak, N. (1977) *The Visual Perception of the Built Environment*, Delft University Press, Delft.

Protzen, J.P. (1980) 'The poverty of the pattern language,' *Design Studies*, **1** (5), 291–295.

Purcell, T., and Heath, T. (1982) 'The two communities: Is there a common focus for designer–researcher collaboration?' in *Knowledge For Design*, Proceedings of the Thirteenth International Conference of the Environmental Design Research Association (Eds. P. Bart, A. Chen and G. Francescato), EDRA Inc., pp. 3–15.

Pye, D. (1964) *The Nature of Design*, Studio Vista, London.

Rapoport, A. (1969) *House Form and Culture*, Prentice-Hall, Englewood Cliffs, NJ.

Rapoport, A., and Watson, N. (1968) 'Cultural variability in physical standards,' *Transactions of the Bartlett Society*, **6**.

Reynolds, J. (1769–1790) *Discourses on Art*, Collier Books edn. 1961, New York.

Reynolds, I., and Nicholson, C. (1969) 'Living off the ground,' *Architects Journal*, 20 August, 459–70.

RIBA (1967) *RIBA Handbook of Architectural Practice and Management*, RIBA Press, London.

Richards, I.A. (1934) *Coleridge on Imagination*, Kegan Paul, London.

Rittel, H. (1972) *On the State of the Art in Design Methods*, DMG Occasional Paper No. 1: DMG Fifth Anniversary Report, The Design Methods Group, pp. 5–9.

Rittel, H., and Webber, M. (1974) 'Dilemmas in a general theory of planning, in *Systems and Management Annual* (ed. R.L. Ackoff), Petrocelli, New York, pp. 219–233.

Rosen, H. (1980) *The Development of Sociomoral Knowledge*, Columbia University Press, New York.

Rudofsky, B. (1965) *Architecture without Architects*, Academy Editions, London.

Russell, B. (1946) *History of Western Philosophy*, George Allen and Unwin, London.

Sax, J. (1970) 'The search for environmental quality: The role of the courts', in *The Environmental Crisis* (ed. H.W. Helfrich), Yale University Press, New Haven, pp. 99–114.

Schein, E. (1965) *Organisational Psychology*, Prentice-Hall, Englewood Cliffs, NJ.

Schon, D. (1963) *Invention and the Evolution of Ideas*, Social Science Paperbacks, London.

(1971) *Beyond the Stable State*, Penguin Books, edn. 1973, Harmondsworth, Middlesex.

Seagrim, G.N. (1968) 'Representation and communication,' *Transactions of the Bartlett Society*, **6**, 11–23.

Sharp, A. (1966) *Modern Architecture and Expressionism*, Longmans, London.

Sharp, A. (1970) 'Appraisers appraised,' *Architects Journal*, 28 January, 204–205.

Simon, H.A. (1970) 'Style in design,' in EDRA 2 *Proceedings of the 2nd Environmental Design Research Association Conference* (Eds. J. Archea and C. Eastman), Dowden, Hutchinson and Ross, Stroudsbury, PA, pp. 1–3.

Smith, A., and others (1962) *The Architect and his Office*, RIBA Publications, London.

Snow, C. (1956) 'The two cultures,' *New Statesman*, **52**, 413–414.

Sommer, R. (1974) *Tight Spaces: Hard Architecture and How to Humanise It*, Prentice-Hall, Englewood Cliffs, NJ.

Starr, M.N. (1963) *Product Design and Decision Theory*, Prentice-Hall, Englewood Cliffs, NJ.

Stern, R. (1977) 'Drawing towards a more modern architecture,' *Architectural Design*, **47** (6), 382–383.

Stevenson, A., Martin, E., and O'Neill, J. (1967) *High Living*, Melbourne University Press, Melbourne.

Stone, P.A. (1976) *Building Economy Design, Production and Organisation: A Synoptic View*, Pergamon Press, Oxford.

Stringer, P. (1974) 'Individual differences in repertory grid measures for a cross section of the female population,' in *Psychology and the Built Environment* (Eds. D. Canter and T. Lee), The Architectural Press Ltd., London, pp. 96–104.

Sturt, G. (1923) *The Wheelright's Shop*, Cambridge University Press, Cambridge.

Thompson, M. (1977) 'The architects dilemma,' *Design Methods and Theories*, **11** (1), 11–16.

Thorne, R., and Purcell, T. (1976) 'Environmental effects on the subjective perception of level of arousal and the human body temperature rhythm', *International Journal of Biometerology*, **20** (4) 318–324.

Townsend, R. (1970) *Up the Organisation*, Michael Joseph Limited, London.

Turner, V.F.C. (1976) *Housing by People*, Marion Boyars, London.

Van Zanten, D. (1976) 'Le systeme des Beaux Arts,' *Architecture d'Aujourd'-hui*, No. 187, October/November, pp. 97–106.

    (1977) 'Architectural composition at the Ecole des Beaux-Arts from Charles Percier to Charles Garnier,' in *The Architecture of the Ecole des Beaux-Arts* (Ed. A. Drexler), Museum of Modern Art, New York, pp. 111–324.

Venturi, R., Scott-Brown, D., and Izenour, S. (1972) *Learning from Las Vegas*, MIT Press, Cambridge, MA.

Viollet-le-Duc, E. (1863–72) *Entretiens sur l'Architecture* (trans. Von Brunt Boston, 1875, as *Discourses on Architecture*).

Vitruvius, M. (20BC?) *The Ten Books on Architecture* (trans. M.H. Morgan), Dover, New York, 1960.

Von Danniken, E. (1967) *Chariots of the Gods*, Corgi edn. 1971.

Wade, J. (1977) *Architecture, Problems and Purposes*, Wiley-Interscience, New York.

Weber, H. (1973) 'The evolution of a place to dwell,' *DMG-DRS Journal*, **7**, 207–212.

    (1975) 'A contextual dwelling cell morphology: Discourse for participation in residential design,' *DMG-DRS Journal*, **9**, (2), 171–176.

White, R., and Lippit, R. (1968) 'Leader behaviour and member reaction in three social climates,' in *Group Dynamics: Research and Theory*, 3rd edn. (Eds. D. Cartwright and A. Zander), Harper and Row, New York, pp.

318–335.

Wilensky, H. (1964) 'The professionalisation of everyone?', *American Journal of Sociology*, **70**, 137–158.

Williams, R. (1958) *Culture and Society 1780–1850*, Chatto and Windus, Penguin Books Ltd., edn. 1961, Harmondsworth, Middlesex.

Wolfe, T. (1966) *The Kandy-Kolored Tangerine Flake Streamline Baby*, Jonathan Cape, London.

Woodford, G., Williams, K., and Hill, W. (1976) *The Value of Standards for the External Residential Environment*, DOE Research Report No. 6.

Wools, R. (1970) 'The assessment of room friendliness,' in *Architectural Psychology*, Proceedings of the conference held at Dalandhui, University of Strathclyde (Ed. D. Canter), RIBA Publications Ltd., London, pp. 48–55.

Wordsworth, W. (1800) 'Preface to the "Lyrical Ballads", in *The Poetical Works of Wordsworth* (ed. T. Hutchinson; revised A. de Selincourt), Oxford University Press, 1946, Oxford.

Yancey, W.L. (1971) 'Architecture, interaction, and social control,' *Environment and Behaviour*, **3** (1), 3–21.

Zangwill, O.L. (1966) 'Psychological defects associated with frontal lobe lesions,' *International Journal of Neurology*, **5**, 395–402.

Zeidler, E. (1974) *Healing the Hospital McMaster Health Science Centre: Its Conception and Evaluation*, The Zeidler Partnership, Toronto.

Zeisel, J. (1981) *Inquiry by Design: Tools for Environment–Behaviour Research*, Brooks/Cole Publishing Co., Monterey, CA.

Zwicky, F. (1967) 'The morphological approach to discovery, invention, research and construction,' in *New Methods of Thought and Procedure: Contributions* (Eds. F. Zwicky and A.G. Wilson), Springer-Verlag, New York, pp. 273–297. (Symposium on Methodologies, sponsored by the Office for Industrial Associates of the California Institute of Technology and the Society for Morphological Research, Pasadena, California, May 22–24, 1967.)

Name Index

General Index